RETRACKING AMERICA

John Friedmann

RETRACKING AMERICA

AMERICA

A Theory of Transactive Planning

ANCHOR PRESS/DOUBLEDAY

Garden City, New York, 1973

ISBN: 0-385-00675-6
Library of Congress Catalog Card Number 72–89308

To My Father

1891–1970

ACKNOWLEDGMENTS

My deep appreciation goes to the Centro Interdisciplinario de Desarrollo Urbano y Regional of the Catholic University of Chile, where I spent some of the most productive years of my life; to its students and staff, with whom I argued many of the more controversial points of the present volume; and to Guillermo Geisse, the Director of the Center, who proved to be not only a good friend but a loving antagonist as well.

In the fall of 1970, I taught the substance of this book to a class of graduate students in the Urban Planning Program at UCLA. Barclay Hudson, who joined me in teaching the course, was a constant source of fresh ideas and illuminating criticism. His keen, inventive mind, no less than his friendship, helped me through many difficult stages of writing.

William Glennon, Beth Earwaker, John Felstiner, Barbara Stuckey, Sharon Kaufman-Diamond, and John Graiwer volunteered to read portions of the manuscript. I have greatly benefited from their comments on both substance and style.

Connie Bishop prepared the final manuscript with great diligence and skill.

John Friedmann

Brentwood
June 1971

CONTENTS

All things are in movement.
—Heraclitus

Shortly after the liberation of Paris in World War II, Jean Paul Sartre, philosopher and hero of the French Resistance, was interviewed by the press. His words electrified the world. While bulbs flashed and cameras clicked, Sartre made his ultimate pronouncement. "Gentlemen," he said, as though he had just returned from the funeral, "God is dead."

Although this book is about planning, I am tempted to make a similar declaration. Our inherited notions of planning are dead. We are thus constrained to reconsider what we need and on the basis of this need to rethink planning from the start.

The planning with which most of us are familiar today was invented nearly one hundred years ago by the originator of scientific management. This is the thesis of Rexford Tugwell and Edward Banfield:[1]

In the early eighties of the last century Frederick Winslow Taylor was a young man working in the shops of Midvale Steel. Through a series of accidental changes in a life which might normally have followed a routine middle-class course, he had become a foreman. He was, however, a new species of that all-important animal. For he did not believe in foremanship, at least of the old-fashioned kind, and almost at once he set out to displace the foreman's rule of thumb with a scientifically arrived at "one-best-way." He intended to reduce the functions of the shop to clearly and precisely stated locations, quantities of materials, forces applied, motions to be gone through, and output to be expected. These would then be the terms in which a planning office would set out the job to be done. The directions would be precise. And foremen—in the old sense—would be eliminated. He called it, later on, scientific management. Actually it was planning.

Taylor's scientific management was meant for a world in which growth was set equal to development, the ends were clear, and the environment was controlled. Its rationality was concerned with the fitness and efficiency of means. Its purpose was to reach a given production target at the least possible cost. It was authoritarian and directive planning. Some called it human engineering.

Frederick Taylor's legacy is still with us in its contemporary forms of operations research and systems analysis. To be sure, important changes have been introduced. March and Simon, for example, distinguish between programs of routine performance and strategies of change.[2] They explicitly relate the concept of planning to the latter. Planning, in their view, is linked with innovation and with actions that cannot, in principle, be programmed for repeated use. The new planning, then, is addressed to novel elements in the environment of organizations. It is concerned with producing change and with maintaining organizational stability under conditions of change.

Taylor was truly a child of his century. Progress was writ large across his horizon: he was sure of where he wanted to go. He shared the certainties of Darwin, Spencer, Queen Victoria, and "Teddy" Roosevelt. There were civilized and heathen peoples, and the former had a moral obligation to protect the latter and, if possible, to raise them to the threshold of civilization. Obviously civilized men, the scientific managers of Midvale Steel maintained a tight grip on their environment. Within their four-square world, the "one-best-way" would lead to increased output and greater profits. The inheritors of Taylor's wisdom applied these simple beliefs to society at large. They, too, were believers in the efficacy of central management. They were specialists in the construction of five-year plans as blueprints for the future. All that was needed were the commands to implement their plans. The future of society was reduced to a set of simultaneous equations.

The Soviet Union was the first country to apply the principles of scientific management to the national economy. Though their experiences largely contradicted the premises of Taylorism, Soviet planners refused to deviate from principle.[3] A succession of five-year plans poured out of the labyrinthine machinery they had devised for this purpose, were passed into law, and ordered to be carried out. Soviet production lurched forward; indeed, it made spectacular gains. But there is substantial doubt that these gains were achieved at the least possible cost to society (efficiency was a fetish of scientific management) or that the plans were instrumentally related to the outcome. As Professor Ehrlich has suggested, the system grew almost in spite of itself.[4]

However confident the planners of Midvale Steel and the Soviet economy may have been in their ability to construct the future according to a plan, we who have inherited the results of their planning have lost the optimism of our innocence. The post-industrial world into which we have stumbled is filled with terrifying uncertainties. We are no longer sure of the course we must take. The environment has become murky. The inefficiencies of centralism have become apparent to nearly everyone. Yet it is precisely under such conditions that some form of planning is needed. We have no assurances that the spontaneous workings of the

private and public economy will lead us into a world we
would wish to call our own. And so it behooves us to rethink planning in terms of the conditions, understandings,
and needs of our time.

An effort of this sort must include a look at the past of
planning, at its origins, assumptions, and working principles.
It must include some formal models for the empirical study
of planning in the present. And it must include a forward
look at the possibilities of planning in the future. This last is
the most difficult of all the operations. The view into the
future must conjure up a reachable utopia, sufficiently idealistic to be worth doing, and capable of being realized. The
reachable utopia of my imagination, elaborated in the last
three chapters of this book, is set forth in the belief that
any fundamental change in the society must be worked
from below. It must originate with those who are without
substantial power.

It is inevitable that a book such as this should bias its
interpretations toward the future and the values that we
hope to bring about. Under the kind of planning Taylorism
inspired, the individual person was treated as an instrument for the attainment of an extrinsic goal. He was reduced
to complete passivity: his behavior was to be engineered to
conform with the plan. The transactive planning of the future, on the other hand, is deeply rooted in face-to-face,
person-centered relations within small groups. If Taylor's
discipline was the ratio of resources to final product, the
discipline of transactive planning is the radical openness
required by dialogue. In dialogue, the object, man, disap-
pears and is transformed into an active subject, the pro-
tagonist of history. The limits of this dialogue can be ex-
ceeded only at the risk of abrogating the transactive relation
itself and substituting for it a manipulative relation. With
this, however, we step back into the self-destructive world
of human engineering.

One of the major premises of this book is that the process

of societal guidance is too important to be left entirely to experts. Guidance activities must reach down into school, farm, factory, office, and neighborhood, where they will draw increasing numbers of people into a direct engagement with their society. By this I mean something quite different from what I take to be the meaning of the currently popular ideology of participation. Almost always this signifies participation in someone else's plans. But by direct engagement with society, I mean acquiring a sense of competence *at the level of the group* in tasks set largely by the group itself but related to the larger enterprise of which it forms part.

This book, then, is informed by a highly personal vision. It is also an attempt to outline the elements of a theory of societal guidance in which historical, logico-empirical, and utopian aspects are brought into conjunction. Because of this, I thought it appropriate to start with a chapter devoted to the intellectual odyssey that led me from the Taylorism I was taught in the classroom to the transactive style of planning I am advocating now. This chapter will succeed, I hope, in exposing the values that underlie the remainder of the discussion.

With Chapter 2, I turn to the more formal aspects of the argument. The theory of societal guidance was born in the disciplined imagination of Karl Mannheim, a German sociologist, whose writings during the nineteen-thirties and -forties laid the basis for all subsequent thinking on the subject. Until recently known to only a few specialists for his pathbreaking contributions to the sociology of knowledge, Mannheim's profound insights into the workings of modern society and the conditions of planning were largely neglected. The chapter is intended to be a synthesis of Mannheim's basic ideas and to show how the various strands of his thinking evolved and came together in a systematic approach to societal guidance.

Chapter 3 is chiefly taxonomical. Its purpose is to furnish

a vocabulary for discussing planning and, at the same time, to draw a logical distinction between forms and styles of planning. Two forms are identified: allocative and innovative planning. The specific manner in which these forms are actualized depends on their social context. The resulting styles of planning are shown to vary systematically with the distribution of power in the society.

Chapter 4 carries the analysis of social context still further. It examines the conditions of valuing and knowing in post-industrial society, and, from this analysis, draws certain conclusions concerning the planning style most appropriate for our times. The major characteristics of transactive planning are identified, foreshadowing the more complete discussion of this style in Chapter 8.

The conditions of knowing are further analyzed in Chapter 5, which concerns the ways in which we commonly relate our present thinking to the future. Our thinking is shown to depend primarily on the values we project ahead and our subjective expectations concerning what will be. Ideological and utopian thinking are contrasted. The former is seen as the perfection of an existing system of social relations, whereas the latter projects images of a future that differs radically from the present. These values, in turn, inform our current actions. Planning is seen as a time-binding activity in which scientific knowledge (based on the recent past) is brought into conjunction with expectational knowledge concerning the near future, hope in the longer-range historical future, and faith in utopian possibilities of a time realm beyond history.

Chapter 6 is pivotal to the structure of my argument. Here, growth is distinguished from development, a distinction that the scientific managers of Taylor's time refused to see. Where development refers to structural change, growth relates simply to an increase in quantity within a given system of structural relations. Many of our current crises are the result of growth straining the limits of existing arrangements in the society. To meet this challenge, planning must become more innovative than it has been in the past. A methodology of innovative planning is proposed. The blueprinting approach of allocative planning is abandoned. Its place is taken by a broader concept of societal guidance.

Having established the basis for a radical critique of planning, I pass on to consider the possible (and desirable) future. Chapter 7 discusses transactive planning in terms of such concepts as mutual learning and dialogue. In mutual learning, the processed, scientific knowledge of the planning expert is joined with the deeply personal, experiential knowledge of the client. Where mutual learning occurs, this confrontation of two quite distinct modes of knowing gives birth to new knowledge capable of guiding the client's present actions.

This micro-analysis is succeeded in Chapter 8 by an attempt to design a scheme of societal order in which the transactive style may flourish. I call this scheme the learning society; in contrast to the hierarchical model of organization, it is based on a system of cellular structure. The basic elements of this structure are task-oriented working groups (or learning cells) which, in turn, are organized into larger systems, called assemblies. Working groups are small, temporary, self-guiding, and accountable to the assemblies. Transactive planning is maximized within the cellular structure of problem-solving groups.

In Chapter 9, finally, I come to the question of how a learning society may be brought about. The answer to this question is both extremely simple and complex. On one hand, we have the exhortation, addressed to anyone, to start a learning cell in the hope that enough learning cells will grow together into the transforming tissue of a new society. On the other hand, and eschewing a head-on confrontation with entrenched interests, the longer-term solution requires a broadly gauged effort to re-educate man so that he may become an actively contributing member of a learning society. Four abilities must be strengthened: the ability to question existing reality, to draw general lessons from concrete experience, to test these lessons in practice, and to examine the results sincerely. The effort to develop these new faculties should start during the formative years of childhood. It is by developing the abilities necessary for a learning society among children that we prepare ourselves for the tremendous challenges that lie ahead.

And when the foundation of politics is in
the letter only and in custom, and
knowledge is divorced from action, can we wonder,
Socrates, at the miseries which there are,
and always will be, in States? Any other
art, built on such foundations and thus
conducted, would ruin all that it touched.

PLATO

CHAPTER 1

ENCOUNTERS

The chapters that follow grew from a series of personal encounters, each of which brought my own ideas into direct confrontation with situations incongruous to them. These encounters took place over a period of twenty years, starting with my student days at the University of Chicago. They included years of work as an economist with the Tennessee Valley Authority, as technical advisor and development specialist with the U. S. Agency for International Development in northeastern Brazil and the Republic of Korea, as professor of regional planning at the Massachusetts Institute of Technology, as research associate of the M.I.T.-Harvard Joint Center for Urban Studies on a project in Venezuela, as director of a Ford Foundation-sponsored advisory program for urban and regional development in Chile, and as professor of planning at the University of California at Los Angeles.

Each change in my employment involved drastic adjustments in my activities, accustomed ways of living, and social relationships. Yet, wherever I went, whether talking with students, statesmen, administrators, or technicians, I was compelled by circumstances to deal in quite specific terms with the question of how, through conscious choice, society may guide the future course of its development. I came to see this as a central issue of our time, and dealt with it both intellectually and practically. With each major encounter, my answers underwent a decisive change; yet beneath the changing surface flowed a current of thinking that made for continuity.

Karl Jaspers once said that we study history to know better what we may become. The present chapter is written in this spirit.

Masters and Students

In the fall of 1949, I enrolled as a graduate student in the recently opened Program of Education and Research in Planning at the University of Chicago.[1] Among my teachers was a remarkable group of men that included Rexford G. Tugwell, Edward C. Banfield, and Harvey S. Perloff. Tugwell, who had recently served as governor of Puerto Rico, was appointed the first director of the program. To his new assignment, he brought a powerful theoretical mind joined to a rich fund of practical experience. Unquestionably, it was he who set the unconventional directions of the Chicago program, where planning was taught as a form of applied social science. Tugwell conceived of society as a complex organism and of planning as a central function—similar to the brain and central nervous system in the human body—specifically concerned with co-ordinating its diverse elements for the benefit of the whole. Planning, he taught, was to be set up as a "conjunctural institution which, through gradual and experimental change, may come to dominate social drift."[2] Through the proper exercise of forethought and the formulation of attainable objectives, planning would make the future relevant for present actions. "When the future is laid out in clear and objective—even if tentative—terms, the result is equally unacceptable to politician and businessman. Both live by uncertainty. Neither can survive exactitude. Yet it is in this clear understanding that the public interest has its best chance to prevail."[3]

Although students crowded into Tugwell's lectures, they left puzzled and disenchanted. His organismic metaphors, his loving descriptions of the social life of bees and ants, his apocalyptic warnings of an approaching doomsday caused by man's ill-considered uses of the natural environment, his quite unrealistic claims for planning as a fourth branch of the government, all expressed in a manner that was patrician and aloof, led to his having less influence on his students than his truly remarkable ideas deserved.

Edward Banfield was just then setting out on an illustrious career as a political scientist. Originally one of Tugwell's disciples, he soon came under the spell of Professor Milton Friedman's brilliant lectures on neoclassical economics. In contrast to Tugwell, Banfield was a persuasive teacher who applied the method of socratic dialogue with consummate skill. In his seminars on planning theory, he introduced his students to the writings of Joseph Schumpeter, Karl Mannheim, Frank Knight, and Herbert Simon. Following Simon's newly published *Administrative Behavior*, he thought of planning in terms of a model of rational decision-making in which the ends were given, and planners laid out alternative courses of action together with their probable consequences.[4] Banfield's empirical studies of the planning process, however, revealed a startling discrepancy with this model.[5] Concluding that planning was an unattainable ideal, at least in the American context, he came to lean more and more heavily on economics, where, it seemed, a rational decision-calculus was operating with reasonable effectiveness through an impersonal market.

Banfield's early flirtations with planning eventually gave way to a deep pessimism about man's condition and the ability of society to deal with its problems through purposeful intervention by central authorities.[6] Nevertheless, his openness to the ideas of his students, and the rigor he demanded of their presentations, contributed to making his seminars among the most memorable in the program and the study of planning worthy of the students' best efforts.

Harvey Perloff displayed a more pragmatic style than either Tugwell or Banfield. His book on Puerto Rico's economic future had just appeared and was considered a pathbreaking study in the new field of developmental economics and policy analysis.[7] Its theoretical assumptions, however, were largely hidden among masses of statistical data and the very down-to-earth quality of his policy recommendations. Here, there were no flights of metaphysical rhetoric, such as Tugwell's "Superpolitical" or Banfield's "Rational Decision-Maker." In his seminars and lectures, Perloff evolved the outlines of what eventually came to be known as the Planning-Programming-Budgeting System. His emphasis on "strategic" or policies planning had a profound influence on the thinking of his students.

More so than in other planning departments, which, at the time, were still concerned primarily with land use planning, the students in the Chicago program were deeply preoccupied with planning in its larger, societal meaning. They tended to regard planning as a vocation, a *calling* in Max Weber's sense. Although accepting Banfield's definition of planning as "rational decision-making," they also moved towards definitions of their own. Many of them saw planning as a process by which social change might be directed —a less "heroic" term might have been *guided*—towards some set of "rational" objectives. During one particular seminar, heated debate ensued on the question whether planning was *necessarily* oriented towards the achievement of specific goals. I argued strongly for the affirmative position against a formidable opposition led by a coalition of my fellow students. I no longer remember the outcome; I do know that I would be more tolerant of the opposing view today. Planning is not merely concerned with the efficient instrumentation of objectives; it is also a process by which society may discover its future.

Planning as Social Process

The first job I accepted after receiving my master's degree was with the Division of Regional Studies of the Tennessee Valley Authority (TVA). From that bleak day in 1952 when I arrived in Knoxville, Tennessee, I found that the TVA was a very different enterprise from what I had imagined it. Instead of a free-swinging agency devoted to the betterment of life in a backward region, it was a tired bureaucracy fighting for its existence, more concerned with saving its budget from a hostile administration in Washington than with innovative action. On a more technical issue, I was surprised that the agency did not have, and, for that matter, had not *ever* had a comprehensive plan for the development of the region's economy. I diligently searched its library for any evidence of an overall statement of developmental policies and objectives, but found nothing except some early statements of euphoria and technical projections of future electric power requirements in the region. To a planner who had been taught that his principal skill lay in the preparation of a comprehensive plan, the absence of one in what was universally regarded as the country's foremost planning agency was a shocking discovery.

With my Chicago experience still freshly in mind, I wrote my first article on planning theory.[8] It turned out to be a rather philosophical essay; nevertheless, a number of themes emerged that are more fully developed in the present volume: the identification of planning with the guidance of change in society; the recognition of the time-binding character of planning; and the view of planning as a social process.

It would appear, then, that planning cannot be concerned solely with economizing, but must also be engaged in creating the kind of future we wish to bring into

existence. Conceived in its broadest terms, planning involves designing the future of a community over time, thus
giving it some rational, meaningful pattern, and the shaping of its history to the extent that control over environmental factors permits. . . . Planning puts within reach of
man the tools for transforming his environment, even himself. It also puts him face to face with questions of ultimate
value.[9]

This was a strong ideological position to take. Following
Tugwell's lead, I treated community as an aggregate of
people holding shared beliefs and values. Planning was
identified with a creative and transforming function in community. The future still appeared as an object capable of
being designed by a central intelligence. Planning, therefore, implied a commitment to the unfolding of reason in
history as embodied in the concrete realization of organized
actions. There was even a faint hint that planning might
produce a change in man himself—an idea taken from Karl
Mannheim and the subject of the final chapter here.

My work with the TVA taught me how planning, exer-
cised through the medium of formal organizations, comes to
depend on the internal dynamics of the bureaucratic process. The early years of the agency had, indeed, been heady
with the excitement of innovative undertakings; in its late
maturity, however, the agency appeared to be most concerned with maintaining itself.

During the early stages of a planning agency we usually
encounter an air of spirited enthusiasm, of experiment
and innovation. Imaginative, creative people are recruited
into the ranks of the organization. It appeals to them, for
it holds the promise of receptiveness to new ideas. The
grooves are not yet cut. Purposes are still fluid, waiting to
be shaped. . . . In time, the agency will become less and
less flexible. It will develop an ideology drawn from its
own experience and buttressed by the need to defend

itself against its enemies. . . . Self-preservation will become its primary aim, and security will be found in its past record of success. . . . As the agency develops its own traditions and habits of procedure, a tight network of internal and personal relationships becomes built up. Since this network may be dislocated by innovations, it constitutes an automatic defense against them. Moreover, the agency will start to look to certain "outside" interests for political support. To keep this support, it must try not to alienate its friends by pursuing a course that might run counter to their interests. In brief, the agency will become less capable of dreaming big dreams, of exploring new solutions, and of influencing the wants of people in the community where the "poverty of aspirations" limits the horizon of what is thought to be possible.[10]

The utopian thrust of planning thus runs counter to the inherent conservatism of mature bureaucracies. To maintain this thrust, I argued, planning may have to be taken outside the constraining framework of bureaucratic organizations.

To be truly successful, planning must become a way of life, a way of feeling, thinking, and acting on all levels of the social process. . . . In the broadest sense, a planning community is a community where thought at the level of planning becomes second nature to every member. It remains a pluralistic community in that it allows full freedom of expression and the pursuit of individual goals within the framework permitted by the continuing interest of the whole.[11]

This was the first glimmering of a learning society, which is more fully described in Chapter 8. It also represented my first explicit break with Tugwell's advocacy of a central intelligence for societal guidance. The article stressed the non-bureaucratic aspects of planning, a theme that was to be more fully developed after I had left America for my first overseas assignment.

Thought at the Level of Planning

I arrived in Brazil in the fall of 1955, initially to teach a planning course in Belém, the economic capital of Amazonia. Here planning carried few of the negative connotations it had acquired in the United States. On the contrary, because it was made equal with *development,* a concept with strong positive connotations, planning was extolled as the universal solution for the problems of economic backwardness.

The article that resulted from this encounter was the Introduction to a special issue of UNESCO's *International Social Science Journal* on "The Study and Practice of Planning."[12] The lead paragraph I wrote for the issue set the theme for the discussion that followed.

> For perhaps two decades the great debate about planning has raged. Now it is over. The question has been resolved. The great protagonists—Friedrich von Hayek, Ludwig van Mises, Karl Mannheim, Barbara Wootton, Rexford G. Tugwell—are silent. The field has been taken over by other men. We no longer ask: is planning possible? Can planning be reconciled with a democratic ideology? But: how may planning practice be improved? The problem of planning has become a problem of procedure and method.[13]

This took planning out of the realm of hothouse polemics into the cooler regions of practice. I wrote:

> Planning . . . reflects the fact that we live today in an age of analysis in which the ancient traditions that gave meaning and significance to our lives have been destroyed, and science has become the chosen road to knowledge and to truth. . . .[14]

This shift enables us to look at planning dispassionately and to analyze it minutely as an activity by which man in society endeavors to gain mastery over himself and to shape his collective future consciously by power of his reason.[15]

Despite its disclaimer, this was a strongly ideological statement, the effect of which was to shift the argument from a narrow conception of rationality—the old decision-making scheme of Simon and Banfield—to the broader, if more ambiguous, concept of reason. Reason was now advanced as the "ultimate weapon" against the apparent randomness of historical events and as a substitute for traditions that could no longer serve as a true guide to action.[16]

The article's major contribution, however, was to elaborate an earlier intuition that planning might best be thought of in terms of its unique *approach* to problem solving. Actually, I had borrowed this idea from Mannheim, who had discussed "thought at the level of planning" as the coming stage of historical evolution.

Provisionally, I named seven modes of thought that, I believed, distinguished planners: scientific objectivity, analysis, synthesis, projection, experiment, utopian constructs, and aesthetic vision.[17] This formulation complemented my TVA discovery that planning might indeed be possible without plan making: "The exercise of planning thought is infinitely more important than a neatly published book entitled: *Six Year Plan*. If we agree to accept this view, planning appears as flexible and sensitive an instrument as reason or thought itself, adaptable to any situation, capable of dealing with any contingency that may arise."[18]

This passage was followed by a strong defense of what, following Perloff, I called framework planning—the formulation of guidelines for more detailed and explicit program development and budgeting. Clearly, I was beginning to move toward a more realistic assessment of the planning process.

> The main elements of planning are two: forethought and reason. Through the use of both, the future is made relevant to the present; it imposes itself upon the present as an imperious demand for action. In the course of planning, the social good becomes defined, although its exact nature may change with changing circumstances. Present decisions lead to actions, and planning continues to arrive at ever new decisions by means of an evaluation of the effects of effort and a continuous assessment of the available resources, conditions, and ends-in-view. Thus, the cycle of planning is closed, while society moves from situation to situation along a path of rational action.[19]

I had not yet come to grips with the question of how decisions are translated into actions. On the other hand, I now had a description of the process view of planning in which goals and means are continuously adjusted to each other "along a path of rational action." Only much later did I make the connection of this path with the process of learning.

Subsequently, I dealt with some of the limitations on the workings of reason in history. First, I discussed limitations that I took to be conditions of, rather than obstacles to, planning, such as tradition, uncertainty, and individual values. All three, I thought, were compatible with the application of reason to problem situations. More serious constraints followed: the difficulty of reaching agreement on ends in a pluralistic society (no longer Tugwell's organic community), the orientation of the political process to the short run, and political ideology. Finally, I thought I saw an inherent contradiction between planning and revolution. Revolutions are events of pure action. Thought at the level of planning had little to contribute until *after* the revolution had been accomplished. This dilemma is more fully stated in Chapter 5.

The End of Ideology

Four more years would pass before I tried my hand at yet another attempt to lay out a theoretical structure for planning. Meanwhile, I had served for a period in Korea and was now back in America, teaching regional planning at the Massachusetts Institute of Technology. The essay I wrote there in 1960 (published six years later in a Canadian planning journal) bore the title "Planning as a Vocation."[20] It represented a kind of summing up of my thinking and at the same time, yet another step in the direction of a more realistic appreciation of planning. I started by differentiating several categories of planning, drawing a major distinction between means-oriented and ends-oriented planning—a distinction whose importance had been stressed by Karl Mannheim. I regarded the former as a purely technical function, while the latter would establish an area of independent action for the planner in "the twilight zone which separates the politician from the bureaucrat."[21]

The article also contained a major effort to debunk the traditional ideology of planning. This section was personally painful to write, as it meant parting with many ideas to which I had become deeply attached. I described the ideology in terms of the planner's adherence to utopian thinking, his norm-setting role, his espousal of rationality as a form of thinking superior to feelings and intuition, his belief in the value of order, and his secret dream of power by which ideas would be translated into practice.[22] I then set out systematically to undercut this ideological position by contrasting it with the actual practice of planning.

Planning practice is chiefly concerned with incremental decisions and planners generally avoid taking the long view.

. . . Planning is conservative, and planners are ordinary
bureaucrats who crave, as much as any official does, the
security of a career, the promise of regular advancement,
and the prospect of eventual pension. . . . Political action
is usually opportunistic in its design. It takes account of
the public interest only to the minimum extent required
for the maintenance of the organization or where the objectives are simple, clear, and widely shared. . . . Planning
that is functionally rational with respect to means for given
ends is infinitely more prevalent. . . . It can scarcely be
claimed that planning in organizations is noteworthy for
its scientific approach. . . . From the perspective of a planning office, the view that planning is an instrument for
bringing the historical development of man under the guide
and influence of rationally formulated and rationally chosen
goals appears sheer nonsense. . . . The technical planner is
compelled to view most of reality, including potential reality,
as 'given'—he cannot hope to change it even if he would. He
consequently sees himself as occupying a rather modest
position in the organizational hierarchy, unable and certainly disinclined to move human destinies and to make
the really "big" decisions.[23]

This bottoms-up view of planning led to the statement
that "planning as a vocation has been reduced to the dimensions of a job." Only one way seemed to be left for rescuing
it as a personal calling—shifting the focus from planning as
an activity of professional planners to planning as a process
of social systems, the concern of every man.

A planning society is one in which planning belongs to
the very essence or structure of its thought processes. In
such a society, only certain elements of planning would
be centralized; most planning would be done by small
fragmented decision-making units which are dispersed
throughout the social body. . . .
Under these conditions, it might well be asked whether
anything remains of planning as a vocation, whether the

separate identity of planning is not simply being swallowed up. The question cannot be answered without some ambivalence. . . . The calling of planning no longer derives from an ideology which is untenable in a realistic assessment of the possibilities of planning, but from a sense of participation in the self-articulation of a social system. . . . It is the social enterprise which is now capable of giving to the individual a sense of self-transcending purpose. The planner whose efforts strike to the very heart of the social enterprise . . . will find a justification of his work and a call to responsibility in the enterprise itself. The calling of his work will be found in the seriousness with which he goes about the tasks which lie ahead.[24]

Toward an Empirical Approach

During the preparation of "Planning as a Vocation," I had the good fortune to meet Bertram Gross, who was then a visiting professor at the Harvard Business School. It was Gross who encouraged me to look at planning with a naked eye. About to organize a group of scholars who would study national planning in a number of countries, he persuaded me, since I was already doing some work in Venezuela, to prepare a monograph on that country.

Gross's approach to planning was to look at the empirical evidence. He wanted to study planning not as it ought to be, but as it *is*. He thought that planning would be effective primarily during periods of severe crisis. As a way of dealing with crisis, planning was difficult to distinguish from dynamic administration. He considered the mobilization of resources as important a job for planners as determining their best use. Though he regarded planning as a central activity of governments, he also insisted that its powers were in fact divided among a number of central guidance institutions; over time and with changes in attention to specific issues, the weight of power within this set of institutions might shift, resulting in different policy approaches. The roles of central guidance and, therefore, also of planning, included general leadership, financial management, critical problem roles, special staff roles (analysis of trends, goals, policy, and major projects), and general staff roles such as communication, bargaining, performance evaluation, and expediting. Gross's fertile and inventive mind conjured up a vision that was beginning to resemble something that might be found in the real world. Unlike Banfield, he did not seek the holy grail of rational decision-making.[25]

My Venezuela study was prepared in 1963–64.[26] In addition to providing important historical materials, it led me to formulate a number of general propositions about the origins of planning under conditions of crisis and the uses of planning in the management of change:

> The crisis of frustration [in Venezuela] had two main aspects: the first was of a short-range nature and concerned the economic depression that had settled upon the country in 1958; the second involved more long-term considerations. The depression was tangible and unavoidable.
>
> Income had ceased to grow, unemployment was spreading, capital was being expatriated in huge amounts, the so-called Emergency Plan was only a stop-gap measure that had no lasting effects. The economy stagnated four long years. Yet somehow the belief in planning was not shattered. On the contrary, its prestige was enhanced each year. . . .
>
> The second aspect of the crisis related to the prospects of reaching the long-term goals which were in currency and about which there seemed little basic disagreement. But the depression, prolonged as it was over a period of years, put their attainment in doubt. At any rate, they were no longer seen as the inevitable future toward which the country would evolve. The immense structural problems of the economy would have to be tackled in a co-

ordinated fashion, with priorities carefully worked out. This
clearly called for a kind of technical expertise that only
planning could provide. Planning and development became irrevocably linked. As the crisis deepened, it also
strengthened adherence to the development ideology as
whose champion the new middle class leadership had proclaimed itself.

And so, paradoxically, national planning created its own
conditions for survival. Intended as a crisis-relieving instrument, it also dramatized in "facts and figures" the continuing
gap between aspirations and current conditions. But in this
it succeeded only in stirring the crisis of frustration still
further.

The birth of national planning in Venezuela under conditions of crisis had two immediate consequences. First, it
put a high premium on its effectiveness. At the very
least, this meant that government was willing to give active
support to the establishment of a workable planning process
and would make use of it in ways that seemed politically opportune. Second, it meant that short-term problems would be given priority attention. Long-range speculation on alternative goal possibilities is a luxury which
planners can indulge only when there are no problems of
great urgency to be met or when planners forgo whatever
chances they may have found for influencing major decisions. A second paradox of planning, therefore, is this:
When planning is least needed—as under conditions of
relative calm and stability—it can afford to be "rational";
but when level-headed rationality is desperately wanted—
as under pressure of an extreme crisis—planning is given
the least scope for exercising its manifest function. More
than ever, it becomes then an extension of politics, and
planners find themselves rushing madly about putting out
fires wherever they can. . . .

This raises an interesting issue for planning theory. If the
paradox stated holds true, planning typically occurs—and
receives political backing—under conditions of crisis. The
rationality of planning practice must therefore be a rationality adapted to its conditions: it must sacrifice comprehen-

siveness to the urgency of overcoming specific bottlenecks; it must be more problem- than goal-oriented; it must be piecemeal and fragmented rather than coordinative.[27]

This kind of thinking led to a distinction between the manifest and latent functions of planning. By the former I meant both the pattern of expected performance and the intended contributions of planning to a social project such as economic development, city building, or industrial production. The second described the unintended, more subtle contributions of planning to the social order.

From 1958 to 1964, national planning in Venezuela had scored primarily in five areas: strengthening the presidency; improving the political process; creating a development society; reducing social conflict; and mobilizing national resources. It therefore looked very different from what normative theory had led me to expect. The changes wrought through the latent functioning of planning were much greater than those intentionally brought about. From this I concluded that planning theory would have to be completely reconstituted on an empirical foundation. Gross's encouragement to look at planning without preconception had managed to free my inquiry for explorations along entirely new lines.

Subsequently, Gross organized a conference on national planning research at Minnowbrook in the Adirondacks. In my paper for this conference, I expanded on ideas that had come to me with particular force during my research in Venezuela.[28] The social environment, I argued, would give rise to a style of planning that was adapted to the conditions through which it had to work.

To arrive at this conclusion, I collapsed the well-known decision model of planning with its tripartite scheme of *analysis, plan,* and *action* into a two-part model in which designing the plan disappeared as a separate step, leaving analysis and action as the two principal components of a single process. As my Venezuelan study had shown, the role of the plan was only incidental to effective planning. Coping successfully with the future was the new objective; the patterning of the relevant information flows became central to the art of planning, which was no longer to be separated from action.

Innovative Planning

The next major advance in my thinking occurred when I left M.I.T. in 1965 to take a position with a Ford Foundation-sponsored project in Chile. As a planning advisor, I found myself engaged in activities I had not heretofore associated with the practice of planning. Believing that this required a redefinition of what planning meant, I drew a basic distinction between *allocative* and *innovative* forms of planning.[29] The former was concerned with the distribution of limited resources among competing users; the latter with producing a structural change in a system of societal relations. This distinction is more fully elaborated in Chapter 4.

My earlier ideas were yielding to a more flexible model. I no longer viewed planners as mediators between politicians and bureaucrats, but as *members of an action-team*. The similarity of this idea to that of the task-oriented working groups described in Chapter 8 is evident. Action-teams are temporary coalitions organized for a specific purpose. Their function is not to co-ordinate but to innovate. Although allocative planning is still necessary, the major thrust in planning the non-routine activities of society should be made by innovative planning groups.

These views received a more complete and formal statement in the next article I wrote.[30] I was still concerned with evolving an adequate vocabulary for discussing planning. Whereas my earlier efforts had been largely directed toward formulating a normative theory of planning—how planning *should* be done—I now came around to Bertram Gross's view and talked of a "positive theory of guided system change."[31] This new empiricism would lead to, among other things, a systematic analysis of planning pathologies and, ultimately, I hoped, to a prescriptive theory. Chapter 3 draws heavily on this article.

Societal Guidance and Transactive Planning

The problem of implementing planning was the focus of my next paper, which was written under the impact of the multiple crises then raging in American society. Though I was living on borrowed information thousands of miles from the center of the crisis, I sensed that a major social transformation was in the making; there would be no return to the comfortable pre-crisis days. At about the same time, in 1968, I read Amitai Etzioni's *The Active Society*,[32] which presented a normative model for the renewal of society. Among Etzioni's major contributions was his lucid formulation of a concept of societal guidance. Both his vocabulary and his treatment of the topic suggested links to Bertram Gross's concept of central guidance and to my own thinking concerning the role of innovative planning. Now was the time, I felt, for a radical reconceptualization of planning. The inherited modes of planning had not produced spectacular results. The leading alternative to the new planning style, the classical decision-model, was ready for an unlamented burial.

The idea that planning and implementation are two distinct and separable activities dies hard. Planning, it is said, leads to the formulation of plans; implementation is concerned with carrying them out. The intervening critical step is a decision. Planners prepare the plans and propose them to the relevant deciders who, after due deliberation, choose the alternative preferred by them and take measures that will make their choice effective. If plans fail to be implemented, it is because the deciders ignored the proposals made to them, preferring their own counsel. . . . The widespread notion that plans *ought* to get accepted and that, when they are not, the failure is one of communication, rests on the technocratic fallacy that planners' proposals are inherently superior to actions that result from the un-aided decisions of non-planners. . . . But perhaps the real problem resides elsewhere. If the focus of planning is shifted from decisions to actions, it is possible to assert that any action that is deliberate is also to a certain degree planned. The problem is no longer how to make decisions more "rational," but how to improve the *quality of the action*.[33]

This declaration was followed by a definition of planning to which I still subscribe: *Planning refers to the application of a scientific and technical intelligence to organized actions.* At stake is the quality of the action, which is far from identical with the rationality of the underlying decision process. I qualified this definition by saying that a scientific-technical intelligence applied to action would have to be normative, analytical, future-oriented, and strategic—a faint echo of my earlier preoccupation with "thought at the level of planning." But here the emphasis was less on mental processes than on the *linkages* between thought and action.

The model I had formulated at the Minnowbrook conference several years before was restated. It would fuse "action and planning into a single operation so that the conceptual distinctions of planning-decision-implementation-recycling are washed out. . . . An action will include deliberation and choice as pervasive, on-going activities, but these are not to be identified as distinctive phases *prior* to action: they are inseparably a part of it."[34]

A new concept was introduced with the idea of a *societal guidance system.*

It would be wrong to regard societal action as the exclusive responsibility of a centralized agency. Typically, it involves many actors—individual or organized—performing many roles, some of which are related in complex ways to each other, while others are performed in relative isolation. Each of these roles has a potential but limited capacity for influencing the course of societal change. This will be called its capacity for *societal guidance*. . . . Roles for societal guidance are most frequently embodied in organizations that are linked to each other in a distinctive pattern; this pattern may be called the *guidance system* of a society.[35]

These ideas are further elaborated in Chapter 6.[36]

The same article also grappled with the problem of how to educate the "new" planner whose role would have to be consonant with the action-planning model. I was already contemplating moving to the new Urban Planning Program at UCLA, and the question of how to educate young planners for the changing circumstances of American life was very much on my mind.

Successful planning, I argued, would depend in large measure on the planner's skill in managing interpersonal relations. The qualities he would have to develop included a heightened knowledge of the self; an increased capacity for learning; special skills in the use of symbolic materials, particularly in relating symbols to reality; a heightened capacity for empathy; an ability to live with conflict; and an understanding of the dynamics of power and the art of getting things done. Finally,

. . . if the planner enters the realm of action, his word must be responsible. He is no longer setting forth alternatives (as under the old decision-scheme), but advocating points of view that will affect the lives and well-being of others. His word is that of a professional, and his professional ethics must therefore include an injunction against irresponsibility. This is a question of conscience that each planner must settle for himself. . . . The results of societal action are manifold. But difficulty of measurement should not be taken as a convenient escape from personal responsibility.[37]

This list, it turned out, foreshadowed a theory of transactive planning, a full statement of which was not possible until later (see Chapters 7 and 8). Interestingly, my ideas about transactive planning did not come from the experience of an advocacy planner working in American city ghettos, but from my encounters with the realities of technical assistance abroad.[38]

Basic to the transactive relationship between planner and client, which I now saw as crucial to establishing effective links between knowledge and organized action, was a process of mutual learning. The gist of this new process, completely at odds with traditional professional behavior, was stated in a paper on comprehensive planning I wrote shortly after arriving in Los Angeles in 1969.[39]

With the writing of this paper, all the major themes with which this book is concerned had been stated. The decision and action models of planning, the forms and styles of planning, the social context of planning, the uses of the future in the present, societal guidance and innovative planning, the style and method of transactive planning, the learning society and its organization, and the problem of educating man for active participation in the new society —these form the substance of the chapters that follow. They are preceded by a special chapter devoted to Karl Mannheim, who in his writings clearly identified the major issues of societal guidance long before anyone else.[40]

CHAPTER 2

PRECURSOR: KARL MANNHEIM

To discover the origins of contemporary thinking about societal guidance, we have to turn to the writings of Karl Mannheim. An important German sociologist, Mannheim is known primarily for his original contributions to the sociology of knowledge. His equally pathbreaking explorations into the processes of societal guidance have passed almost unnoticed.[1] Just as he was about to be named UNESCO's first Director for Europe shortly after World War II, Mannheim died in exile, in London, leaving few followers. Yet he posed some of the critical issues with which the present study is concerned.[2]

The Sociology of Knowledge

The sociology of knowledge provided the springboard for Mannheim's leap into the field of societal guidance and planning.[3] Mannheim was the first sociologist seriously to pose the question of the relationship of thinking to action, and he did so in a fundamental, radical way. In *Ideology and Utopia*, his first major study, he showed how ways of perceiving and forms of thinking derive from the position a person occupies in the social structure, an expanded version of Karl Marx's idea that the ownership of the means of production is the determining factor in the political ideology of the bourgeoisie and therefore accounts for its behavior. Because of his exclusive concern with property relations, Marx limited his observation to a single social class and failed to appreciate the multiplicity of structural positions existing in society, some of which have no relation to property or the production process. Any of these positions may influence the ways those who occupy it look at and respond to the world. Mannheim extended Marx's principle to include all social groups but one, an exception to which I shall return later.

The sociology of knowledge has been criticized for its apparent inability to trace, without substantial ambiguity, the social origins of intellectual products such as philosophies, political ideologies, and novels. I am not concerned with these criticisms here, however; I will concentrate instead on Mannheim's intellectual development, from his early explorations in *Wissenssoziologie* to some of his most daring theorizing about the nature and processes of societal guidance.

The basic idea of the sociology of knowledge is easy to grasp. I will illustrate it by sketching the "perspectivism" of four social groups—the European landed gentry, the American business community, the Central European industrial worker, and the American university student. The examples are mine, not Mannheim's, and are intended as general pictures, not as empirically valid descriptions of any particular set of historical facts.

1. Once powerful and prosperous lords of a feudal order, the remnants of which may still be found in isolated regions of southern Europe and Latin America, the *landed gentry* saw the world primarily in terms of their belief in a natural hierarchy of social relationships. Sanctioned by church and state, this order was regarded as divinely ordained. As members of the ruling class, the gentry harbored,

in addition, a mystical belief in the power of the land to influence man's destiny. This belief in a fateful relationship —which endowed the gentry with certain mystical powers that set them apart from the common run of mankind— imposed on them an obligation of stewardship towards the land. The gentry's virtues were the ancient ones of piety, personal honor, and generosity. In government, they defended the rule of an hereditary elite. In political life, they were intensely conservative. In matters of education, they showed a predilection for humanistic studies and for the traditional professions of military science and the clergy.

2. The ethos of the *American business community*, as it evolved during the nineteenth century, was rooted in quite different social conditions. Highly urbanized, this community of interests lacked the vital security of landed estates passed on within the family from generation to generation. Its virtues, therefore, stressed hard work and a frugal style of living, toward the end of amassing some wealth and property. Its members, driven by anxiety for individual achievement, favored an allocation of material rewards according to the product of each man's labor. The distribution of income they believed to be determined by a competitive market that operated fairly within a framework of impersonal rules. Those who failed in this game remained poor but had only themselves to blame. Since the rules applied equally to everyone, a failure to score had to be taken as a sign of personal inadequacy. The outlook of the American business community was secular and pragmatic. The man of business subscribed to the idea that history tells essentially the story of mankind's progress, and he thought of society as, in principle, perfectible. Ideas of fate and destiny—so congenial to the mind of the landed gentry—were altogether foreign to his thinking. In government, he favored a liberal-democratic system capable of guaranteeing the personal freedoms necessary for individual achievement and the observance of the rules of competition. In education, he in-

clined toward the professions "useful" in furthering material progress, such as engineering and science.

3. Contemporaneously with the rise of the American business ethos, *industrial workers* in Central Europe acquired a distinctive outlook that reflected, above all, their dependence on a market in which each man had to sell his labor for a going wage. In contrast to the familism of the landed gentry and the atomistic individualism of the American business community, spokesmen for the industrial workers of Central Europe advocated a social order in which all members would share equally in the fruits of material progress. Glorifying manual labor (but expressing a yearning for more leisure and more opportunity to exercise "higher" mental faculties), they proclaimed human needs as the just criterion of material reward. Obstacles to the realization of an egalitarian order would have to be removed as the first condition of man's liberation from his entrapment in the marketplace. The surplus product of his labor, augmented by means of improvements in the organization of work and technological innovations, might then be used to serve the interests of everyone in the society instead of helping to enrich the few who, by controlling the instruments of production, were able to expropriate this surplus for their own enjoyment.

4. *University students*—especially in present-day America but in other countries as well—have still another perspective on the world. Unencumbered by social responsibilities and as yet imperfectly integrated into society, they are able to extol the absolute values of freedom, love, equality, and justice and to hold them up as standards for judging a world where compromises between freedom and necessity are unavoidable. Prepared to step out beyond the confines of the university, they are ready to champion causes that look towards radical change, and to put their youth on the line in demonstrations and other forms of political

activism to make the world conform to the purity of their vision.

According to the sociology of knowledge, the intellectual products and behavior of each social group reflect those partial and conflicting perspectives on the world in which social position and self-interest are fused with ways of knowing and acting. A single truth does not exist.

Each group's experience confirms it in its outlook. In many Latin American countries, for example, homeless working-class families frequently organize "invasions" of vacant land along the fringes of cities to build up new, spontaneous communities. Because they occur outside the normal market framework, these seizures are condemned by the national bourgeoisie as contrary to the prevailing "rules of the game" and, therefore, illegal. Police are mobilized and sent out to the *poblaciónes* to evict the squatters. Students, persuaded that the workers' cause is just, take to the streets to shout their outrage at injustice and are promptly chased by riot squads called in to restore respect for the social order. Such confrontations, which often lead to bloodshed, tend to engender further demonstrations. In due course, some students become sufficiently radicalized to join revolutionary movements whose aim is to destroy the foundations of a moral order that seems to them unjust and to replace it with a new society more generous and true than any they have known.

Events such as these make headlines in the daily press. They are conflicts caused by the mutual incomprehensions of different social groups.

To Mannheim, the connections between perspectives and social positions—the study of which forms the subject matter of the sociology of knowledge—were part of a fundamental explanation of how social changes come about and history is made. Further to clarify these connections, Mannheim distinguished between *ideological* and *utopian* forms of thought. The former is concerned with the justification of

an existing set of social relationships. Brought together in systematic form, such justifications constitute the basic ideology of those who occupy the seats of power: natural law and hereditary rule for the gentry, free enterprise and majority vote for the urban bourgeoisie. Utopian thinking, on the other hand, transcends the *status quo* at every point. It reaches out into a future in which social patterns are radically transformed. In the examples above, students and workers hold views in contradiction to the established order; each group projects a future that is at odds with existing society.

The principal distinctions between ideological and utopian thinking may be shown in schematic form:

Ideology	*Utopia*
interpretation of what is in terms of the present	interpretation of what is in terms of a projected future
justification of the *status quo*	justification of radical change
held by dominant classes	held by dependent classes
used as an instrument of social oppression by the elites in power	used as an instrument of fundamental reform or revolution by militant counter-elites

It was Mannheim's conviction that these contrasting perspectives were bound to clash. Not only would utopian thought be thrown against the citadels of ideology, but alternative ideologies and utopian systems would compete among themselves for domination. Mannheim's concern, however, was not with the correctness of the contending views, but with the partial and limited character of each. Correct insight into the nature of social relationships, he believed, was impossible for anyone firmly anchored in the social structure. It might be recovered only in a vision that

would encompass the multiple interrelationships of society
in a grand, impartial sweep.

But if everyone necessarily occupies a definite position in
society, is not the urge to see things whole bound to be
frustrated? This possibility was unacceptable to Mannheim.
Writing in the middle thirties, he saw Europe tearing itself
apart in ideological conflict. Between the totalitarian orders
of fascism and communism, on the one hand, and an increasingly ineffective democratic liberalism, on the other,
might there not be a Third Way, capable of restoring a
measure of hope to a continent about to destroy itself
in a general war? Everything seemed to depend on whether
the logic of the sociology of knowledge might allow for an
exception to the fateful partialities of socially determined
perspectives.

Only one group appeared to Mannheim to be sufficiently
detached from the existing social order. Its members lived
on the margins of society, discussing, evaluating, criticiz-
ing, writing. Beholden to no one, they were governed by
a deep commitment to ideas, versed in many disciplines
and subjects, and thus uniquely qualified, he thought, to
look at societal relations without bias. In his transition
from the sociology of knowledge to planning, Mannheim
projected his hopes upon the "free-floating" intelligentsia.
The intellectuals, he claimed, had little or no stake in
the existing order. They were consequently able to swing
freely into the realms of utopia, transcending present reality
and its sustaining systems of belief. On the basis of a
radical critique of the present, they would be able to invent
new futures. Some intellectuals, of course, might choose to
work for the established powers, becoming clerks, in Julien
Benda's cutting phrase. But the true intellectual was loyal
to ideas, and he could not be bought.

This, of course, was pleasant fiction disguised in scientific
jargon, but it permitted Mannheim to formulate some of
his most powerful ideas concerning the nature of guidance

processes. The ability to see things whole was, for him, an essential condition for the survival of society.

Two Forms of Rationality

The Europe of Mannheim's time had entered upon what he called the stage of *fundamental democratization*, chiefly characterized by a decline in the hierarchical standards of value that had provided norms for conduct in the past. Now everyone was entitled to be heard on an issue, and every voice claimed to be equal, regardless of the depth of insight and understanding. This reduction of socio-cultural distinctions had augmented the already prevailing disorder and permitted unscrupulous dictators to emerge as self-proclaimed saviors of society. Through a cunning combination of manipulated mass opinion and brute force, they had managed to destroy the very bases of the democracy they claimed to represent. For true democracy cannot be sustained on massive ignorance posing as knowledge. Where this occurs, the rational element in democracy, so necessary to its survival, gives way to irrational forces and dictatorial forms of social management in which power becomes increasingly centralized in the hands of the state. Mannheim had witnessed the burning of books in Nazi Germany and had seen some of the best minds of Europe perish in concentration camps or political exile.

The other major source of the ominous growth of irrational forces Mannheim located in the growing interdependence of modern social systems. This was reflected in the rising demand for experts in nearly every field of human endeavor. Specialized knowledge was required to make the system work efficiently and to deliver its products on schedule. But the price of greater efficiency was a loss of intelligent insight into complexity itself. More and more people seemed to know less and less, errors multiplied, and national economies were speeding down the track to disaster. The

Great Depression was on; World War II was looming on the horizon.

Mannheim believed that the recovery of a holistic view through planning would lead to greater sanity and order. But if planning signified the rational mastery of the irrational, what meaning might be attributed to rationality? This was a crucial question.

Following Max Weber, Mannheim distinguished two forms of rational thinking. *Functional* rationality, or the efficient relation of means to given ends, was essentially the province of the expert. The expert, say, the engineer, always worked in accordance with his client's wishes. He was skilled in designing solutions for problems given to him; it was not his business to question them. Efficiency was for him a kind of religion.

The second form, or *substantial* rationality, Mannheim defined as intelligent insight into the behavior of complex social systems. This form of thinking might lead to an understanding of the workings of the social system both as a whole, and in its multiple meanings and ambiguities, to the discovery of the forces underlying its dynamic behavior, and to a grasp of its direction. Substantial rationality was concerned with the ends of action, in the same way that functional rationality was focused on the means. Mannheim argued that it takes a knowledge of the total situation to decide, for instance, whether to use a bomb to blast an entire city or, indeed, whether a bomb of such frightening power should be built at all. The experts merely carry out their jobs. One would invent the bomb, another build it, a third carry it aloft, and a fourth drop it, all without questioning the larger implications of their assignments. Each would act cleanly and efficiently, some buttons would be pressed, and a hundred thousand human beings would be pulverized into eternity. Functional rationality, argued Mannheim, was needed to conduct the business of society; but by itself, it could lead only to chaos and destruction.

Although societal guidance had to employ both forms of rationality, its greatest need was for "intelligent insight" into the workings of the social system.

By thus relating the concept of rationality to processes of societal guidance, Mannheim set the terms in which the theory of planning was to be discussed for an entire generation. His cue was taken up especially in the United States, where the concept of functional rationality enjoyed great popularity. During the 1950s, the basic ends of American society were still largely unquestioned, and the efficiency of means seemed to be the only relevant criterion for decision. Or perhaps America was suffering from a surfeit of clerks who lacked the intellectual freedom to explore utopian futures. At any rate, studies in the rationality of choice enjoyed a great vogue. But the emphasis on functional rationality narrowed the discussion to the point of banality. The real issue, as Mannheim saw it, was how the course of change in a society might be guided in accordance with intelligent insights into its patterned complexities.

The Principia Media of Society

In enlarging upon this point, Mannheim engaged in another bit of myth making. The relationship of thought to action, he claimed, had passed through three historical stages. The first was the stage of *chance discovery*, where man acquired new knowledge largely by accident and adapted it pragmatically to his needs. The second stage was that of *invention*, during which effort was directed towards partial ends, innovation became institutionalized as a process, and functionally rational behavior predominated. The third stage, which Mannheim believed about to begin, was that of *planning*, where "intelligent insight" into the complexities of social relationships would gain mastery over society's irrational impulses.

Empirical evidence for this succession of stages was weak; the third stage, in any event, was still in the realm of prophecy. But this vision permitted Mannheim to go on to his next major question, how thought at the level of planning might become effective in society. Given society's immense complexity, how should planners guide the course of its development towards utopian futures?

We come here to one of Mannheim's keenest insights. He proposed that the planner-intellectual probe deeply into the currents of social change until he came upon the *principia media* of society. This new concept was difficult to explain at a time when sociologists were beholden to organic metaphors. Today, we might speak of the *principia media* as developmental processes that lead to structural change within society.

Recent findings of systems science confirm Mannheim's basic intuition. Complex systems, according to Jay W. Forrester, are remarkably insensitive to changes in many of their parameters. But they also have a high sensitivity to changes in a *few* parameters and to *some* changes in structure. These key points for policy intervention are not usually self-evident; they must be discovered through laborious study and analysis.[4]

Mannheim's *principia media* are similar to Forrester's "strategic" system parameters. Although they cannot always be controlled by instruments of public policy, they offer an excellent opening for such intervention, for even small changes in the *principia media* may produce consequences with far-reaching effects upon the structural relations of a social system.

Two examples might help to clarify this concept. In the early nineteen-fifties, economists with the United Nations Economic Commission for Latin America thought they had detected in industrialization one of the emergent *principia media* of Latin American development. The correlation of increasing manufacture with economic and social progress in many Western nations had convinced them that the active promotion of the industrial sector in their own societies would result in similarly dramatic changes. Their studies were reinforced by countless articles and books written at the time in both the United States and Europe, as well as by the dramatic and apparently successful industrialization experience of the Soviet Union. The critical issue, it seemed to them, was how to accelerate production and employment in manufacturing. If this could be accomplished on a substantial scale, national development would be assured.

More recently, a number of social scientists and planners claim to have discovered in the urbanization processes of a society a yet more potent force for structural transformation. A suitably broad definition of urbanization would include the generation and geographic diffusion of innovations, the flows of controlling decisions among cities, internal migration, and the geographical pattern of investment flows. These urbanization processes affect the integration of national societies in critical ways. By acting upon them, national governments may, with an economy of means, effect decisive changes in the spatial arrangements of a society.

I cite these examples, in part, to demonstrate the non-trivial character of Mannheim's insight into the process of societal change. Claims to have discovered important *principia media* in the processes of industrialization and urbanization might turn out to be mistaken, but they are not statements of the obvious, nor are they lightly made. The discovery of the relevant *principia media* in any historical situation implies a major scientific undertaking.

Mannheim insisted that the essential had to be separated from the more accidental manifestations of the historical process. The guidance of societal change had to be grounded in a thorough understanding of its developmental laws. If it were possible to detect *principia media* in their nascent state, the future might be shaped according to a human purpose. But once they came to permeate the entire fabric of social life, opportunities for fundamental changes might no longer be available. Planners would then have to content themselves with making minor adjustments to a process over which they had no guiding influence. *Principia media* could never be reversed, he thought.

One is inclined to agree. If one can promptly seize the principles that operate in specific historical situations and subordinate them to a rational purpose, it might be possible to direct the overall process of societal change. On the other hand, history is more powerful than reason. Once a movement, such as urbanization, has been started, it cannot be turned back. It can be guided and controlled, however. Migration to cities, for example, can be accelerated or decelerated. With effort, migrants may be channeled to certain regions and distributed among cities of certain sizes, even though the structural relations of regions and cities to each other cannot be changed substantially except over long periods of time.

So much for Mannheim's principle of guided change. Its application to social policy proved a more recalcitrant task. Mannheim remained silent on the question of how the planner-intellectual could bring his knowledge and insights to bear effectively. Since planning was for him an alternate model of society, comparable to liberal democracy and fascism, perhaps this was an unimportant question. Mannheim was concerned with the systemic character of planning and the diffusion of planning ways of thinking throughout the society, rather than with concrete illustrations of how the planner might become effective.

Yet he was not unaware of the problem. Planners commanded no resources other than their knowledge and ability to learn more rapidly than others. How then should they proceed when their ideas were resisted by those whose interests they threatened?

It is interesting to note, in this connection, that Mannheim spent the war years living in England, where he came to admire a democratic system capable of putting up effective resistance to Nazism without itself debasing human liberties. He found in English democracy almost none of the corruptions and weaknesses of Weimar Germany and Daladier's Second Republic. While in London, Mannheim fell in with an influential group of Christian humanist thinkers that included, among others, T. S. Eliot, Joseph Oldham, and G. K. Chesterton. Intimate contact with these men over a period of years had profound consequences for his own thinking. He became urgently concerned not only with the question of "freedom under planning" but also with the possible role of education in the reconstruction of society.

Mannheim became persuaded that resistance to constructive change could be overcome only by a lengthy process of re-education. If a new man could be created—autonomous, capable of rapid learning, and responsible—a new society might be brought into being. The *principium medium* discovered by Mannheim in his London years was education!

Because it is not an essential part of my argument, I shall pass over his detailed discussion of educational planning and concentrate instead on Mannheim's theory of social controls. Later writers, such as Kurt Lewin, Robert Dahl, Charles Lindblom, and Amitai Etzioni have carried his ideas much further, but it might be useful at this point to return to Mannheim's basic contribution.

The Theory of Controls

Mannheim distinguished between *direct* controls, to which sanctions are attached and whose immediate, first-order consequences are intentional, and *indirect* controls, whose effect is to structure situations (environments) to which individual actions must be adapted. Economic planners, for instance, acting through the Federal Reserve System, may require banks to raise the rate of interest on capital borrowing. From the standpoint of the nation's banking institutions, this would be regarded as an instance of direct control. But once the interest rate had been changed, it would act as an indirect control on borrowers, who, responding to the new supply situation, could be expected to reduce their overall demand for credit.

Mannheim believed that planners should restrict the use of direct controls to those essential to their purposes and rely, to the greatest possible extent, on indirect controls to regulate the structural relations and developmental processes in the society. In this way, the limited powers of government could be applied with greater effectiveness; information required for planning would be held within manageable limits; and large areas of comparatively free choice could exist.

Mannheim's theory of controls not only implied a theory of systems behavior that by now has become widely accepted—see, for instance, the work of Jay W. Forrester referred to earlier—but also related to his idea of *principia media* as forces capable of inducing structural change in social systems. If complex social systems were, indeed, sensitive to changes in only a few of their parameters, then the points of effective intervention were largely defined by the *principia media* themselves. More precisely, one had to look for pressure points within the social system, where significant influence could be brought to bear. When direct controls were applied at these critical points, waves of consequences would be set off throughout the system. To the extent that these consequences could be predicted, planners might be able, with an economy of means, to guide the course of society's overall development.

Because indirect controls tend quickly to be accepted as part of a "normal" set of constraints on individual action, they are generally hidden from public view. We are not generally aware of them. Advocating their use to produce certain effects on collective behavior (e.g., to reduce the overall amount of credit available in the economy) might thus appear as a move to hand over manipulative powers to a small elite of technocrats. Moreover, because many second- and third-order consequences are unpredictable (or predictable only within very wide margins of error), every use of indirect controls is fraught with great risk. A much more certain and perhaps more honest way would be directly to control all actions that are believed essential to the aims pursued.

This seems to have been the preference of Soviet economic planners. By eliminating the price system as one of the most powerful instruments of indirect control in the economy, and substituting for it a system of "material balances" to plan the volume and quality of production, Soviet planners believed they had discovered a method for rapidly converting Russia's economic backwardness into socialist prosperity.[5]

They were right to the extent that material progress could indeed be induced by a method of direct physical controls. But as the Soviet economy grew in complexity, they were increasingly wrong about the relative efficiency of unrestricted intervention. During recent years, in fact, tentative moves have been made to reintroduce some forms of indirect control into the economy.

One of the least expected consequences of the extensive use of direct economic controls was the necessity it created for coercive measures in many related facets of life. To make the Soviet system work, jobs, location, housing, and consumption had all to be regulated according to a plan, and, as domestic criticism mounted, thought control had to be added.

Viewed from this vantage point, Mannheim's willingness to risk the use of indirect controls appears a good deal more attractive. The skilled employment of indirect controls would, of course, require a detailed and profound knowledge of the behavior of a social system, not only at the start of an action, but over the entire period of its detectable consequences. It would imply a carefully managed system of "feeding back" information to the original sources of the action to allow for a continuous adjustment to its real as compared to its expected consequences.

The relation of knowledge to controls is thus an unexpected one. The less we know about the consequences of an action, the more likely are we to use direct controls to achieve the desired results. But the reverse is equally true: as our understanding of system reactions to intervention increases, we can afford to be parsimonious in the application of direct controls. And from this relationship, yet another may be derived. Knowledge and freedom are correlative terms. The selective use of direct controls leaves open large areas where choices may be free, as planners are indifferent to the outcome. To return to our earlier example, how borrowers decide to use the credit they obtain may be of no concern to planners, so long as the total volume of credit is restricted, and secondary effects on the rates of inflation and employment are of the desired magnitude and direction.

The distinction between direct and indirect controls may be a subtle one; it is nonetheless vital to the health of a society. We think that we choose freely, but our choices are, in fact, limited by controls that are impersonal and are applied to everyone alike. If the limits imposed—such as a rise in the rate at which capital may be obtained—are perceived in roughly similar ways and result in a roughly similar ordering of individual preferences, *average* behavior will fall into definite patterns. For example, the total amount of investment will decline, with only those borrowers obtaining capital for whom its possession is worth the increased cost. This is the intended effect. But the decision to borrow or not is left with the individual; it remains, in a sense, free.

It might, of course, be argued that this freedom is illusory. The borrower's choice has been "rigged" because certain alternatives previously open to him have been eliminated. While this is unquestionably true, it does not follow that freedom of choice is an illusion. Every choice is made from among a given set of alternative possibilities. These alternatives may be the result of conscious planning, or they may be cast up by the social process in ways that no one had specifically intended. But the question of freedom under planning would seem to have little to do with the degree of intentionality; it is exclusively concerned with the number of alternatives available. In the extreme case, when choice is limited to either the strict observance of innumerable rules or death, the implied degree of freedom is minimal. A society so limited in its options can no longer be called free.

But what of the planner who knows that his actions will inevitably restrict the number of available options for at least a part of the population? Within the new set of constraints, choice may still be free (and for many the range of available choices may even be wider), but does not the planner himself bear a moral responsibility for limiting the choices of some while perhaps increasing the choices for others (e.g., easing the terms of credit for large borrowers, while tightening the sources of credit for everyone else)? The answer is not clear, and Mannheim was troubled by his inability to resolve this question. A knowledge of probable consequences, he thought, imposes moral responsibility for them. If this is so, however, does it not follow that all who are likely to be affected should have a voice in whether to choose these consequences over some other set? This perplexing issue led Mannheim to touch on several phenomena that are still very much with us. Although he contributed little to our understanding of the decentralization of power and participation in bureaucratic decision-making processes and actions, it is to his credit that he recognized them early as basic questions in societal guidance. I shall return to them later, in a different context.

A Scientific Politics

Mannheim's writings on societal guidance are fragmentary throughout. At times, they reflect the prewar pessimism of a German intellectual and Jew, at other times the forward-looking posture of British socialists and humanist thinkers preparing for the postwar world. He never allowed his ideas to freeze into the dry sterility of doctrine. His mind, open to all experiences, yet rigorously trained in the disciplines of science and philosophy, was at the same time skeptical and consequential, pursuing ideas with a rare persistence. It was also to a very high degree creative. Mannheim invented the idea of democratic planning. Weaving into his invention both empirical knowledge and moral passion, he never arrived at a grand synthesis. Most of his books are collections of essays that chart the intricate paths of his own thinking. Yet, through his writings there runs a unifying theme and sense of purpose. The course of human events, he believed, could be decisively influenced by rational thought without a loss of freedom.

The basis for this belief was by no means obvious. Thinking lay embedded in social structures, only occasionally able to free itself to gain a multi-faceted perspective on the world. Political actions stemmed from impulses that were often irrational from the standpoint of the social system as a whole. Reason was not applied to the definition of purpose; societal relations remained opaque; power sought only short-run advantage and was blind to any but the most immediate consequences; fundamental democratization had destroyed the foundations for judging right from wrong and good from evil. Under these conditions, could a scientific-technical intelligence be joined to politics? Could politics itself be made into a science?

This question started his search. Today, it seems no longer quite so startling in its juxtaposition of seemingly contradictory terms. National governments have instituted planning at the highest levels. Development programs are charted as the basis for political action. Chief executives have their permanent staffs of technical advisors. Budgets are increasingly related to longer-term programs. Though politics has not become a science, public policy is rarely made today without the active participation of technical experts. It is not clear, of course, whether the results of such policies are always superior to those that might have ensued without the benefit of expert counsel, and whether the linkage of knowledge to action has always been as close as it should be. Political realists might argue that the scientific analysis of policy is a luxury, not a need. In reply, it might be argued that the planner's job is simply to provide facts which politicians are free to use in any way they please.

The idea of a division of labor between politics and planning has a respectable pedigree. In Mannheim's time, it had been most precisely formulated by Max Weber, who held that the social sciences should "tell it as it is" and keep personal and political values out of scientific discourse. Translated into methodology, this meant that planners—who might be considered technicians of science—should never venture beyond the formulation and presentation of alternatives for action. The choice was to be left to the "technicians of values" or, more plainly, to the politicians. Whether this described a *possible* relation between planners and politicians was not at issue. It was a *logical* relation that, in turn, was based on certain philosophical assumptions concerning the conditions of knowing. The belief in a value-free social science, closely related to the idea of rationality, restricted social science's role to the efficient relation of means to ends. The ends of action were considered extra-rational, if not irrational. Since objectives were regarded as the products of political struggle and compromise, they had no place in the model of rational choice.

Mannheim's studies in the sociology of knowledge led him to contrary conclusion, however. Scientific work, he thought, could not produce "pure" facts but only a selected emphasis and perspectivist interpretation of them. Scientific analysis had to begin either from a given position in the social order or, for the free-floating intelligentsia, with insight into the hidden forces of societal change. A moral judgment lay at the root of both kinds of knowledge: either you defended the system of social relations because it served you well (ideology), or you criticized it from the vantage point of a possible future (utopia). Facts without values were meaningless; an array of data such as might be contained in a census publication revealed nothing until subjected to disciplined analysis and interpretation. The intellectual, even though he was detached from the social structure, could not remain without moral commitments. His task was more than to measure and record; it was to understand reality, to reveal the subterranean forces working for change, to point out the directions in which the system was moving, to signal dangers in the present situation, and to advocate the measures required for reconstruction on the basis of new sets of values.

This position placed Mannheim outside the predominant empiricist tradition of sociology and led him to reject the Weberian dichotomy of fact and value. He argued that the scientist and the politician must work together. This implied a dedication on the part of planners to search for morally valid purposes of action and, on the part of politicians, to search for scientifically valid knowledge. This symbiotic relationship could never give rise to a rigidly doctrinal plan—a blueprint of the future—but it could result in a self-correcting process of societal guidance. A sense of valid purpose would give direction to this process, but the continuing quest for knowledge would keep the system radically open to new insights and discoveries.

The clear division of task-related roles envisioned by Weber was thus impossible, and the autonomy of a value-free science an illusion. A strictly objective science would be either irrelevant for public action or used for short-term, partisan advantage. In both cases, the scientific enterprise would end by being irresponsible. Like any other human activity unrestrained by moral judgment, it would affect the social order essentially in random ways and so contribute to its instability and possible decomposition. A scientific politics, by contrast, would be a morally responsible endeavor.

In his method, Mannheim proceeded much as a physician would, beginning with a diagnosis of the illness and then prescribing the necessary steps for a recovery. Doctors do not define the state of health to which they hope to restore their patients, and Mannheim never spelled out his particular vision of the future. He was more concerned with the process of recovery than with the ultimate order of society. In this, Mannheim set himself apart from Marxist thinkers, who spent much more time elaborating the nature of the just society than considering the ways of getting there. Run-of-the-mill Marxists naïvely believed that the destruction of the capitalist system would automatically produce a system of full communism, in which the state would disappear and everyone would give according to his ability and receive according to his need. More realistic Marxists admitted the need for a transitional dictatorship and the sophisticates among them wrote treatises on the planning of socialist production. But Mannheim's utopias were immersed in the stream of historical change. They were not models of ideal society but instances of a continuously moving intelligence, its bearing set upon the future. Mannheim refused to fall into the trap of objectifying states of social order whose time had not yet come.

In this he distinguished himself also from the average bourgeois reformer, who spent much of his time designing the future while ignoring the processes by which present social actions might be redirected. Faced with the practical problem of how to move from here to there, the desperate wisdom of both Marxist and bourgeois planners was to control everything in sight. The former sought to do so by establishing production targets to which specific sanctions were attached, while the latter relied primarily on social legislation. Neither method proved very successful. The dynamics of communist society did not conform to the initial expectations of its planners, who were surprised to find the Soviet economy lurching awkwardly from crisis to crisis.[6] Planners in capitalist countries, on the other hand, discovered that controls such as land use zoning regulations could, at best, slow down the avarice of speculative enterprise; they were ineffective in giving form to a life-sustaining physical environment for man.[7]

The lessons these failures might have taught have seldom been correctly drawn. An exclusive concentration on the future will generally lead to conclusions that are irrelevant for societal guidance. What is needed is rather a simultaneous consideration of the ends and the available means, and the application of the instruments of policy in a process that involves the monitoring of the results and the continuous scanning of the actual behavior of the system and its environment. Mannheim was never quite that specific about the mechanics of societal guidance. But he laid out a framework for thinking about these processes that pointed in the right direction. Societal guidance, according to Mannheim, was a conjunctive act that involved technical expertise and political action. The problem that remained was how such a linkage might be accomplished.

Today we know a great deal more about the possibilities

of planning in this sense. In subsequent chapters, I shall therefore consider Mannheim's propositions in the light of the contemporary situation in America. Some of them will have to be modified and perhaps even rejected. But before doing so, it is essential to have a close look at the ways of joining scientific knowledge and a technical intelligence to action.

Appendix: Mannheim's Influence on Planning Theory

The direct influence of Mannheim's writings has been small. The few critical evaluations of his work refer exclusively to his treatment of the sociology of knowledge.[8] Although there was general accord on the intuitive validity of what I have called perspectivism, the relevant empirical evidence was difficult to bring together. Mannheim's contributions to the theory of planning have been almost completely ignored. His insistence that scientific effort be placed on a normative foundation rendered his views unpopular with mainstream sociologists. And economists, who soon pre-empted planning studies, preferred to devise structural planning models rather than to study the nature of guidance processes themselves.[9] Holding to the Weberian view that facts should be kept apart from values, economists displayed no interest in Mannheim, who, in addition to his professed normative orientation, belonged to a different scientific fraternity.

Nevertheless, Mannheim continued to be read after his death. His books were translated into English, and the more theoretically oriented sociologists all became familiar with his work. But while they agreed that Mannheim was one of the important sociological thinkers of his generation, they did not quite know how to relate his idea to their own. He fell outside the compass of an establishment sociology that was generally hostile to societal analysis, preferred a focus on the behavior of individuals and small groups, prided itself in its use of quantitative methods, shrank from value judgments and "diagnosis," and was not the least bit future-oriented. Major textbooks managed completely to ignore Mannheim's existence.

Nevertheless, some of Mannheim's ideas were further elaborated by a number of American writers. Though few of them admitted to this influence on their own work, they had evidently read his books and seized upon those topics they found congenial.

The general theme of planning was taken up by several authors. Robert Dahl and Charles Lindblom came closest to Mannheim's original formulations.[10] Covering much of the same ground, their collaboration gave special emphasis to the theory of social controls, to which they made a distinctive contribution of their own. Their book stands as a landmark of applied social theory.

Rexford Tugwell's work is less well known. In several brilliant, if controversial essays, he developed the idea of planning as a conjunctive act.[11] His doctrinaire insistence that planning should be organized as a fourth power of government unfortunately discredited his views. There was no chance whatever that such a central directive body could come into being in the United States. As a result, Tugwell's extremely stimulating writings on the planning process have been forgotten. Tugwell was not directly influenced by Mannheim; indeed, most of his major statements on planning appeared before the publication of Mannheim's books in English. But his approach to planning is so closely related to Mannheim's that it deserves to be mentioned in the present context.

More recently, a third major contribution has been made by Amitai Etzioni, the title of whose book, *The Active Society*, suggests Mannheim's own orientation to action.[12] Etzioni devotes two chapters specifically to planning, but restricts its meaning to the rather narrow and sterile context of decision-making. Most of his book is concerned with the guidance institutions of society and problems of social participation. It is a representative work in what has come to be known as the New Sociology, which has broken away from the dominant tradition and deals boldly with major problems of society. The father and acknowledged leader of this faction is C. Wright Mills, who pioneered the field of radical social diagnosis in the United States. After his untimely death, Irving Louis Horowitz assumed the mantle of his leadership.[13] But while the New Sociology of Mills, Horowitz, and Etzioni is unquestionably *engagé*, only Etzioni has made the leap into the field of societal guidance. The others have been content with critical analyses of present-day society. Like Mannheim, they did not shy from normative science, but their practical influence has remained small. To pass on to more specific topics, the discussion of rational decision-making dominated writings on planning theory for an entire decade. Two authors stand out: Herbert Simon and Charles Lindblom.[14] Both agreed that in practical affairs a simple model of means-ends rationality was an insufficient guide for public choice. Simon suggested a decision criterion of "satisficing" (i.e., of choosing an alternative that, while it did not maximize utilities, was "good enough" in view of the costs involved in obtaining more complete and reliable information). Lindblom proposed to abandon social rationality altogether in favor of what he called a process of "disjointed incrementalism," in which the interests of society emerged as the by-product of the mutual short-term adjustments of partisan actors.

Neither of these authors explicitly considered the question of substantial rationality, which had been central to Mannheim's discussion. Simon assumed that values would somehow emerge out of the political process and so were "out of bounds" for rational analysis, while Lindblom was unwilling to recognize the existence of society-wide objectives. Social systems, according to Lindblom, maintain themselves fairly well even without explicit objectives. Any failures in the mechanism of mutual adjustment that might unbalance the system would soon be corrected by small measures taken in response to immediate crisis situations.

Dahl and Lindblom's contribution on the subject of social controls has already been mentioned. A rather different orientation to this question was chosen by Kurt Lewin and his followers. A psychologist, Lewin may be credited with the formal elaboration of a theory of indirect controls applied specifically to small group behavior.[15] Subsequent writers have extended Lewin's theory to a new field of applied social psychology that has enjoyed considerable success in large business organizations and in government. The literature on this subject is very large, and it will suffice here to name only one of its best-known contributors, Warren G. Bennis.[16] No one writing in this field, however, has come to grips with the problem of guidance on a societal (national, regional, or city-wide) scale.

Finally, recent work in the policy sciences must be mentioned. This term was originally the title of a book edited by Daniel Lerner and Harold Lasswell, who wished to dramatize the relevance of the social sciences to problems of policy analysis.[17] After a lapse of nearly two decades, the discussion has been reopened, with a number of significant contributions published during the past few years. Although the subject is quite close to Mannheim's concept of a scientific politics (in German, the word *Politik* stands for both politics and policy), the more recent publications mention his name only in passing. Among the more important works are those by Yehezkel Dror, Raymond Bauer and Kenneth Gergen, and Warren Ilchman and Norman Thomas Uphoff. Lindblom has also written a small volume in which he extends some of his earlier theories to the field of policy formulation.[18]

CHAPTER 3

THE FORMS AND STYLES OF PLANNING

Years ago, a freshly minted Ph.D. from the University of
Chicago, I taught a course on regional planning in the
Brazilian city of Belém, a medium-sized provincial capital
on the Amazon River delta. My students were young professionals working for the newly created Amazon Development Authority. To round off six months of rather dreary
classroom study, we decided to hire one of the steamboats
that plied a leisurely trade between Belém and Manaus
two thousand miles upstream. Our intention was to pay
brief visits to some of the development sites in the region.

In order to enliven a journey that took us through long
stretches of monotonous landscape composed of sky, water,
and equatorial forest, I conducted a series of informal seminars on planning theory. Our very first meeting began with
what I thought would be a simple and straightforward
question. "What is planning?" I asked. But the simplicity
was more apparent than real. Overnight the question became a byword among us. Hotly, but inconclusively, de-
bated at all hours of the day and night, it was greeted with
peals of laughter when anyone dropped the phrase, now
teasingly, now as a challenge. Some thought that planning
was identical with economic development. Others believed

it to be a way for making decisions more rationally. Yet a
third faction emphasized its instrumental character. A
fourth group preferred to view it in the context of control
and order. A fifth group saw it as a way of blueprinting the
future. Many factions were formed during the sweltering
two weeks of our journey. Suspended between sky and
water, we experienced a strange sensation. Here was a
group of practicing young planners unable to define the
nature of their calling.

I have subsequently sprung this question on many other
groups of students. Suppose you wanted to study planning
in the city of Los Angeles, I might ask them, where would
you look? What would you study? Would you include only
those offices which carry "planning" in their titles, such as
the Los Angeles City Planning Department, or would you
study other activities and agencies as well? Questions such
as these turn out to be extremely perplexing. They point to
a major conceptual weakness in the study of planning.

My intention in this chapter is to propose some distinctions that I have found useful in looking at the behavior
of planners and planning agencies. The first relates to the
forms of planning. I shall discuss here the ways in which
scientific and technical knowledge is related to organized
actions that help to (1) maintain a given system in a state
of equilibrium or balance and (2) induce major changes in
its performance. The second major distinction refers to *styles*
of planning and explores the ways in which planning is influenced by the instruments and methods of control available
to planners as well as by the social and institutional environment to which it must adapt itself to be effective.

The following discussion is somewhat technical and abstract. It will equip us, however, with a set of concepts and
a vocabulary that will be used throughout the remainder of
this book. I therefore ask the reader's indulgence.

The Forms of Planning

Societal guidance encompasses both the maintenance and the change of social systems. National planners, for example, may be concerned with holding to a given rate of growth in production, or with keeping unemployment down to politically tolerable levels. Such objectives, which may be basic to the health and vigor of the economy, can be achieved only by holding a set of critical relations, such as consumption and investment, exports and imports, and the several production sectors of the economy in a dynamic balance. But central planners may be equally interested in changing the overall economic performance of the system, accelerating its long-term rate of growth, for example, or altering the proportions of income received by different sectors of the population. These changes can be accomplished on an enduring basis only by appropriate changes in the institutions that generate a given growth rate or a particular distribution of income.

Urban planners face quite similar tasks. They must see to it, for instance, that a city continues to function adequately under conditions of steady economic and demographic expansion. People want to move about the city without excessive loss of time, and the basic demands of the population for land, housing, public services, education, and recreation must be met. In this case, the problem is principally one of adding to existing facilities and of making a series of adaptive changes in those conditions that affect the degree of efficiency in city life. At the same time, however, urban planners may also need to bring about major improvements in the city performance. The need for these *qualitative* changes may derive from an accumulated inability to keep public services abreast of urban expansion, or from a change in values that renders earlier performance standards obsolete, or from demands for new services, such as mass transit, public housing, and pollution management. To respond to these demands, planners will have to think of altogether different ways of guiding the city's development; they will have to innovate on a substantial scale.

These two facets of societal guidance—maintaining a complex social system in balance and, *simultaneously*, inducing new performance characteristics through changes in some of its structural relations—interpenetrate in many ways. Innovations may be needed, for example, to restore a system to a healthy balance: to create conditions of full employment in an environment subject to rapid technological change and skill obsolescence, or to invent new forms of governance for cities that have grown into a tangle of conflicting jurisdictions. On the other hand, a measure of balanced order may be prerequisite to the introduction of planned innovations. In times of crisis and social turmoil, basic innovations are difficult to make; all efforts are instead directed to coping with the immediate troubles—putting out a fire, recovering from the ravages of civil war, restraining runaway inflation, or feeding a famished population. Imaginative solutions to these problems may be improvised but, as a rule, they do not constitute structural and, therefore, lasting innovations. A minimum of order must be restored before the basic institutional changes that will diminish the probabilities of future conflagrations, civil conflict, hunger, and inflation can be accomplished.

In spite of the difficulty of distinguishing actions aimed at maintaining systems from those designed to change them, two forms of planning have evolved, one addressing itself primarily to maintenance, the other to change. I have chosen to call them allocative and innovative planning.

By *allocative planning*, I mean the distribution of limited resources among a number of competing users. This is typically regarded as the major task of central planners and, for many people, it is planning's only proper function.

The well-known Planning-Programming-Budgeting System (PPBS) that was introduced into the operations of the federal government, following a successful experience in the Department of Defense, represents a clear instance of allocative planning. Elsewhere, central planning agencies are principally engaged in efforts to rationalize the allocation of investments to promote such ends as economic growth. The cost-benefit studies used by the U. S. Army Corps of Engineers and the Department of Interior in the selection of water resource projects are a type of allocative planning. Even a master plan for a city is best thought of as an instrument of resource allocation, the resource being, in this case, limited urban space.

Whatever the level on which it takes place, allocative planning shows certain distinctive characteristics. Four of these will be described.

1. *Comprehensiveness.* Allocative planning must be comprehensive with respect to at least the following sets of interdependencies: (a) all explicitly stated objectives; (b) major alternative uses for the resources available; and (c) projected external conditions that may modify the setting of intermediate targets.

With regard to the first set, the logic of allocative planning requires that the system over which resources are to be distributed have a single set of comprehensive, system-wide objectives, so ordered that the more inclusive, overriding objectives are placed at the top and the more narrowly conceived, instrumental ones at the bottom. This requirement has led planners to the notion of a general or *public* interest, reflecting a consensus on the society's relevant values. Since a full description of the public interest in this sense is hardly ever formulated by political decision makers, planners themselves have had to attempt to identify and order the relevant values. This, in turn, has prompted planners to assume a model of society in which a stable consensus on the relevant values is not only attainable but also predictable. They postulate a society in which enlightened citizens, acting on complete information, will maximize the welfare of the community of which they form a part. In the bird's-eye perspective of central planners, therefore, society appears harmoniously ordered; conflict and struggle are either absent or subordinated to the superior wisdom of a collective mind (i.e., a central planning agency).

Complex modern society fails to correspond to such a model. Special interests predominate, and where the planner's values threaten powerful and self-regarding groups, the latter are generally capable of frustrating the intentions of the plan. Since planners are not so naïve as to believe that their own preferences can prevail over those who exercise effective power in society, they will be careful to couch their version of the public interest in terms that are acceptable to the powerful. Allocative planning serves primarily the interests of those who are already strong.

Regarding the second set, planners are constrained to employ criteria capable of harmonizing the competing claims of potential resource users. The principal criterion is that of marginal efficiency, in which social benefits accruing from the last dollar spent in any particular use must be equal to the social benefits in all potential uses. This criterion highlights a certain ambivalence in allocative planning. The method of marginal analysis is incremental. Alternative uses for relatively small units of resources must be compared to detect the social productivity of each. This puts the emphasis on short-term options.

But the productivity of resources cannot be properly evaluated without a long-run view. And this suggests the need for allocations that commit the society for long periods ahead. Every allocative plan, therefore, strives to formulate a model of future society that is different from the present in some important ways. This model, implying a given pattern of resource allocations over time, is necessarily a statement of what society ought to become. But marginal analysis has nothing to contribute to a choice among alternative futures. Moreover, insofar as central planning acts as a handmaiden of the dominant interests in the society, any long-range statement will simply be a projection of prevailing interests and, consequently, will usually point to only minimal changes.

This ambiguity cannot, in principle, be resolved. It has contributed to a schizophrenic turn of mind among planners who champion marginal analysis as a method but wish to work for a society where basic changes are at least conceivable. Unwilling (or unable) to act as technical brokers in a political process, allocative planners have had to be satisfied with rather makeshift and logically indefensible solutions.

The third set of interdependencies refers to external conditions that may significantly influence the setting of intermediate targets. Here, allocative planners have claimed a special, trained ability to predict the future. The commitment of resources to particular uses can be justified only by the claim that the results of doing so will meet the future "needs" of the society as these are currently foreseen. But not only may perceptions of need change with time; other conditions, such as the availability of critical resources, may do likewise.

A comprehensive approach to allocative planning clearly requires abilities in long-range forecasting. These forecasts must be quite precise, including the timing of foreseeable changes, year by year, in order to furnish an adequate informational base for long-range planning. Central planners inevitably try their hands at forecasting future conditions, such as the size and composition of the population, the volume and distribution of income, external assistance, evolving price structures, the differential rates of inflation, technological innovations, changes in values, etc. But, as we shall see in Chapter 5, their ability to predict these changes is severely limited. Except where very short periods of time are involved, central planners are operating either on the basis of wrong assumptions or simply in the darkness of their ignorance.

The requirement of comprehensiveness in central allocation, therefore, gives rise to a series of logical inconsistencies that contributes to making its system-balancing role a precarious undertaking. None of the inconsistencies mentioned above permits of an easy solution that would leave the principle of central allocation, as presently understood, intact.

2. *System-wide balances.* The criterion of optimal choice, which is the intellectual foundation for allocative planning, requires a balance among the various components of the system, to permit the precise calculation of the results of incremental change. The models with which allocative planners work are thus expressed in terms of equilibrium relations. Planned investments must not exceed the system's capacity to save; total imports must not exceed projected exports plus other external sources of financing; employment gains must not be less than the projected increase in the labor force; electric power production must meet the projected levels of consumption. The proper magnitudes must be determined with considerable precision if they are to serve as targets of the economic system.

This approach to planning has implications for the behavior of allocative planners. It makes them reluctant to consider innovative actions that are risky and might upset the delicate balances they have projected. It diverts their attention from strategies for change as they struggle to make their equations balance to the satisfaction of hypercritical peers, who are more likely to be impressed by sophisticated models than by the actual substance of the plan. Finally, it makes them singularly reluctant to identify priorities for action, for that would mean devoting single-minded attention to certain critical elements at the expense of a comprehensive look at all the relevant variables. Allocative planners tend to be unduly impressed with the incapacity of systems to adjust themselves automatically to internal and external changes. They are prone, therefore, to suggest policies for each and every element in their equations, implying that intervention is needed at all points simultaneously to keep the system in a proper balance.

3. *Quantitative analysis.* Neither a comprehensive account of major variables nor system-wide balances can be achieved without the help of quantitative models. These models allow for a study of the system under quasi-experimental conditions and are capable of leading, through a process of trial and error, to logically consistent solutions. The most frequently used models of this type include national economic accounts, input-output matrices, simulated systems, and linear programming.

In general, it may be argued that allocative planning concentrates more on a description of possible system states than on the process of transforming the existing society, and this is specifically true of these models. They are usually divorced from the society's institutional and legal constraints and, therefore, do not take into account the actual limits upon the instruments available for implementing actions. Useful as learning devices, quantitative models tend to divert the planner's attention from the need to formulate his plans in terms of the real world. Though highly abstract, they come to stand in the planner's mind for the reality they purport to describe. This inclines him to believe in the persuasiveness of his own logic and to ascribe greater rationality to the actors of a system than they are likely to display.

4. *Functional rationality.* Allocative planning is an attempt to make decisions functionally rational. As I suggested earlier, planners prefer to think that the major value premises of their work are independent of "rational" analysis. Their calling, they will be quick to tell you, is to work out the practical implications of the implicit norms of a society. As a well-known economist explains it:

The tendency now is to abandon the effort to determine through economic analysis, what is the best form of economic organization or the "best" set of economic policies, and to accept goals established through the political process and stated by governments—full employment, price stability, more rapid economic growth, elimination of pockets of poverty or distressed areas, and the like. For the most part, such goals seem reasonable to economists, but by starting their analysis at the point where government policy is already determined, they avoid value judgments of their own. They may point out inconsistencies among goals, or worry about such dilemmas as rising cost of living and increasing unemployment side by side, but choice between goals is left to the government, as is the establishment of priorities. Usually some set of measures for achieving goals— once priorities are established—can be suggested, even if there remains doubt as to whether they constitute the best set of measures.[1]

Such thinking is an exercise in self-delusion. On the one hand, planners like to present themselves as exponents of a morally neutral science; on the other hand, they lay claim to a special knowledge of the public interest. Though clearly in conflict, these two positions are frequently upheld as though they were in no way incompatible. The only logical defense would be to say that the public interest can somehow be determined scientifically, or that its formulation is itself an act of pure reason. Neither of these defenses is very convincing, however. Allocative planning cannot be based on rational grounds alone. It inevitably includes a major normative component, reflecting someone's, not necessarily the "public's," interests.

These basic traits of allocative planning have become deeply ingrained in the minds of professional planners. Nevertheless, the influence of central planning on the processes of societal guidance has been relatively small, and the institutions which have been developed to exert it have remained relatively ineffective. Nor is this judgment confined to central economic planning. It is equally valid for the physical planning of cities which works through such allocative devices as the master plans or, more recently, general plans for urban development. The principal purpose of these plans is to divide the physical space of the city among existing and potential users.

The continued support of some kind of central planning suggests, however, that it may meet some needs that have little to do with its intentions. International agencies, for example, no less than the federal government, insist on the preparation and submission of comprehensive development plans as the basis upon which they make project grants to interested governments. This gives the granting institution the satisfaction of supporting a "best" course of action, *even where a firm political commitment to this course may not exist.*

Central allocative planning, we may conclude, has not lived up to its initial promises. The desire to be comprehensive has produced the illusion of an omnipotent intelligence; the method of system-wide balances has led to an overemphasis on stability; quantitative modeling has encouraged the neglect of the actual conditions governing policy and program implementation; and the claim to functional rationality has made planners insensitive to the value implications of their work.

Innovative planning has fared considerably better. It may be regarded as an approach to institutional development that is expected to produce a limited, but significant change in the structural relations of an existing system of societal guidance. According to one author, innovative planning "creates wholly new categories of activity, usually large in scale, so that they cannot be reached by increments of present activity, but only by initiating a new line of activity which eventually leads to the conceived result."[2] In innovative planning, different kinds of technical experts apply their skills directly to the development of new organizational responses to the needs perceived. Rather than preparing elaborate proposals that are preliminaries to action, *they achieve a fusion of plan-making with plan-implementing activities during the course of the action itself.* In innovative planning, plan and action become coterminous.

Examples of innovative planning are not difficult to find. Typically, the effort is directed at the solution of a major problem, such as structural unemployment, rural backwardness, urban decay, or persistent failures of the educational system. New institutional arrangements are introduced to change the direction of the stream of ongoing events or the rate of its flow. As the pace of institutional innovation accelerates, the rhythm of societal development will quicken. Or, as Bertram Gross has observed of Mexican planning,

> A new institutional infrastructure was needed. To build it in small pieces, however disconnected, seemed infinitely superior to the piling up of a vast hierarchical bureaucracy in a small number of ministries. It provided more upward career channels for people with ability and ambition. By placing scarce eggs in many baskets, there was more room for trial and error, more protection against failure. Promotion of new institutions took precedence over their coordination.
>
> This kind of institution building has a pulse rate of its own. The more successful it is in getting things done, the more problems the new institutions create. This leads to increasing pressure to pull things together a little more tightly. . . . But then the effort to get important things done leads once again to new spurts of decentralized institution building. Central promotion of decentralized institutions once again races ahead of central coordination.[3]

To underline the distinctions between innovative and allocative planning, I shall describe three salient aspects of the former: a predominant concern with institutional change, a basic orientation towards action, and a special emphasis on the mobilization of needed resources.

1. *Institutional change.* Innovative planning is fundamentally concerned with translating general value propositions into new institutional arrangements.

Imagine a simple case. Faced with a crisis of rising unemployment among young people, the government decides to undertake a vast program of public works, but wishes to limit the latter to rural conservation and environmental improvement. The program is intended to enroll unemployed young men and women in an Environmental Conservation Corps, which would join with local citizens in the recovery of eroded hillsides, the construction of flood control works, and large-scale reforestation. The budget set aside for this purpose equals about 15 per cent of the current budget for the Department of Agriculture, which, logically, should manage a program of rural betterment. But Agriculture, concerned with its ongoing and more or less routinized programs, is unable to absorb an additional project of this magnitude. Moreover, its long-standing rival, the Department of Interior, has expressed an interest in assuming charge of the new program, while several other departments have let it be known that they too would like to be dealt into the game. Under these conditions, the easiest solution is to establish the Environmental Conservation Corps as an independent agency of the government.

A skeleton staff of agronomists, soil conservationists, engineers, medical doctors, psychologists, educators, and professional administrators is recruited to draw up the details of the program, establish suitable selection procedures, propose a list of priority locations, negotiate with state and local governments to begin operations, and start to work on a program budget for the next few years. Regional offices are set up, and work begins on the construction of work camps at various sites around the country.

This entire process, from initial conception to the full-scale operation of the program, may be included under the concept of innovative planning. The concept ceases to be applicable only when the program has become a matter of routine administration.

This example serves to emphasize several important characteristics of innovative planning. First, the Environmental Conservation Corps is addressed to a single set of problems. It makes no pretense of being comprehensive. Its area of impact is limited and focused. Second, it represents an attempt to improve the performance of a guidance system that has produced a certain volume and type of unemployment in the past. The change introduced is a structural one in the sense that it is meant as a permanent addition to the guidance system so that, in the future, a given proportion of the young unemployed members of the labor force will automatically be channeled into productive work that also involves a measure of re-education and social integration. This particular attempt will not itself reduce the incidence of unemployment among the young, but it will offer them an alternative to remaining unemployed.

Third, the Environmental Conservation Corps represents a non-incremental change in budgetary allocation (at least with respect to existing conservation work). This is typically the case, with the result that the social productivity of innovative planning cannot be evaluated by the usual methods of marginal analysis. The establishment of the corps is a political decision. Nevertheless, its consequences may be analyzed in advance by technical experts who, as active participants in a decision process, are probably not indifferent to its outcome. That this approach introduces significant biases into their analysis is undoubtedly true. But the relative loss of objectivity on the part of the individual analysts can be, and frequently is, balanced out in the confrontation among their diverse value positions. The pretense of a morally neutral science has thus no place in innovative planning.

Fourth, the Environmental Conservation Corps is a reformist rather than revolutionary innovation. Since revolutionary changes tend to occur faster than information about them can become available, a scientific-technical intelligence applied to revolutionary activity is superfluous; it can make its analyses only *after* the fact. On the other hand, where a number of independent innovative planning efforts occur simultaneously, they may eventually link up and, *together*, bring about a substantial transformation of the social system as a whole. Whether such a change deserves to be called revolutionary is a question that cannot be answered here.

2. *Action orientation.* Purpose and the realization of purpose are indistinguishable in innovative planning. It is, of course, true, that the invention of a program may be regarded, in purely instrumental terms, as a means in relation to an explicitly formulated end (e.g., reducing unemployment). It would be more accurate, however, to think of innovative planning as a creative social response to problem situations that are often vaguely understood. The Environmental Conservation Corps is designed to cope with large-scale unemployment among the young. It may reduce unemployment among this group, but it may also have important side effects. Not all of these effects may have been foreseen at the outset, but as they become apparent it is entirely conceivable that the original objectives will be reformulated. Their prior specification is therefore less important, and certainly less essential, than in allocative planning. Objectives are evolved during the course of the action itself, as a self-image crystallizes, the genuine options for action are discovered, and practical results become apparent. Substantial rationality is thus joined, in innovative planning, to a search for the means of effective action.

Related to this continuous search for the relevant objectives of action is a central concern with strategy. In successful instances of innovative planning, two related strategies will be employed. The first is primarily concerned with matters of institutional development, such as approaches to funding agencies, questions of internal organization and governance, relations with other agencies and institutions, and the building of a base of political support. The second is more concerned with achieving the evolving purposes of the institution. Going back to our earlier example, it would seek responses to such questions as: What criteria and methods should be used to recruit members into the Environmental Conservation Corps? What programs should be developed, in what sequence? Where should the programs be initiated? How should local communities be approached? How can the active support of government agencies be obtained? The two kinds of strategy are often joined: the development of an institution becomes an inseparable part of its ability to carry out its mission.

The imperatives of action are primary. Strategies are evolved "on the run" and are frequently not even recorded in formal documents. Innovative planning is, to a large extent, an ephemeral process that leaves its traces primarily in telephone conversations, the minutes of meetings, and floating memoranda. Formal documentation appears to be important only in connection with retrospective official reports and the need to obtain resources for the continued operation and expansion of the innovation.

3. *Resource mobilization.* Innovative planners perform an entrepreneurial function in mobilizing and organizing the use of institutional resources. Allocative planners, by contrast, are almost exclusively dedicated to the task of distributing resources among competing users. Because innovative institutions are new, and their continued existence is not yet assured, their management staffs will usually spend much of their time attracting resources to the organization. Their success in this will be reflected in the organization's budget, which, at least during the first few years, is likely to show large annual increases. From the standpoint of already existing institutions competing for the same resources, the

innovative agency will appear as a predator on the scene. For this reason, the innovative institution will have to take care not to expose itself unnecessarily to criticism. A good part of its activities may, therefore, be shrouded in relative secrecy until a loyal clientele is built and the first concrete (and, it is to be hoped, successful) results are reported.

Planning has for so long been identified with central resource allocation that its innovative thrust has, for the most part, gone unnoticed. Yet innovative is undoubtedly the more prevalent form of planning. Imagine a country where nothing ever happens. From year to year, public resources are allocated in roughly the same proportion to the same users. Small adjustments may be made from time to time, correcting random errors in the system, but these do not produce significant changes in the country's economy. In such a country, planning is clearly superfluous; its planners—if they existed—would simply copy last year's plan. Admittedly, this is an extreme example. But it serves to underscore the point that allocative planning is needed only when important changes are occurring and balance must be artificially restored.

Imagine now the opposite extreme, a country so overwhelmed by change that the whole system becomes wildly unbalanced. Clearly, one would argue, it is precisely under these conditions that some form of central guidance is needed. Yet it is, in fact, unlikely that allocative planning would be used in such a situation, for the government would lack both the knowledge and the power necessary to make its decisions effective. The only possibility of salvaging the country by means of planning would be to carry out a large-scale program of institutional innovation.

Summarizing, we arrive at the unattractive conclusion that, *where allocative planning is most feasible, it is superfluous, and, where it is most needed, it is unfeasible.* Innovative planning, on the other hand, is both needed and feasible in the two cases described: in the first, to get the country moving, and in the second, to build up the new structures without which the country would fall into chaos. Most countries are located between the two extremes and, therefore, practice both forms of planning. But innovative planning—being change-oriented—generally predominates.

Innovative planning occurs at a limited number of inter-sections in a system of structural relations, where the new institutions that are brought into being constitute relatively isolated "enclaves of modernity." Impulses of change ripple outwards from these points to other parts of the system. In-itially, these innovations are not co-ordinated with one an-other unless central allocative planners wield, in fact, more power than they normally do. But once a given institutional development reaches a certain level of consolidation, efforts will be made to adjust its transactions with its environment in ways that will allow the institution (and its programs) to operate more smoothly and effectively, on an increasingly routinized basis. New allies and bases of external support will be sought, especially among other recent innovators, until a network of innovative institutions comes into being, establishing a new "plateau" from which a second genera-tion of innovations may arise.

Innovative planning, then, is an initially unco-ordinated and basically competitive form of planning. It contrasts sharply with central allocation, an activity pre-eminently concerned with balances, co-ordination, and the implementa-tion of a consensual public interest. The top leaders of the Israeli government, for example, have:

> deliberately nourished the institution-building, empire-con-structing, resource-grabbing, expansionism of organization in all sectors of society, including science and education as well as the trade union movement, political parties, and private business. This has meant the promotion of sectoral planning. The result has been more and more high-pressure planning and implementation by competitive institutions. Under such circumstances, clear-cut coordination by com-

mand of central authorities has neither been feasible, essential, nor desirable.[4]

Relations between allocative and innovative planning are thus inevitably in a state of tension. System balances must be maintained, but change in desired directions is also needed. Although both forms of planning are generally required, innovative planning tends to be relatively independent of central allocative mechanisms. It manages its own resources and aggressively seeks to enlarge the scope of its influence and power. For a considerable time, its results can be known only in fragmentary form, rendering evaluation of its use of resources impractical. Innovative planning may eventually acquire its own base of political support. Its managing staff will tend to be selected more for their entrepreneurial talents than for their skills in bureaucratic management.

In all these respects, innovative planning is likely to run into the opposition of central (allocative) planners, who will strain to reincorporate the innovative effort into normal bureaucratic molds, limit its claims upon central resources, and improve its reporting and accounting systems. For central planners have responsibilities quite different from those of innovators. They must worry about the critical ceilings of resources expenditure and make certain that other essential functions of the system are not impaired by the reckless actions of innovative planners. While they may accommodate change up to a point, allowing some flexibility in the management of the subcomponents of the system for which they have responsibility, central planners must not lose sight of indicators that will tell them whether the system is holding to a steady course.

One of the major differences between innovative and allocative planning, however, has nothing to do with this classical struggle between demands for greater autonomy and subordination to general rules. Innovative planning, as we have seen, is largely a self-executing activity; the formulation and carrying out of plans constitute, in this case, a single operation. But with allocative planning, there is always the problem of how the general plan is to be carried out. The failure to make planning effective, in the sense of producing real effects visible in the society, is a frequent, popular, and justified complaint. The usual attempts to explain this failure refer to a gap in communications between planners and decision makers or to the "irrationality" of a political process that doesn't take into account the system-wide perspectives provided by the plan. In a more constructive vein, allocative planners will assert their need to be located as close as possible to the sources of formal authority, usually the chief executive. But experience has shown that, unless the chief executive has a keen personal interest in using his planning staff to make the basic resource allocations, the effectiveness of central planning is likely to be low.

A more fundamental explanation appears to lie in the decision model that central planners have consistently used to describe and, at the same time, to justify their professional roles in societal guidance (Figure 1).

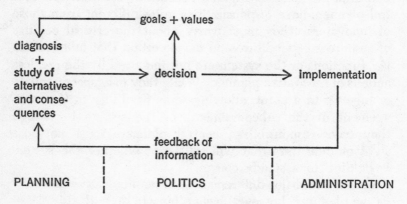

Figure 1. The Classical Decision Model of Allocative Planning

In this model, planning, political decisions, and implementation appear as sequential steps. Decision makers provide the planners with goals and values. Once these norms have been established, planners carry through a general diagnosis of the situation, identify the alternative courses of action that will maximize the decision makers' values, and examine the probable consequences of these actions. The final array of alternatives and consequences is then presented to the decision makers, who, upon reviewing the information, select a course of action. This decision is then communicated to the administrative bureaus, which are dedicated to carrying out the designs of their political masters. As results start to materialize, a stream of information is generated that is channeled back to the central planners, who carry out a continuous review of the plan.

According to this model, planners, politicians, and bureaucrats are engaged in distinct and separate activities, each doing essentially one thing: planners analyzing and proposing, politicians defining the objectives and choosing, and bureaucrats implementing the selected programs. Theoretically, planners have little need for contact with bureaucrats except to receive the information that the latter supply them as a matter of routine. The climax of the entire process is a dramatic moment of political decision. Implementation, on the other hand, is seen as nonproblematical. The model assumes that the needed resources will somehow be forthcoming, and that sufficient powers exist to co-ordinate the necessary actions. Or, more simply, the model assumes that once a decision has been made, a simple command is all that is needed to make it a reality.

No model, of course, can ever provide an accurate description of the real world. This particular model reflects the prevailing bias of allocative planners towards functional rationality, their desire to remove planning from the contaminating influence of pragmatic action (i.e., from the exercise of effective power), and to surround it with an aura of scientific objectivity. To the extent that planning is influenced by this model, it becomes oriented to the system's political objectives more than to the needs of implementing agencies. The reason for the inconsequential nature of much allocative planning therefore resides in its failure to take into account the basic difficulties of implementing decisions.

Styles of Allocative Planning

How much power a system has—or is willing to use—will determine both the choice of implementing strategies and the probable outcomes. If I have money, I can hire a contractor and build whatever housing suits my needs. If I don't have money, I may be able to borrow some, but then the banker may wish to impose certain restrictions on the quality of the design. And if I cannot even borrow the amount I need, I will be forced to keep on living where I live.

The relation between effective power and the kind of results that may be obtained from using it would seem an obvious one, yet it is rarely acknowledged to exist in allocative planning. Where it is heeded, so that the capacity to plan is linked directly with implementing processes (taking into account all existing limitations on the uses of power), a unique *style* of allocative planning results.

Implementing processes are, to a large extent, determined by the distribution of power in a system.[5] Theoretically, therefore, it is possible to distinguish among systems where power is strongly centralized, weakly centralized, fragmented, and dispersed. Associated with each type of system is a particular method of implementation and style of allocative planning (Table 1). These relations do not, of course, completely characterize any existing system. But the typology is useful for exploring the interconnections among planning styles that give rise to the complex systems of societal guidance we can actually observe.

TABLE 1

A Typology of Allocative Planning Styles

Distribution of power	Strongly centralized	Weakly centralized	fragmented	dispersed
Method of Implementation	compulsory targets	mixed field controls • general rules • inducements • information	bargaining (few negotiators: corporate structure)	participation in decision processes (many participants: community structure)
Predominant Forms of Control	sanctions	restructuring of the decision environment	normative compliance	voluntary compliance
Predominant Orientation Toward	plans	policies	processes	processes
Characteristic Role of Technical Experts	bureaucratic specialist	advisor	negotiator and broker	organizer and advocate
Style of Allocative Planning	command planning	policies planning	corporate planning	participant planning

Four major planning styles emerge from this typology: command, policies, corporate, and participant planning. The first, or *command planning,* is associated with strongly centralized systems of governmental power. In such systems, a bureaucracy exists for the purpose of meeting compulsory targets, and appropriate performance is required of its members. Sanctions, such as fines and prison terms, may be imposed to secure compliance with the plan, but various forms of moral pressure and persuasion may also be applied. In command planning, the technical expert is accustomed to fine divisions of labor and the tasks of information processing are highly specialized.

The command system comes closest to the formal decision model of allocative planning. Its information requirements are extraordinarily demanding. Complete, accurate, and timely information must be obtained about all aspects of the system to be planned, and the controls must cover all the variables relevant to achieving specified performance levels. Subunits of the central planning office must therefore be established throughout the administration, down to the lowest functional and territorial levels. No element of the system can be exempted from participating in a process which, to produce the results that have been blueprinted in advance, must join planning and administration in ways that will erase all practical distinctions between them.

Control figures are used throughout the command system to establish targets and to provide a carefully calibrated measure of performance. They may also be used to increase pressures for compliance, and may frequently be set above the levels actually believed feasible. Ultimately, however, the system's successful performance depends on a generalized fear of the sanctions that may be imposed if performance should fall below the expected target levels. Because of this—and because the command style of planning is subject to enormous errors of fact, calculation, and judgment—extralegal means are widely used to correct the results of planners' miscalculations, and graft, lying, and corruption become intrinsic to the system.

Policies planning is less demanding in its requirements for information, organization, and control. Associated with weakly centralized systems of government, its method is to induce appropriate actions through statements of general guidelines and criteria for choice, the provision of material incentives, and the dissemination of information for decentralized planning. In each case, the emphasis is on indirect or field controls. Policy announcements, inducements, and information have the primary purpose of *restructuring the environment for decisions of the relevant actors.* Policies, for instance, are meant to make some allocative choices impossible while increasing the probability of other, more desirable ones. A tight credit policy will make money unavailable below a certain rate of interest. An industrial location policy, applied through a system of licensing and subsidies, can prevent locations in areas not scheduled for expansion. Both have the effect of making certain choices more, and others less, attractive. The effect of providing information, on the other hand, is primarily to reduce the uncertainties involved in any choice and, consequently, the risk of economic loss to actors.

The use of policies planning frequently requires some form of direct control to reset the boundaries of choice. But such controls must be applied selectively for maximum impact (e.g., control over the banking rates of interest; a compulsory licensing system) and thus leave substantial areas of freedom where planners are indifferent to the precise results.

The expert role characteristically associated with policies planning is an advisory one. Most central planners are to some extent active participants in formulating policies. As advisors, they stand somewhat outside the normal rules of bureaucratic conduct, however, and therefore rely on personal ability to influence decisions more than on official position or professional title. Policies stand a greater chance of being implemented than comprehensive plans for resource allocation, because policies are usually responses to urgent political demands and are backed by political commitments. Policies are also easier to manage than central resource allocations. Generally, they focus on a single issue only, such as low-cost housing or the fisheries industry, and are concerned more with introducing specific changes into an

ongoing situation than with maintaining system-wide balances. Policies planning is often the prelude to a concerted
effort at innovation.

In *corporate planning*, process tends to be stressed more
than the ultimate product and may even come to be valued
in its own right. More specifically, the results of negotiations
through which corporate planning is sustained are not determined in advance; they crucially depend on the distribution of effective power among all the participants in
the bargaining process and on their comparative skill in
using this power.

Corporate planning occurs in situations where the structure of power culminates in a small number of influential
organizations, such as industrial and business conglomerates,
farmers' associations, labor unions, the church, and universities. Where power is so organized, each major corporate
entity is able to exercise a veto with respect to any action
affecting its own area of influence. No policy can therefore
be implemented without the consent of those entities that
will be most directly affected. Wage policy has to obtain
the prior consent of both industrial employers and labor
unions. Farm policy must be approved by farmers' associations. And so forth. In situations where power is so divided,
the government is no longer an autonomous agent. Nevertheless, it may retain some freedom of choice to the extent
that it can bargain effectively among the several contending
interests. The perspective of government planners will therefore differ from those of the individual corporate entities,
whose range of immediate interests will be more narrowly
conceived.

The stakes are high in corporate planning. At the very
least, all participants wish to preserve the existing balance
of power among themselves. They are also looking for
marginal advantages in the allocation of public resources.
And finally, they hope to benefit from the knowledge
obtained during the course of bargaining. Because of the

multiple intercorporate balances involved, corporate planning is not likely to result in long-range commitments to action. Each issue, as it arises, must be negotiated separately, with the result that the process of corporate planning appears as a continuous web of bargaining sessions and mutual consultations at the technical level. This continuity is also the most effective incentive for staying in the game. A small concession today may be met by someone else's concession tomorrow, and every participant hopes to maximize his long-run advantage by waiting for these opportunities. Binding long-term agreements are therefore a rare occurrence.

In this regard, the corporate planning process resembles and may even replace the political process. Participation is limited, however, to a small number of powerful actors, each of whom represents an important sector of the social economy. The subjects to be negotiated are generally introduced by the central planning office in the form of draft documents, backed by detailed technical analyses and projections. Major policy changes are not likely to be proposed, however, since they might occasion excessive conflict. Whenever any participant feels threatened, he may disrupt normal proceedings by staging a walk-out or resorting to extra-official means of persuasion, such as massive strikes or demonstrations. For this reason, corporate planning tends to be essentially conservative in its results. Its principal objective is to maintain the existing structure of oligarchical rule.

Corporate planning may be organized formally, as in France, or informally through systems of mutual consultation, as in some American cities. In either case, it will exclude from the processes of societal guidance all interests not directly tied into the corporate structure. The principal role of government planners in such a system is that of brokers among a small number of competing interests, and their further actions reflect the temporary outcomes of the negotiating process. Other technical experts serve the interests of their corporate masters at the bargaining table.

Participant planning occurs under conditions where power to implement decisions resides in community forms of social organization and, consequently, is dispersed. Organizations of this type may be groups of neighbors (village, commune, neighborhood, housing estate), groups of workers (workshops, cooperatives, agricultural settlements), and groups of students and faculty (departments, colleges). In every case, the group must be spatially contiguous and capable of aggregating, formulating, and expressing the interests of its members.

Societies organized solely on this principle possess a rudimentary structure. Community groups always have quite limited resources, consisting chiefly of voluntary contributions of labor and small surpluses from productive activity. If the community is poor, however, its surplus may not be sufficient to meet the common needs, so that efforts to attract outside resources must be undertaken. For this reason, one would expect community groups in complex societies to evolve some system of hierarchical representation to ensure an adequate hearing at the city, district, and national levels of decision-making. A recent experiment in Chile, for instance, allows for the organization of neighborhood councils, associations of such councils at the municipal level, a small number of provincial federations, and finally a nationwide confederation. In principle, such a confederation will be controlled by its participant membership from below, but it will also exhibit the characteristics of traditional corporate entities, and its functional role in planning will in many ways be similar.

The source of ultimate control, however, is not unimportant. Corporate groups are traditionally controlled from the top. Community groups, on the other hand—located at the base of the organizational pyramid—usually share in all important decisions concerning the use of their resources as well as in the implementation of some of these decisions. In this process, the role of central authorities is restricted to that of providing relevant information and technical assistance. A neighborhood group will decide on programs for housing improvement, street maintenance, the location and construction of parks and playgrounds, necessary social facilities, and the like. A workers' co-operative might deliberate over a program of modernization, social facilities in the factory, and product diversification. University departments organized on a communal basis may decide, in joint deliberations of students and faculty such questions as departmental governance, courses of study, student admissions, faculty selection and promotion, financial support for students and research, and methods for handling field work assignments.

But as these examples make clear, such groups cannot take care of the whole list of community needs, and whenever claims are made on resources controlled by central authorities, higher levels of community organization must be brought into play. In addition to the provision of information and technical assistance other tasks must be performed: mediation among competing interests (similar to corporate planning), central allocative planning to provide for system maintenance, and the distribution of funds according to the agreements reached in the negotiating sessions at the level of community confederations.

The process of participant planning is, at least at the lower levels, not very demanding in terms of information (most people know the environment in which they live), but extraordinarily demanding of time. Participation cannot be delegated, for unless at least a representative sample of the community is active in it, the process has no legitimacy. Procedures will be democratic, and decisions will be made, in small groups, on the basis of consensual agreement and, in larger groups on the basis of majority voting.

The old-fashioned New England Town Meeting may serve

as a prototype of participatory decision-making. Larger or more complex population groups necessitate some form of representation, however, with the result that the planning process becomes professionalized and probably bureaucratized as well. Not only do full-time representatives of community groups have to be paid, but the greater complexity of the issues and their greater distance from immediate experience make professional expertise essential. Planners working in a participant process need skills not unlike those that predominate in corporate planning. Among other things, they must be effective advocates of their clients and politically sophisticated negotiators.

Professional planners at the local level, however, must, in addition, be able to rally the community around the common tasks, help its members to learn about the problems they are facing and the available methods for dealing with them, and provide a constant stream of information about those relevant aspects of the external environment. On important issues, the higher levels in the pyramid of community structure will wish to consult the membership at the base. An uninformed, untutored membership lacking "intelligent insight into the structural forces of change" in the society may be unable to arrive at the substantially rational understanding of its condition that is needed for effective system guidance.

The typology of planning styles I have discussed so far has a number of characteristics to which attention should be directed. First, it is based on a continuum of power distribution that runs from strongly centralized to dispersed. A number of traits are stylistically associated with different points along this continuum. For example, the interpersonal element in planning increases steadily as one passes from command to participant planning, just as an orientation towards the preparation and processing of planning documents decreases. Interpersonal skills are of considerable importance to the advisor, but they are crucial to the community organizer.

Innovative planning is related to styles of allocative planning in less systematic fashion. It lacks an independent role under command planning, where it is simply incorporated into the general structure of command. It occurs frequently under policies planning, but only rarely in the conservative, slowly moving system of corporate planning. Under participant planning, innovation will occur principally in the guise of organizing the planning process itself. The earlier discussion of the conflicting relationships between central allocative and innovative planning must therefore be modified to take prevailing planning styles into account.[6]

Interrelations among Planning Styles

Each of the four styles of allocative planning described may be thought of as one component that must be joined to others to make a guidance system work. Command planning cannot dispense with policies, and policies planning is impossible without involving the principal power centers through which the plan must be carried out. In other words, policies planning implies a measure of corporate planning.

This is where matters stand at present. But increasingly, there is pressure for a wider involvement of society in the processes of societal guidance. Old-style authoritarian planning is no longer acceptable in many parts of the world; it is certainly not in the United States. The responsiveness of guidance systems must therefore be heightened by extending the planning process to more dispersed groupings of effective interest representation in the society.

Certain relationships among components are more probable than others (see Figure 2). Three sets will be described: the linkage of command to policies planning, of

policies to corporate planning, and of corporate to participant planning. In a complete guidance system, these three
sets would be forged into a chain, with transactions flowing
in both directions, relating a small number of command
structures to the myriad participant units in the society.

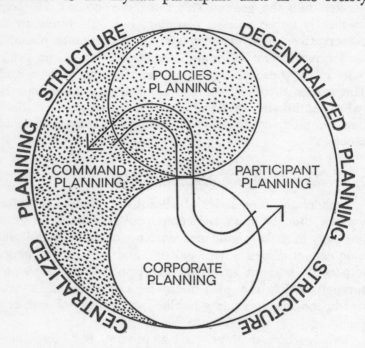

Figure 2. Probable Interrelations among Styles of Allocative Planning

1. *Command and Policies Planning.* This is the combination of planning styles most frequently encountered. No
command system can expect directly to control every action
necessary to the achievement of a given purpose. Where the
powers of central government are weak, the extensive use of
indirect controls is particularly essential. But even in totalitarian societies, reliance will be placed on policies plan-

ning in the measure that knowledge about the relevant conditions improves. For where the consequences of an action are known and understood, controls can be selectively applied. Properly used, policies planning is thus not only considerably less demanding than command planning in terms of information processing; it also gives the citizen a sense of greater freedom and reduces his fear of central sanctions. So long as desired performance levels can be reached, these are not insubstantial gains.

2. *Policies and Corporate Planning.* Unless the central government is powerful and corporate entities in the society are weak, corporate planning must be grafted onto the system of central controls (command plus policies). The relation of corporate to command planning appears more logical via policies planning than by way of a direct connection. Conducted by means of bargaining and negotiation, corporate planning is more likely to result in general statements of policy than in sets of detailed control figures to which specific sanctions are attached. These policies will tend to focus on the definition and uses of central inducements intended to bring about a certain type of corporate behavior. Industrial trusts, for instance, may argue in favor of export subsidies, while business interests may support a large freeway construction program that will bring consumers from outlying portions of the city to the center. This sort of negotiation may result in a bargain involving mutually contingent decisions. Industrial trusts may then promise to raise export levels by a certain percentage so long as government can guarantee a subsidy for exports, but the subsidy decision may, in turn, depend upon industry's proving its ability to increase total exports. Corporate planning joined to a policies framework can work only so long as there is mutual confidence that any bargain made is likely to be kept.

3. *Corporate and Participant Planning.* The urge to take an active part in the decisions and actions that affect one's life is one of the major sources of the current crisis not only

in the United States but in many other countries as well. The formation of high-participant community organizations is sometimes encouraged and aided by central authorities; at other times, it is a more spontaneous process. Students battle for a voice in the management of change in universities, workers wish to take part in the management of industries, neighbors organize to improve conditions in their own communities. Participant planning has been raised to quasi-corporate levels only in a few cases, as in Yugoslavia and perhaps Israel. The worker-controlled industrial trust is still a rarity, and the national confederation of neighborhood councils that has been under discussion in Chile has yet to be created. Nevertheless, the general trend appears clear. With the passing of time, an increased volume of planning will take the form of transactions between corporate and participant structures. Bureaucratic, hierarchical controls imposed by central authorities are no longer acceptable. On the other hand, the extreme dispersal of power among very large numbers of participant units leads to their impotence and makes it imperative that they be brought together into larger, self-managing corporate systems. A small participant unit in society may be able to block a local action, but in most cases, it will be unable to influence its immediate environment in any positive sense. Strength sufficient to influence policies on a continuing basis is attained only through active participation in the management of corporate affairs.

The model that emerges from a consideration of the probable connections among planning styles is that of an "active" society which articulates its own objectives and guides the course of its development by employing a scientific-technical intelligence to the maximum extent possible. In this model, the activities involved in societal guidance are no longer the prerogatives of a small elite, whether it be democratically elected, hereditary, or maintained in power by brute force. They engage an active minority (and possibly even a majority) of the total population for whom the processes of governance and guidance are inseparably a part of life.

Summary

It is my intention in this book to lay the foundations for designing guidance systems appropriate to the conditions of America in the remaining decades of this century. In the present chapter, I started by drawing a basic distinction between allocative and innovative forms of planning. Although innovative planning will generally predominate in a developing society, both forms are necessary and depend upon each other for their effectiveness. Pure system maintenance will result in stagnation; pure innovative activity—without the balancing effort made possible by allocative planning—will lead to increasing disorder.

A further refinement was then introduced with a discussion of the styles of allocative planning. A typology of planning styles was evolved, using the distribution of power in society as the principal criterion. Viewed abstractly, each of the resulting styles forms a part of a composite design for societal guidance. The most probable relations of such a system were shown graphically in Figure 2. A number of important questions, however, remain to be resolved. Among them are the following:

1. What institutional arrangements will establish effective connections among the different styles of allocative planning?

2. Should any particular planning style have preference in the overall guidance system of society?

3. How may a scientific-technical intelligence be linked effectively to each style in the guidance system?

4. How may the learning capabilities of the entire guidance system be enhanced with respect to its environment?

5. How may the guidance system's stability be assured under conditions of multiple internal and external stresses?

Much preliminary work remains to be done before we can return to consider these questions. Specifically, there is a need to look at planning as an adaptive process within the broader context of societal relations. The design of a guidance system that includes planning must be attuned not only to the conditions of power, but also to those of valuing and knowing in society. Since we are primarily interested in guidance systems for America, we now must take a closer look at some of these conditions.

CHAPTER 4

THE CONTEXT OF POST-INDUSTRIAL SOCIETY

The established style of planning in the United States is as sober and rationalistic as the engineering design for a bridge. It involves an enormous amount of data processing and modeling; it proceeds in linear sequence from problem statement to solution. Because the guiding value judgments are implicitly accepted, planning assumes a posture of objective aloofness. Surrounded by the antiseptic walls of his office, the planner measures, analyzes, and projects. The less the outside world intrudes upon his calculations, the happier he is. He strives to reach determinate solutions. Under the steady white light of his austere environment, submerged in his think tank, the planner totes up costs and benefits, laboriously extracts conclusions from his print-out sheets, rearranges whole cities by a flick of his wrist, assigns resources among sectors and programs, and drafts bold statements of public policy. Telephone calls will occasionally intrude upon the tranquil flow of his cerebral existence. But the reality, he will insist, lies hidden in the data tapes with which he works and not in the confusing babble of the outside world. Statistics are patient; they don't talk back. The planner prides himself on the reports that issue as the final product of his labors. From chaotic complexity, he has precipitated order; a least-cost path has been charted into the future. Only the ignorant will fail to see the beauty of his plan, appreciate the infinite care that went into its construction, embrace the policies the plan contains, and carry them through so that the future may be made according to a central will and purpose.

But the style of the age is altogether different. Bathed in psychedelic, strobic lights, it flickers across the multi-paneled screens of vision, and it blows the mind. Reality is filtered through the mocking sensibilities of Roy Lichtenstein and Andy Warhol. Even language has become explosive, incoherent, seeking to express the inexpressible in hopes of gaining entrance to some transcendental reality beyond the measurements of logic. Colloidal has replaced linear thinking; the unrelated is suddenly related; tomorrow and yesterday can happen NOW.

A vast chasm of mutual incomprehension separates the style of the rationalist planner from the frenetic style of the contempo mod. Young people regard the bureaucratic planner as a living fossil. And what if they are right, and the planner's books land on the shelves unread, and the world continues to spin through its gyrations, and the future simply happens—NOW, what then? Shall we build a wild bonfire and cast the books into the flames? Or shall we try to think through everything afresh, search for a style of planning that will capture something of the essential vitality of the age and be attuned to its desperate search for meaning?

The task is not an easy one. I shall attempt to analyze some aspects of the social context with which planning in America must come to terms. For styles of planning are determined not only by the distribution of power in society, but also by a host of other conditions. The crisis we are experiencing is one of valuing and knowing. This chapter is devoted to a study of them both.

The Crisis of Valuing

1. *A philosophy of scarcity in an era of abundance: the emerging realm of non-utilitarian values.* From the beginnings of time, man has lived under conditions of scarcity. Historically, except on rare occasions, he has always been poor. Often he went hungry, and he died young. As a nation, America has never known the extremities of poverty that we find in most parts of the world today, in India or in China, for example, or even among the native Indians and the rural blacks of our country. But still, until recently, scarcity has been the rule. For while America held out the promise of enormous stores of untapped wealth, we came upon these shores to do a job: the destiny of our people was to hew a nation out of the wilderness, and make it powerful and great. It was a stirring enterprise, and we lived frugally to make it possible. Three and a half centuries of hard work have formed the character of our people.

Surrounded as we are by luxury and wealth, it is difficult to remember now what it was like. I was not born in this country, and I have vivid recollections of my childhood in Vienna in the thirties. It was a childhood lived within a typical economy of scarcity. Meat was eaten once a week, on Sunday, and the rest of the time you filled your stomach with potatoes, bread, and beans. In the corner grocery, the man would ladle sauerkraut out of a barrel and wrap it carefully in newspaper. At home, the lights were turned on only after dark and only where you needed them; the rest of the house was left in shadowy obscurity. The same was true of heating. There was an oven in each room, but the fire was kindled only where the family was gathered. And as for sleeping, one did not need a heated room, but crawled beneath the feather beds and threw the windows open to the cold. Clothing was patched and darned. One good suit was kept for years and years, protected against moths and dust, and worn only on festive occasions. When buying, you looked for sturdy quality, not style. To get around, you walked or took the tram. Only doctors had cars, we thought, and fat industrialists.

In all of this, one thing stands out with clarity: whatever one did, one would first compare the usefulness of this to that. One budgeted most carefully the little money one had —and always saved a bit, because saving was a hedge against the future.

The science of economics was born in the Era of Scarcity. It raised to the level of a scientific principle what everyone already knew from everyday experience. Utility was the cardinal standard according to which commodities, services, labor, and time were to be measured and compared. In the marketplace, all things were assigned a value according to their capacity for satisfying wants, while resources were allocated so that the net return in satisfactions for the final dollar spent would be the same from every use. The idea was that, as one accumulated more and more of anything of value, the appetite for it would be gradually satiated and finally stilled.

The tyranny of the principle of utility was total. Nothing could escape it. Man, for instance, was reduced to his role as a resource in the productive process, as worker, student, clerk, politician, or farmer. His worth was calculated by the present value of his discounted future earnings. And his earnings were dependent on the price his labor brought him in the marketplace. What useful things could he do? What functions could he perform? And how effectively? And that was all there was to man—a walking bundle of utilities wrapped up in flesh and bones. The logical corollary of the measure of utility was to treat everyone according to his economic worth. It was never a question of *who* you were but *what* you did. Utilitarians did not speak of persons but of individuals, of functional units interacting in functional ways. And interactions were regulated by time, which was regarded as being external to man, as something to be used and, therefore, useful. And so time had to be allocated carefully, according to the rules of the cardinal standard.

Along with an economy of scarcity went an appropriate ethics. Be thrifty, said the moral philosophers, work hard. Save and accumulate. Invest in the productive plant of the nation. In your dealings with others, be honest; don't shortchange them; use proper weights. But don't pay more than they deserve to get. Be temperate in your judgments; calculate your risks before you launch upon new enterprise. Respect the labor of others; take satisfaction in a good day's work. Measure progress by an index of how much you produce. Above all, do your work responsibly and well. The system depends on what you do.

But the Age of Utility ended by becoming the Age of High Consumption. Resources such as man and time and all the rest—minerals from the mountains, produce from the soil, machinery, organization—were to be used to gratify consumer wants that were increasing without apparent limit. When creature comforts were satisfied, one continued to accumulate utilities in terms of power and status. And lest one's appetites should flag, a whole new propaganda sector was invented to lure one into buying more.

In the Age of High Consumption, the old values have become irrelevant, and worse; they have become counterproductive. The hag of scarcity has fleshed out into Mother Bountiful. Our larders are full. The sauerkraut no longer comes in newspapers but tins, and what one does not need, one packs into the freezer. Walking is outmoded; one drives a car. And science has created so many wonders—journeys to the depths of the ocean and journeys to the moon and to the planets beyond—that anything that might be wanted seems to lie within man's reach. We seem to have moved into a realm of freedom where choice no longer need be closely calculated with an eye frozen on utilities and sheets of profit and loss, but can be free to explore the unlimited possibilities of human experience, from aphrodisiacs to Zen. Playfulness has replaced the standards of the counting house. Sensuality is sought in violence as well as love. The motorcycle has become the ambiguous symbol of both. Youthfulness is artificially prolonged by make-up, dress, and wigs to heighten the accumulating pleasures. From the lush undergrowth of the contempo culture is heard a cacophonous chorus celebrating life.

In all this confusion of contending values, in this sheer randomness of appearances, in this babble of tongues, where shall we find the values to guide the future course of the society? In an era of abundance, where all directions seem equally seductive, which shall we take? Values have become fragmented, and neither efficiency nor growth—the great touchstones of the past—is any longer accepted without serious question as a criterion for choosing. Why efficient, if not also beautiful and life-enhancing? Why more growth, if we are unable to manage it and only ruin our environment? The "quality of life" is held out as a substitute, but who determines what the quality of life should be? Post-industrial America has lost the fundamental consensus that has sustained the nation from its birth. In the decades ahead, the meaning of living in America is up for grabs.

2. *The cracked melting pot: rising cultural pluralism.* Mainstream America—the idea of a common race in the New World—has always been held in veneration. E PLURIBUS UNUM proclaims the great seal of the nation, and this refers not only to the federation of the states but also to the forging of a single people out of many, and the building of a culture shared by all.

The immigrant discovered it. To become American—to "americanize"—no other country has a word describing a similar process. There is no way for a Greek to become German, a Korean to become Japanese, an Italian to become Yugoslav; there is no word to describe "becoming

French." One can become *like* any of these nationalities, but never one of them. But one CAN become American, if not within the first, then in the second generation. While the older people huddled together in the national ghettos of our large cities, their children wished only to disappear among the millions of anonymous faces, forget the embarrassment of their origin, dress alike, eat alike, enjoy the same jokes, speak the same language, worship the same god, and weave fragments of historical folklore into a national myth. There was equality for all, they learned, no matter what their "race, color, creed, or national origin." Everyone was free to make the money that he could and say his piece. One might begin as office boy but, if one worked with diligence and cunning, one might someday become bank president. July the Fourth was the great rallying day. People waved the Stars and Stripes, had their myths rededicated, and settled to a picnic on the green.

Memories of the old country blurred quickly. In certain quarters of the city, one might still hear the old folks talking Yiddish or Italian, Armenian or Greek, Polish or German, drawing thin lifeblood from the past. On Saturdays, mainstream America came down to them, to rummage through their curio shops, breathe the exotic air, and click its tongues over a tantalizing meal. But returning uptown late at night, mainstream America knew in its heart this quaintness could not last. The children would eventually learn to speak American and to salute the flag; they would turn their backs upon their parents, and leave their parents' memories behind. They would grow up, the boys playing baseball and the girls cheering on.

And then, overnight, it was all different. And then, overnight, BLACK BECAME BEAUTIFUL. To be different became beautiful. To spit upon mainstream America became beautiful. And the beautiful people became Wasps, an uneasy majority among minorities.

It happened so fast that we are still reeling from the

shock. The Great Seal cracked, and we saw again the color of people's faces, the shape of their noses, the curling of their hair. The strange talk of the harmless folk moved right into the center of the city, but now it was the young who spoke it loud and aggressively. And it was no longer quaint.

We even felt a new mood blowing through the temples of the city, as many people reasserted their own faith and mode of worship against the tepid hymn singing issuing from mainstream pews. Church militant was on the march throughout America. Strange sounds, strange sights, strange tastes. Soul music and soul food; natural hairdos and Indian headbands. Old names were once again pronounced with pride: Aragon, Sullivan, Uyemori, Finkelstein. Hassidic Jews, in garb no more exotic than the rest, stepped from the pages of a novel by Isaak Bashevis Singer to recruit new members in the Student Union of the University of California . . . what was this all about? And what was happening?

It started with the blacks, Black Power and Black Pride, with the idea of a Black Nation, asserting their identity. They climbed out of their invisible slums, came to be seen, to be heard, to be respected, and to force the white majority to deal with them in terms of all their differences and grant to them the right to live among them as a nation, free from the ancient terrors. They wanted to be separate, but equal. The movement was truculent, its rhetoric was weird. Also, it was successful beyond all reasonable expectations. The blacks had shown the way; they had taken the trip and had come back.

The others were to follow soon: the browns, the reds, the yellows—Mexican Americans, American Indians, Japanese and Chinese Americans—the great minorities. But also Puerto Ricans and Jews, the Hippies and the Woodstock tribal nation, Hare Krishna monks and Women's Liberationists. Each group proclaimed its right to cop out from mainstream America and to be itself. The wish was to return to the tribal commune and share what could be shared—traditions and feelings, thoughts and beliefs, memories and hopes, but above all, pride in one's own way of being alive. Do YOUR OWN THING, said the philosophers of abundance. FIND YOURSELF, said the philosophers of America's new tribal nation. Join with those who are like you; discover yourself in the face of your brother.

And suddenly it was no longer wrong to live apart in separate enclaves. The territorial imperative took over. Neighborhoods proclaimed their right to be neighborhoods. Those with money to afford it moved out into the countryside, put up a wall, and sat beside their heated swimming pools in languid, isolated splendor. The blacks stayed behind in the smoggy wastelands of the city and told the white man to keep out. Students had their traditional preserves. An Indian tribe stormed Alcatraz and pitched their tents inside the former prison yard. And almost anybody might lie down to stop the bulldozers and so prevent the freeways, parking lots, and office towers that followed in their tracks from being built. And they would all raise a great ruckus, clenching their fists: *let no one come to change what we have built without consulting us! The community is us. The community is sacred. Stay out until we ask you to come in—on our terms.*

Mainstream America was gripped in fear. The dream had blown away so fast. Can there be really more than *one* America? Shall we withdraw, each group behind its castle walls, and put a gun beside the bed? Shall we melt down the Great Seal of the nation to stamp out little badges for each tribe? Shall we gild the ghetto, or integrate and level down, cast out the spell, enlarge the prisons, and push the bulldozers across the prostrate bodies? *Shall we plan for unity or for diversity? Shall we plan with people or against them? How?*

3. *The spreading sense of alienation: toward an active society.* The pervasive diffusion of utilitarian values through-

out America caused your person to be used by others for ends not necessarily your own; the connecting link was generally money. The highly differentiated roles you were asked to play made it difficult to integrate them around an adequate conception of the Self. The prevailing philosophy of functionalism did not encourage personal encounters through which you might discover who you were. In your dealings with others, you were not supposed to reveal the hidden recesses of your soul. *The system had bought only your role; it did not want your person.* Instead, it taught you how to bathe your relations with others in the bland oil of superficial friendliness and banter. It taught you how to "personalize" your services, but not to be a person. You were supposed to smile, adopt a casual and noncommittal posture, but keep your real feelings locked behind a door of steel.

Who were you then? When someone asked, you were expected to explain your job. But even this you did not fully comprehend. How did it actually relate to other jobs and to the enterprise that claimed so large a part of you? You worked, and you got paid for it, but how did it all add up? Someone, you thought, would surely know, high up above you in the spheres of corporate management, where all the facts were on computer tapes, where planners moved around abstract relations, and bureaucrats made choices that would filter down to you as orders. Perhaps the orders were not good, and then you grumbled. But, generally, you kept the grumbles to yourself. The shadowy authorities had probably good reason for choosing to keep you ignorant; they had a more encompassing responsibility. And, after all, how could you ever hope to reach their ear? You scarcely knew them by their names. There were suggestion boxes in the hall; if you were fortunate, the gods might listen to your mortal voice and send you a reward from heaven. But normally you sent the buck up till it stopped. Uncomprehendingly, you stood before the Moloch; the proper thing to do was not to question anything and do your work.

Your mind had thus been severed from its ancient moorings in feeling. Across the icy gap, relation to your dwarfed Self was impossible. You craned your neck, squinted your eyes, but the black empty hole of your Self remained empty. You were incapable of knowing either what you did or who you were. Life had become devoid of meaning.

But in their cunning, the managers had taken care of even this contingency. They offered the wild orgasm of consumption as a substitute for meaning and held out status and a share in power for those who dared to be ruthless. As for the rest, their minds were drowned in a barrage of images that were intended to amuse and entertain and sell, but not to make you think. They told you, look, it's happening NOW. You are already late. Climb up and join us for the trip; it's guaranteed to bring you instant satisfaction.

But the media also brought you news about the world outside the pleasure palaces. And what you finally made out, sorting the random images ever so cautiously, was weird. One by one, the storybook fables of childhood came tumbling down; your classroom teacher had not told you right. All the benefits that held you propped up in society flicked on as monstrous shapes upon the tube. The billy club, the looting mob, the starving children's bellies, the assassin's gun, the black man gagged and tied down in the Hall of Justice, the burning monk, the wasteland squalor of the city, mocked. Democracy, equality, justice? Peace? Beauty? Love? The words that flowed mellifluously from politicians' lips lacked credibility. From six to midnight every day, American society stripped off its clothes, its ugly sores exposed—a pious fraud.

Not everybody saw the show this way, of course. They were bewildered, yes, but refused to think that everything had changed in fundamental ways: AMERICA: LOVE IT OR LEAVE IT, their car stickers commanded. And they gave their votes to those who thought the nightmare that disturbed their sleep could be dispelled by increasing the dose of law and order. For the most part, they were older people, who had brought the world to this but could not face its implications.

But the young turned away from the system. In small but growing numbers, they chose among three paths. The first, *withdrawal:* the words appropriate to it have been incorporated into the language—turn off, cop out, drop out. Those who withdrew hit the drugs until the drugs became a menace to themselves. They wandered off as gentle hippies, no longer of this world, in search of love and kindness. They donned the saffron robes of Buddhist monks to beg and chant strange canticles in the streets. Others were wanton in their violent, destructive acts: the ritual murders of the Manson clan, black magic, and the havoc wrought by motorcycle gangs.

A second, *acid comment,* the Rabelaisian theater of the absurd. Mad happenings were staged: a naked female cellist playing Ave Maria to an enraptured audience; public copulation; mock funerals complete with dirges in the humid night. They invented a machine that, as it worked, gradually destroyed itself. They set up a thousand cans of Campbell's soup in a museum and called it ART. Their bitter jokes tore savagely into the establishment. Obscenities raged; nothing was holy.

The third, *revolutionary change* in every possible direction. The Yippies laughed and ran a pig for President. Black Panthers spat out their hatred of the white society and whipped the masses into fury with their rhetoric. The SDS engaged in confrontation politics, presenting non-negotiable demands. Hard-hat construction workers marched; riots ensued; the city burned.

The utilitarian society that had failed to hold the allegiance of the drug freaks, the black comedians, and the student militants showed some concern but did not panic. Deal with them firmly, said the voices of authority; co-opt them when you can, and law and order will be re-established in the land. But what they did not see was that a counter-culture was gradually taking shape among the exiles from America's mainstream. The prophets of the counter-culture recruited massive followings among the young. Their values contradicted the establishment on all essential points; but they appealed and gathered strength because they held out hope for a recovery of existential meaning.

Find your way back to the discovery of the Self, the prophets said; reassert your value as a person. Don't be afraid to show your feelings as they are. Be angry when you are angry, confused when you are confused, loving when you love. Let your thoughts merge with what your heart feels to be true. Don't shut the heart off from the mind; so isolated from each other, mind becomes sterile and heart overflows in boundless and destructive fury. Accept the ones with whom you live, help them in their discovery of who they are, and do not be afraid. Commit yourself to what you do, the prophets said; be credible. Fit actions to your words so that they may confirm each other. Work to redress the grievances of your society; do not accept what you cannot accept, but don't impose your views; learn from each other.

Build up new forms of the collective life, the prophets said; create new person-centered institutions. Avoid the large scale; work in small groups; let others truly share in tasks that you yourselves decide upon together. Hold down bureaucracy to the bare minimum you need for central guidance and strengthen non-hierarchical relationships that reach out to other groups. Do not engage in what you do not understand or, understanding, don't believe in doing. Take active part in the decisions that will shape your life.

These are the major values of the counter-culture. They are the values of a growing portion of the college generation that will rise to the controls of American society in the remaining decades of this century. They are new values for a society that, until recently, was based chiefly on the ideas of scarcity, mainstream culture, and a mechanistic social order in which each individual fitted as a replaceable and standardized part. But in an era of abundance, these bases tottered.

In place of them, the prophets of the counter-culture proposed to put a sense of non-utilitarian freedom, a richly patterned tribal culture, and a social order that had a place for persons relating to each other out of the plenitudes of their expressive selves. These values may be new today, but they are ancient in their origins. They represent a forward thrust into a timeless order. Utilized, depersonalized, mass man is a recent and perhaps ephemeral phenomenon of history. His powers are impressive and immense, but they are dwindling now. In the world foreshadowed by the counter-culture, rationality is no longer linear and stable, emanating from a central and all-knowing intelligence. And the planning of the future must adapt its style to this reality.

The Crisis of Knowing

1. *The growing scale and complexity of socio-technical systems: antinomies of knowing.* Planning concerns the use of knowledge in action. As part of a process of societal guidance, however, it concerns only those actions that have a bearing on the maintenance and change of structural relations in society. To be effective in this sense, planners must possess a relevant knowledge of the society. The question may therefore be raised: Can we obtain such knowledge about the inner workings of the world's first post-industrial society? Or are there limits to what can, in principle, be known about a large and complex system such as ours? Few national societies are as difficult to know as the United States, and few present such awesome challenges to planners who want to make their knowledge count. What is the nature of this challenge, and what conclusions may we draw from

it for the design of a more congruent system of guidance than that we now possess?

It will be useful, at the start, to distinguish between direct, personal knowledge, based on the experience of the knower with the facts at hand, and indirect, or processed, knowledge, which is based on other people's measurements and systematic observations.

Personal knowledge is limited to the experiences that one has had. Because of this, it is inadequate as an exclusive basis for action. In the first place, most of what we need to know must be obtained at second hand, by word of mouth, by reading, or by systematic study. Personal knowledge is encapsulated in contexual knowledge derived from other people's observations. This knowledge generally remains unexamined, constituting a web of myths that tempts us to extrapolate from personal experiences to broad generalizations. Secondly, personal knowledge is perspectivist, being slanted not only to the knower's position in the structure of society, but also, and more pertinently, to his particular involvement in the situations from which his experiences are drawn.

This bias is difficult to correct. From the standpoint of the knower, the only valid test of what he knows is a pragmatic one: personal knowledge either works or it doesn't. But even successive contradictions by events may leave its form essentially unchanged. For personal knowledge tends to be so closely identified with the knower that any challenge to its cognitive validity may be regarded as a threat to his integrity as a person. And thus it will be resisted.

Except as an account of what has taken place, told in straightforward and expository language, personal knowledge is prone to misuse on two accounts. Since it can offer at best a first-level and relatively superficial explanation of an event, misuse occurs when this personal view is accepted as the only possible account. Another sort of misuse is the transformation of a singular experience into a general statement through the medium of a mythological (i.e., unexamined) context.

We commit both kinds of error almost daily, because it is intellectually comfortable to do so. Critical, self-reflective thinking is both personally demanding and technically difficult. An example: we drive to the ball park and get caught in a monstrous traffic jam on the way. A first-level explanation of this event might be: too many cars converged upon a single area simultaneously, or the freeway exits were poorly designed, or not enough police were on hand to direct the traffic, and so on. (A more complete explanation might require us to explore a complex pattern of relationships that includes the location of the ball park itself, the timing of the game, the various approaches leading to the area, the traffic control system in use, the design of the freeway, and similar variables.) Furthermore, we may then raise our first-level account to the level of a general principle by furnishing a social context that is spun essentially out of myths. Freeways, someone might venture, are the result of a capitalistic system that exploits the poor for the benefit of the rich. Traffic jams are a product of social injustice. The myth itself—relating traffic congestion to a system of economic relations—is not further explored; it may be based on hearsay evidence ("There are no traffic jams in Moscow") or on deductive reasoning (socialism→public transportation→ smooth-flowing traffic) which is accepted as conclusive proof of its validity.

Myths such as these are necessary if we are to make any sense out of our everyday experiences. There is no time to subject the context of each experience to an exhaustive, critical analysis. But this fails to alter the conclusion that personal knowledge, projected into statements that claim to be true in a general sense, is usually in error.

This makes it clear that personal knowledge can never become the exclusive basis for societal guidance. On the other hand, for all its shortcomings, neither can we do without it. We shall shortly see why this is so.

Processed, in contrast to personal, knowledge is built up from symbols that stand for particular dimensions of reality, and is expressed in the form of models that can be formally communicated, critically examined, and revised on the basis of new observations. The principal characteristics of these models and their consequences for what we know about the world may be summarized as follows:

a. Models of processed knowledge represent a constructed reality; they are proposed as a theory *about* reality that is subject to scientific verification. But for every set of facts, more than one theory is possible, contingent on researches that will attempt to falsify the theories and to propose new explanations. As a result, most scientific theories about particular phenomena enjoy only a brief span of life. They represent a fleeting knowledge of the world.

b. Most models show a set of elements in a relation of equilibrium to one another. The stability of the model is assumed; the relationships described are valid only if the conditions in which the model is embedded do not change. Processes may be derived from this structure, but they are powerless to change it. Processed knowledge is conservative knowledge.

c. The larger the system that the model seeks to explain, i.e., the more encompassing the theory, the smaller will be the relative number of variables considered, the simpler will be the relations identified, and the greater will be the amount of relevant information filtered out. A magisterial input-output table of the economy can be represented as a matrix of twenty or two hundred sectors on a single sheet of paper. But it will tell us nothing about the nature of the industrial processes that are implied, the location of the productive firms, the forms of economic organization, the efficiency of management, and so on. Simply, but convincingly, it will show the sales of all the sectors to each other.

As such it may be useful, but it will bypass most of the essential data. A model such as this conforms to the rule that if you see the whole, you cannot see the parts. The inverse of this rule is also true. As a result, if you wish to see both part and whole, you have to look sequentially: first at the part, then at the whole, then back to the part, in a continuing sequence of observations out of which a composite image can emerge. But this image cannot be communicated, except again sequentially, as in the chapters of a book; it can never be communicated as a single, integrated whole. Processed knowledge is sequential knowledge.

d. Models are either presented as general theories, without explicit reference to time, or as particular theories where historical time is explicitly taken into account. If they are of the first kind, they are bound to be grossly in error whenever they are used to predict a specific event in a grid of time-space co-ordinates. But if they are of the second kind, their explanatory powers are quite limited, and usually they remain unverified, since the number of particular cases is unlimited, while the resources for research are always scarce. Both kinds of theory are necessary and useful; think, for example, of (1) the general theory of photosynthesis and (2) a special theory of smog formation in the Los Angeles basin. Their relationship will be tenuous and the resulting knowledge incomplete.

e. Models are necessarily partial and selective. They seize upon those elements of reality that are susceptible to modeling and about which information can be obtained. The frequency of models is therefore greatest where the largest amount of processed knowledge has accumulated in the past. In a sense, they endeavor to explain what has already been explained. In any event, processed knowledge leaves huge gaps of ignorance awaiting further exploration. Whenever a new model is dipped into reality, new variables are drawn out, and a new theory results. These theories float about, as it were, quite unconnected with each other. Sometimes they are quickly forgotten. At other times, they have a longer life-span and may attract the interest of scientists, only to lead eventually to more "exciting" models. The partial models are rarely brought together into a general theory. Processed knowledge is a fragmentary knowledge of reality.

f. Models use aggregated data. Each aggregate represents an abstract value for a number of elementary observations. To obtain such values is a licit enterprise. But in adopting this procedure, we are left in ignorance about the total range of observations and the particular form of the statistical distribution that underlies it, although this information may be every bit as interesting as the reality that has been modeled. A key datum in many planning studies is the total population of an area. But every area, having a spatial extension, can be broken down into smaller and smaller spaces, until the individual household in its habitat is reached. To say that country X has so much population will, therefore, tell us very little by itself. But the figure will be entered into models valid at the national level, as if the entire nation were compressed into a single point. Models are powerful to the extent that they achieve simplifications of this sort. But this achievement is possible only because they are cast in the form of probability statements. For instance, if we figure the population density per square mile in country X, we are forced to assume that it will roughly correspond to the actual densities that will be found in a random sample of selected subareas of the nation. Processed knowledge is probabilistic in its structure.

g. Models are essentially concerned with past relationships; they are incapable of generating innovations. An innovation is an element newly introduced into a given situation. The emphasis is on its newness with respect to the system into which it has been introduced. But *what* innovation will be introduced, and *when* and *how* and *with what consequences,* we cannot know in advance of the fact itself. Most models are internally consistent; that is part of their beauty and renders their results determinate. But innovations engender conflict, and the few conflict models that have been tried are indeterminate in their conclusions. Moreover, such models tend to be quite general in form; applied to the specific case, they do not lead to accurate predictions. Processed knowledge is oriented towards the recent past; the validity of its projections, whenever they are sufficiently concrete, is strictly limited to the near future; beyond that, it ceases to be knowledge and becomes prophecy.

h. Theories that model complex relationships usually make quite extraordinary demands on data. Brought together in the model, these data are subjected to certain quantitative manipulations in their relationships to each other. However, the original data may contain some error, and the rules of transformation in the model may themselves not be precise. Although there is a tendency in such a process for errors to cancel each other out, the greater their number or scope, the more likely it becomes that they will not, that instead of diminishing they will blow up. Futhermore, since models are frequently used to project future values, or to make comparisons with the past, the value of the change observed may itself be attributable to nothing more than error. A well-publicized example of this problem is the calculation of national income accounts. The rate of change in income from one year to the next is usually quite small, but major policies are often based on it. Yet, when it is small, say only 1 or 2 per cent, even the sign may turn out to be in error, so that an apparent increase may actually be a decline in the economy. One is forced to conclude that processed knowledge is prone to large and undetected error.

i. Models are symbolic representations of reality. Frequently, however, they serve as substitutes for a reality inaccessible to personal experience. The power of models to create images of the real world is very great. Their logical consistency, their conceptual precision, their quantitative implementation all conspire towards this end. Yet the real world is somewhere down in the relations among people, social groups, and institutions. It is a gross distortion of reality to accept the model as the thing in itself; to do so can have disastrous consequences. There is no way to correct this distortion when reality is inaccessible to personal knowledge. A model of changes in settlement patterns is a case in point. There is no way to learn about changes in settlement except through quantitative-geographic analysis. You can wander through a thousand streets and pass through all the villages and towns of the nation, and still not have a sense of how the pattern as a whole evolved historically. This pattern reveals itself only in charts, maps, and statistical tables. We accept these images and act accordingly. But images can be misleading, and the actions based on them may be inappropriate. Processed knowledge creates distorted images of reality.

The crisis of knowledge in America derives partly from our modes of knowing the world. When the society was small and rudimentary, one could learn most of the relevant facts about it and form appropriate images that served one well in guiding actions. But as society expanded, what we could know about it became more problematical each day, even as the need for conscious guidance became a condition of its survival. This failure to understand, and the consequent inability to provide even minimally effective guidance has led, with rising frequency, to what some observers have called a "turbulent" environment in which individual and collective actions produce negative and unpredictable results for others, even for the originator of the action himself. Many people tend to experience American reality as the outcome of randomly operating forces, and what is happening no longer seems to add up.

Personal knowledge is totally inadequate as the sole approach to system guidance, yet processed knowledge is also severely limited in what it is able to do. It is, as I have tried to show, ephemeral, conservative, sequential, tenuous, incomplete, fragmented, probabilistic, oriented towards the recent past, prone to large and undetected error, and likely to generate images that are reality-distorting. It is not what many people think it is—a stock of verities, solid and permanent, true knowledge of the whole, deterministic and complete, a seamless web, pressing forward into the future, an honest guide to action. If it were all these things, central guidance would be easy, and personal knowledge would be clearly revealed as an inferior form of knowing. But it is not, and we are therefore obliged to find some way of relating personal to processed knowledge on quite equal terms, using each to correct and supplement the other. And we must find a way to introduce into systems of societal guidance a mode of knowing that values the use of a diversity of models, an approach that is frankly experimental and self-correcting. Models are useful and perhaps the only tools we have for learning rapidly in complex situations; but they reflect fictitious and distorted images of reality. In societal guidance, they must become connected with personal knowledge so that both, those who know primarily from experience and those who know about the world chiefly through the prismatic images of models, may increase their capacity for learning. I shall refer to the resulting process as *mutual learning*.

2. *Accelerated rate of change: disrupted continuity.* It is impossible to document the rate of technological and social change in our time, and consequently impossible to support the statement that it has been accelerating. Attempts have been made to show a geometric increase in the number of scientific publications or inventions. But these figures do not convey the *sense* of super-rapid change in the environment in which we live. Someone returning from an extended stay abroad, who has been cut off from the daily news at home, would scarcely recognize his coun-

try. Old cities have been torn up and rebuilt; the language has changed and is spiked with colorful expressions whose meanings are still unrecorded; new social movements abound; fifth graders are shown movies about the effects of using drugs; obscenities have become a public attraction; new technological marvels have appeared; pictures of the moon landing are televised to Earth; the scientific verities of yesterday have become obsolete. Within a single decade, we have advanced from the New Frontier through a racial revolution and a war against poverty, to a national concern with environmental degradation, unemployment and inflation. One sometimes feels that only the war in Vietnam is still around.

The present rate of change is overwhelming. Almost nothing is fixed; everything appears to be in movement. The impressions accumulate in unstable heaps that tumble down, disintegrate, when the pile becomes too high, only to build up again to dizzying heights and then collapse once more. Interpretations count for almost nothing any more. Intellectuals are working overtime to detect some pattern in the shifting sand, but to little avail. Everyone sees something different, and no sooner is one theory proposed than another one appears, blowing the first into oblivion. Even the statisticians cannot keep pace. They scarcely know what to count next. Riots? The Pill? Group Sex? Murder? Black Professionals? Sensitivity Training Groups? Freeway Miles? Smog? And who would need to know and to what purpose?

Among planners, there has recently been a good deal of talk about the need for "social indicators," for useful measures of society's performance, but the practical results so far have been disappointing. Without a theoretical framework to tie the indicators back into the structure of society, we are unable to devise efficient strategies of intervention. Indeed, we are unable to provide a satisfactory explanation of the multiple changes we observe. The indicators do not indicate. What does a rising crime rate index, for example, tell us except that crime is increasing or that the police are perhaps doing a better job of reporting crime than they did before? It does not lead to helpful conclusions. On the contrary; it may succeed in creating an atmosphere of panic in which people are inclined to grab a gun and shoot at sight.

Out of this sense of cognitive disorientation has come at least one strong conclusion. What was yesterday cannot serve us as a guide to what will be tomorrow. We have little to learn from the past. The ragpickers of history cannot tell us anything about the Age of Now, the age of total, but fragmented sensations. And of what value are even the reports of statisticians, mulling over the old data that no longer describes what is, but only what has been? The world is being shaken up like a kaleidoscope. Nothing remains the same but for a few seconds. Tomorrow, looking at the tube, reading the paper, we will be living in a different world, and after that in yet another world, and after that. . . . The exciting heady stuff dissolves the moment that we try to shape it into knowledge. We are left with a few fragments and do the best with them we can. But we are stammering.

In desperate search for a foothold on firm land, a few daring spirits have set out to explore the future. They are a bunch of hardy pioneers. But this much is clear from their efforts. To the extent that the future is different in its structural relations from the present, it is incapable of being known. Since it has not occurred, it cannot be known except as it is already lodged in the present, but even then we do not know which of the myriad possibilities that are contained in now will eventually materialize.

And so, in the temporal aspect of history, in the external movement of everything, speeded up almost beyond endurance, the knowledge we have appears as but a flimsy covering for our ignorance. The past is irrelevant; the present is known only in fragments, leaving huge voids; and the future cannot be known. Under these conditions, what shall we do? Is planning still possible? Can knowledge still be linked to action?

Even the poor man survives, miraculously. He makes the best of what he has. He wakes and struggles for survival. His wit is quick to grasp at opportunities. He does not think too far ahead. He avoids major commitments when he can. He looks for openings and for routes of escape. Every day, the poor man recovers the future from the scrap heap of the past. And perhaps he will continue to survive.

In our poverty of knowledge, we are all very much like him. The little that we know, we must use well. We have to make the future as we go along.

3. *The growing gap between experienced and observed reality: the incommunicability of expert knowledge.* Our ignorance is great, but our need for knowledge even greater. We stand in awe before the man who knows. He has gained access to the information on which our lives so desperately depend. His words fall in austere cadences that mean little to us. Yet we believe in the efficacy of his incantations to dominate the spirits that, invisible to all but him, rule our lives. This spirit world is far from the experienced world of common sense. Removed from time and place, the expert moves about in realms without dimension, communicating in a secret language with other members of his caste spread out over the globe. His values reflect the code of his craft no less than what he knows. He works while others sleep. He seems remote and unapproachable to ordinary men. His words project authority. He is the lord of processed knowledge.

We are prepared to give him all the social recognition he demands, yet we are rarely willing to lend an ear. A yawning gap of non-communication separates his world of learning from the world of acting. The rules that govern the behavior of these two worlds have nothing in common. The *requirements of learning* bind the expert to the constant examination and re-examination of his data at the level of theory and of experiment. The *requirements of action* bind the potential client to pragmatic tests of what will work. And so, each must obey the laws of his calling:

–the expert, to work with models abstracted from the real world and operating under controlled environmental conditions: the actor, to work with models of the real world under the variable conditions of a shifting environment;

–the expert, to work without regard to an existing power distribution and to be unconcerned with outcomes in the real world: the actor, to take the distribution of power as the starting point of his analysis and to consider, first, the means through which a course of action may be carried out;

–the expert, to search for certainty in results by means of continuous exposure to critical views: the actor, to take on normal risks of action and keep opponents ignorant of his own strategies;

–the expert, to be content with general solutions within the assumptions of the model: the actor, to seek deterministic answers to the problems of a special case;

–the expert, to interpret the past: the actor, to make the future;

–the expert, to work without limitations of time: the actor, to work under the pressure of time;

–the expert, to specialize in one branch of knowledge at a time: the actor, to demand a general expertise, capable of taking many branches of knowledge simultaneously into account;

–the expert, to look for success in academic recognition: the actor, to look for practical payoffs in terms of profits and power.

These two modes of behavior, one oriented to the acquisition of knowledge, the other to the acquisition of power, seem to be growing further apart. They have become mutually incompatible and incommensurable. The accelerated pace of scientific enterprise fosters increasing specialization. Each expert hoes his own row; he calls across to a few neighbors laboring within earshot. Problems are formulated in ways that men of action do not understand. The normal language of scientific discourse is ever more conceptual and mathematical, removed from primary experience. How should the mayor of a city understand the meaning of an economic landscape, an interaction surface, or the differences between wavelike and hierarchical diffusion processes? These concepts, on the frontiers of knowledge, may take a decade to filter down to the layman at the frontiers of action. Meantime, what is the actor to do? Accept on trust the expert's counsel? Remain stranded in the lagoons of his personal knowledge? Or should he turn his powers over to the lords of processed knowledge and put his faith in the geometries of reason? How is the gap in knowledge to be bridged?

The solution seems to lie in the forging of a personal relation between expert and client actor, in the adoption of a "transactive" style of planning. Processed knowledge would thus be joined to action through a series of personal transactions that would bring the rules of the two worlds into conjunction. Each world would thus be modified in turn. The moral values of the planner and his client stand at the center of this new relation, so that advice and its acceptance will be based on the degree of confidence one has in the position of the other. Personal would come to be connected with processed knowledge in the planner's mind, just as the client's mind would be enriched by reasoned judgment based on expert study. Problems would be formulated jointly and solutions studied for their relevance to action. In time, the planner's models would be cast into new molds, but in the urgencies of action, he would rely upon his gifts for disciplined invention as much as on a formal statement of the probable results. Transactive planning rests essentially on the ideas of human worth and reciprocity. It is the only process through which effective learning can occur.

A Planning Style for Post-Industrial Society

The context of post-industrial society—the crises of values and of knowledge we have unfolded in these pages—sets the conditions under which both allocative and innovative forms of planning must be made to work. The emerging realm of non-utilitarian freedoms, rising cultural pluralism, participant democracy, the antinomies of knowing, disrupted temporal continuities, and the growing difficulties with the communicability of expert knowledge will either forge a style of planning that is adapted to the new environment or leave the choice of society's actions to the limited, non-adaptive perspectives of personal knowledge, unaided by a scientific-technical intelligence. What lessons for the new style have we learned?

The crisis of values has taught us:

–to regard the future as open to choice and experimental action;

–to place the person as a source of moral values in the center of any action;

–to search for participant forms of social organization and to accept the perspectivist views of each of these as a valid foundation for societal planning;

–to enlarge the scope for autonomous group action by reducing the influence of bureaucratic organizations, effectively decentralizing power, and linking the new communitarian forms of social relations into larger participatory structures capable of sharing effectively in the processes of societal guidance.

And the crisis of knowledge has taught us:

–to put the emphasis on a transactive style of planning;
–to stress, within this context, the importance of mutual learning;
–to turn planning increasingly to the interests of individual client groups and organizations;
–to facilitate a rapid learning process through an efficient system of information feedback to the centers of societal action;
–to concentrate attention on the near future; and
–to plan for actions in no greater detail than our knowledge of the probable consequences will allow.

These stylistic features will serve as the criteria for the design of a new guidance system appropriate to post-industrial society and capable of supporting those values which are now competing for attention. In general, they suggest a guidance system in which innovative planning—with its emphasis on institutional development, involvement in actions, the mobilization of resources, and a selective focus—will be applied at the key points of intervention for the construction of a new society, while allocative planning—designed for system maintenance—will link participant with corporate, and corporate with policies planning. The pervasive style will be transactive.

Before embarking on this new design, we need to look more closely at two salient aspects of societal guidance. The first relates to the value of the future in the present (Chapter 5). All guidance efforts are necessarily oriented towards the future. But is the future to be regarded simply as a container into which we pour the consequences of present actions? Or are we drawn into the future by the values, goals, objectives, and utopian constructs we have put there ourselves? Or is the future wholly contained in the present and, therefore, predictable? What is the nature of the special relationship we have to future time?

The second aspect requires a look at systems of societal guidance, their influence on collective phenomena, and the role of innovative planning in the development of a society (Chapter 6). The failures of planning in the past can, in large measure, be attributed to a methodology that was based on a deterministic model of society. A change in this assumption will have far-reaching implications. Specifically, it will assign to innovative planning a far more central role in guidance systems than it has had till now.

CHAPTER 5

THE USES OF THE FUTURE

The process of societal guidance occurs in the present, but its real object is the future. With respect to the future, planners typically ask three questions: What is likely to happen without specific intervention? What should happen? And how can the desired future state be brought about? The first question demands a prediction and is addressed to scientists. The second is essentially moral in content and is addressed to politicians. The third, which is concerned with means, is addressed to technical experts.

The questions are valid, but they hide the complexities of dealing with the future behind an oversimplified concept of the division of labor. The future is a completely different dimension of time from the remembered past or the experienced present. How it is interpreted will decisively influence the design of a system of societal guidance. Let me attempt to clarify this by examining some important characteristics of the future.

The future appears to us as an objective dimension of metric time. We count it in hours, days, months, years, and centuries. These units of measured time follow each other in an irreversible, arithmetical sequence independently of our senses. The future thus appears as an external, objective order whose laws are determined by the movement of the planet.

The future appears to us as a projected dimension. Like an arrow, it moves forward from the past and present along a linear path. Time does not curve back upon itself. The future is a projected reality capable of being viewed only from the perspective of the present; it is neither the fantastic, timeless world of children's fairy tales, nor a palpable reality that we have lived.

From the perspective of the present, the future may be viewed in two ways. As future history, it is continuous with the past, and appears either as a logical extension of, or in dialectical opposition to, past events. As utopia, it is projected as an ideal state discontinuous with the past but capable of informing and inspiring present actions.

The future appears to us as a dimension of yet unrealized possibilities. We tend to regard the future as an empty container that can be filled with the quasi-reality of projected images. Some projected futures we believe (or *expect*) to be more probable than others; we also prefer them to a greater or lesser extent, that is, we *hope* that they will or will not come about. The relations between these psychological propensities can be visualized in the form of a two-by-two matrix:

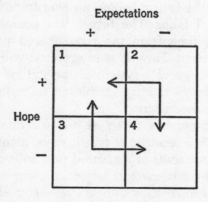

Figure 3. Expectations

Square (1) includes projected possibilities we like and can probably achieve; square (2) includes those things we wish for but probably cannot achieve; square (3) includes what we would rather not see happen but probably will happen anyway; and square (4) includes everything we do not want that is, in any event, improbable.

Both expectation and hope are subjective states of mind; we have no way of verifying either. Also, they are difficult to keep separate. Strong positive hopes will lead us to discount low expectations, so that a projected image we greatly desire will seem more probable than it would if it were less desirable (2→1). Strong negative desires, on the other hand, will lead us more willingly to accept forecasts that show a low probability for the occurrence of a specific event (3→4).

The reverse of this situation is also true. Low expectations tend to discourage hope (2→4), while high expectations tend to strengthen positive feelings about events that appear probable (3→1). As a result, the possibilities we project into the future are nearly always some mixture of hope *and* expectation.

The future appears to us as a dimension of change. A completely unchanging social system (possible only in the imagination) would have no future, only an eternal present. Nothing would move, no external forces would intrude, no forms would change. The universe would be completely lifeless; in the language of physics, it would have reached a state of complete entropy of randomness in the distribution of energy.

But life, as we experience it, is not at all like this. Historical changes may be exceedingly slow, as in the case of certain cultures arrested at a primitive level of development, but they do occur. Through contacts with the outside world or through inventions, metric time acquires a special set of meanings and is transformed into historical time.

The future appears to us as a dimension of choice. Choosing means having the power to make one's wish effective, to

take the steps that will bring the future into some con-
cordance with the choice. This is not to say that we are free
to *will* the future. Our powers are always limited, and our
knowledge of functionally efficient relations is imperfect.
Through the actions flowing from it, every choice results in
consequences only some of which can be foreseen. Because
of this, we do not choose the future once and forever, but
many times over, as information about consequences becomes available, as we adjust to other changes within the
system, and as our attitudes and values change. The choice
of the future is, in reality, a kind of exploration or, better
yet, an *experiment* that involves a series of sequential steps
and is corrected by a continuous stream of information flowing back to us. Essentially, it involves a process of learning.

*The future appears to us as a non-homogeneous dimen-
sion.* The near appears more determinate than the distant
future. For the near future, we assume the relative stability
of existing structures in the environment. Our behavior is
based on the expectation of continuity and order. So important is this assumption to our lives that we normally act "as
if" things would not change substantially, even when they
patently do. Adjustments in normal behavior are made only
under critical conditions when the assumption of "as if" is
clearly no longer tenable. Thus the possibilities for choice
with regard to the near future appear to be severely restricted.

The further we project the future from the present, however, the less we believe that things will stay the same, and
the more liberty we seem to have to choose a future that we
like, regardless of the facts. Past events may shape the future
for a hundred years; nevertheless, as we project life's possibilities farther and farther ahead, we act as if we expected
our choices to become increasingly free from past constraints.

The future appears to us as an unbounded dimension.
We regard it as a dimension essentially without limit and

without a preordained goal, which will terminate only with the disappearance of the human species. Some mystics and philosophers, such as Teilhard de Chardin, see history evolving toward some finite point, an Omega, a touching of the human spirit with the Divine.[1] But regardless of our metaphysics, we act in the world "as if" the future extended indefinitely forward in time.

These conceptions of the future, and the importance accorded them, are peculiar to the Western mind. In the biblical tradition, they presuppose free choice and center this choice in man. Only one constraint is imposed upon the exercise of our freedom: a knowledge of good and evil, and the responsibility we consequently bear for the outcome of our actions.

In Western thought, the future appears as something distinct and separate from us that is to be subdued, managed, and made to serve our needs. Our attitude toward the future is Faustian in its overweening pride and its separation from nature.

This differs radically from the time conceptions of other cultures. Complete belief in predetermination, for example, implies subordination to the Eternal Will of God, forever inaccessible to human reason (Islam). A philosophy that regards man as an integral part of nature subjects his future to the rhythmic movement of the elements (Taoism). A view of the world as essentially chaotic implies that we appease the spirits and supplicate their favors (Aztec). Yet the Western conception of time is being increasingly accepted by non-Western peoples, and is now predominant.

The Desired Future

Two major kinds of intellectual orientation suggested by Karl Mannheim profoundly influence our projections of the desired future: ideological and utopian.

Ideological thinking is rooted in the established order and

is used to affirm and justify it; utopian thinking is rooted in the moral imagination and is used to transcend the established order. Our desired futures incline toward one or the other pole, and each orientation tends to provide moral justification for the actions we undertake in its name.

The differences between the two are decisive. Ideological thinking trusts in the gradual unfolding of the possibilities inherent in an established system of order (political, economic, social, and cultural). It takes for granted that the system, however imperfect, can be brought closer to its ideal form. As a result, ideological thinking is basically reformist. It does not challenge the system's structural relations, but seeks only to modify some of their effects.

Utopian thinking, on the other hand, believes in the necessity of a sharp break with the established order and the creation of an altogether different reality. It is concerned with total entities, the one existing and historical, the other projected into an indeterminate future. Where utopian thinking is related to action, it appears as a revolutionary movement. But whether or not it is linked to action, it has an important influence on ideological thinking because it strengthens the latter's desire for change and accelerates urgently needed, if partial, reforms within the existing system.

Utopian thinking is subject to an internal contradiction, however. So long as it does not seek to move into the realm of action, it is an important corrective to ideological thought. But when it acquires the features of a revolutionary movement, the exigencies of action inevitably take precedence over the long-term requirements of the new order. What matters now is the subversion of the existing bases of power in the society. To the revolutionary, the future is immediate and replete with narrow, pragmatic choices. It ceases to be in any sense utopian.

But the moment he succeeds, his thinking becomes ideological. For now that he has acceded to power, a new social order must be built up and perfected. Old utopian ideas must make room for practical considerations and the compromise has to be defended against opposition. His thought no longer attempts to transcend an existing reality; it now serves merely to justify it. The successful revolutionary inevitably becomes conservative. And with the passage of time, the new society will generate its own adversaries who will question its tarnished reality in the name of a new utopian future.

Utopian thinking is, therefore, effective only when it occurs within the matrix of the society it rejects. It can never become an action orientation in its own right. The foundation of practical action has always been ideology, while utopian thinking has served as leavening in the process of perfecting a given social system.

These relations are illustrated in Figure 4. I do not mean to suggest that the sequence shown in this diagram is, in any sense, inevitable. Some societies may avoid successive revolutions by either absorbing major elements of utopian thinking or repressing counter-movements with brute force. Other societies may be overthrown from without or made tributary to some external power by more peaceful means. But the diagram does show, in a rather general, schematic form, the leavening influence of utopian thought on going societies (expressed here as a conflict relation, $i_1 \longleftrightarrow i_2$), the conversion of utopian into ideological thought that comes as the result of successful revolution ($u_2 \rightarrow i_2$), and the relation of one social order to the next ($s_1 \rightarrow s_2 \rightarrow s_3$). It should be added that the physical superposition of S curves in the diagram is not meant to convey a progressive forward thrust in history. Each system is different, but in an historical perspective none is necessarily "better" than the preceding one.[2]

If this line of reasoning is correct, utopian thinking may be laid aside, at least for the time being, and we can concentrate on how ideological images of the future may be related to present actions. Technical planners have frequently claimed that the alternatives for present choice can

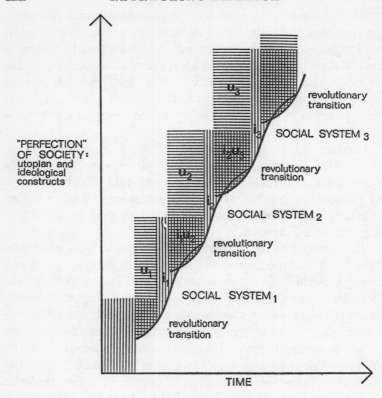

Figure 4. Ideologies, Utopias, and Revolutions in the Transformation of Societies

be deduced in logical form from the major value premises of the society by a process known as goal reduction (Figure 5). This process posits a hierarchy of objectives, where each level may be deduced from the next higher one on the basis of both functional and logical relationships that are known (or can be discovered) to exist.

This hierarchy has the form of a truncated pyramid, so that the number of "actions" is necessarily much larger than the number of major societal "goals" from which they are derived and towards which they will presumably be directed. Each level in the hierarchy, moreover, is both a means and an end, except for the two extremes: actions, which are purely instrumental, and general societal values, which are taken to be the ultimate ends of the society.

Some planners claim that they are able to prepare just such a table of hierarchically ordered social values. Their claim is false, however. For the hierarchical arrangement of values is not merely a functional and logical but also a *temporal* ordering, which moves from the near future at the base (actions) to the distant future at the top. This creates problems that, even in terms of the planner's own assumptions, make the whole enterprise of goal reduction unrealistic.

To start with, choice among alternative objectives is not simply a technical question. A number of equally plausible routes (sub-objectives) may lead to each level in the hier-

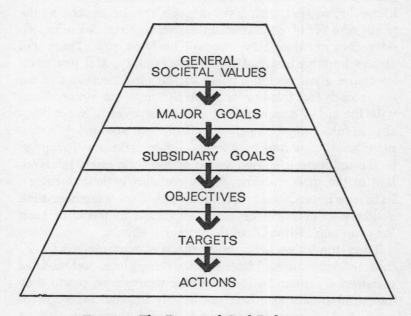

Figure 5. The Process of Goal Reduction

archy of goals, and different social valuations can be attached to each of these routes. These valuations can be
made legitimately only through a political or quasi-political
process, however. Such processes exist in every society for
deciding on current or *immediate* actions; they do not exist
for making choices about potential actions that are still in
the remote future. Yet unless these choices are made (and
the planners cannot make them, except by substituting their
own values for those of future political processes—a highly
suspect business, at best), the goal-reduction process breaks
down. There can be no gaps in the chain of consequences
and actions that is deduced in a reverse order of time from
distant general objectives down to the level of present action.

The other difficulties with the concept of goal reduction
are no less instructive for our purposes. The ability to engage in goal reduction presumes a thorough knowledge of
the functional relations connecting the several layers in the
hierarchy, so that each level of goals can be treated as the
result of a set of actions taken earlier in time. Such knowledge does not now exist, nor is it likely to exist. There will
always be large areas of doubt, uncertainty, and just plain
ignorance about society's behavior. This is especially true for
the second- and third-order repercussions of an action. Even
with the aid of computerized simulation models, we are unable to take complex feedback effects into account. We simply do not know how people and organizations will respond
to the unforeseen consequences of someone else's intervention in the social process. Every complex action, therefore,
has large unpredictable and unintended consequences that,
as likely as not, will be more important in terms of their
long-run implications than the intended effects.

Then, too, there is the appearance of more or less "spontaneous" innovations whose nature, time, place, and mode of
occurrence cannot be foreseen and whose repercussions on
the social system are therefore largely unpredictable. Yet a
good deal of planning revolves around these innovations

and their effects, as society attempts to accommodate to them in advance. To leave them out of account, as one would have to do in the process of goal reduction, would mean to arrive at irrelevant conclusions. A similar effect is caused by changes that are external to the system but impinge on its internal structure. Such situations are seen very frequently in planning practice. Usually, they lead to a reordering of the priorities for action and, in many cases, to a reassessment of the situation and the definition of new problems.

For all these reasons, goal reduction in the sense of a scientific analysis-in-reverse, proceeding from distant goals to present decisions and actions, is a logical as well as a practical impossibility. Precisely the same reasons can be advanced to show that, except in a highly restrictive sense, the process of *forward analysis* or forecasting is equally impossible.

In planning it is not enough to predict the outcome of an action in which the context does not change. This is essentially the procedure of experimental science. Planners, however, often find it necessary to project a total set of historical conditions that are, in turn, subject to the influence of a multiplicity of ill-understood forces, both internal and external to the situation. History, unfortunately, cannot be projected in this total sense except as pure imagination.

In practice, the context of the situation that is to be altered by a specific act of intervention is usually assumed to remain constant; in other cases, alternative "scenarios" of the future may be constructed, based on different assumptions about the "external" environment. Neither approach is entirely satisfactory. Holding the environment constant may leave out of account some of the most important variables for altering the future, while the scenario method fails to provide a criterion of choice among alternatives. Because the relationships among elements composing a scenario are at best plausible, incapable of being verified, the construction of scenarios is not a scientific enterprise at all, as it is sometimes claimed to be, but essentially a *moral* one. The attractiveness of future scenarios for planning lies not in the accuracy of their prescriptions for specific actions, but rather, as it were, in their ability to *import values* from the future into the present, providing political actions with a moral foundation.

In most societies, several images of the desired future compete with one another, clashing whenever one group tries to impose its particular vision to the exclusion of some or all of the others. So long as the competition occurs within the framework of ideological thinking, conflicts can and usually will be resolved by negotiation. That is partly what politics is about. Where there is widespread agreement on the meaning of the good society, the differences will be chiefly over emphases, priorities, and rate of change. Given a sufficiently flexible political system, a way will be found in which the priorities of the most vocal groups can be accommodated over time. Utopian constructs, on the other hand, are non-negotiable. They break into history as an absolute force, and where they have strong support among sizable groups of the public, they create a serious problem at the political level.

The Expected Future

A flat assertion was made in Chapter 4 that we cannot have *knowledge* of the future but only *beliefs* about the probable occurrence (or non-occurrence) of future events. I would now like to elaborate upon this statement.

It is a generally accepted idea that the aim of science is to arrive at statements about phenomena that lead to reasonably accurate predictions concerning their behavior. This is certainly true for the natural sciences, and despite some methodological controversy it is also true for the social and behavioral sciences, particularly economics. What is usually left unsaid is that predictive statements are extremely formal—relating, in the experimental sciences, to the behavior of a few variables under highly simplified and rigorously controlled conditions and, in the historical sciences, to the behavior of certain variables under conditions that are *assumed* to remain unchanged but cannot be controlled. Thus I may have a theory that asserts that the economy of a region will grow as a function of increasing its exports to other regions. Exports create "multipliers" within the region, which ultimately lead to an increase in the regional product that will be greater than the initial export effect. But to make this statement historically valid for any particular region, a number of additional variables must be considered, including the nature of the exports, the ownership pattern of the export industries, the number of workers employed relative to the capital used, the workers' place of origin, the existence or non-existence of urban markets in the region, its geographical relation to nearby markets, the ability of local entrepreneurs to respond to new demands and challenges, the settlement pattern, the export sector's demand for raw materials and intermediate products and the locations of the industries producing them, the economics of interindustry relations, and threshold sizes of new industries and services in terms of market demand. The simple prediction based on theory, that increases in regional exports lead to greater than proportional increases in the region's product, is true as far as it goes. But it does not adequately explain the behavior of particular regional economies and is of little use in predicting their reaction to specified increases in exports. For this last can be done only on the assumption that everything else will remain constant, and this is evidently not the case.

Predictive statements are therefore always cast in a form of "*if* this, *then* that." Nevertheless, there is a lingering belief that our inability accurately to predict the future states of social systems is due primarily to the immaturity of the social sciences. As I have suggested, a faith in the eventual capacity of the social sciences to predict the course of history underlies all traditional notions about planning, especially the classical decision model (see Chapter 3) with its reliance on prediction.

This faith is based on two alternate images of scientific work. According to the more primitive image, scientific workers are engaged in building a huge edifice, rather like the Tower of Babel. The results of their work, brick laid on brick, is cumulative, even though it is not centrally coordinated. Science yields "hard" facts that are incorporated in ever more general and expanding theories. As the tower of theory (composed of sub-theories and facts) rises slowly over the plains of common ignorance, scientists are able to encompass wider and wider areas in their vision that will eventually include the future. It is consequently only a question of time until we have the knowledge that will enable us accurately to predict the future.

According to the more sophisticated image, scientists inhabit the myriad cells of a fly's eye, looking in all directions at once. Each scientist penetrates his own specialized area of knowledge and reports the information he finds (together with his conclusions) to a central brain in the fly's mind, where all the information is collated and synthesized by computer. As more and more information is channeled to this centralized intelligence and something like "total" knowledge is approached, the fly's ability to predict the future increases remarkably. Prediction in this sense is a function of the total amount of knowledge available to the central brain, an image frequently used to justify the creation of so-called data banks, and the basis of all the proposals for a central "intelligence" system (or planning function) that will send the correct messages to the far ends of the central nervous system (i.e., to the operators and workers), instructing them in their individual tasks.

Both these images are misleading. The reasons can be

found in the structure of knowledge and of the future. With respect to knowledge, we can say, based on earlier analysis, that:

–Knowledge is cumulative only within the assumptions of what Thomas Kuhn calls "normal" science, that is, the assumptions of the current scientific establishment.[3] From time to time, these assumptions are overthrown in a process not unlike a socio-political revolution, which replaces an outdated orthodoxy with a new one and establishes the framework for a new generation of scholars.

–Knowledge is not an accumulation of "solid" facts, like a wall made out of bricks, but arises from the interplay of theories and counter-theories, each drawing on its own set of data and making its own interpretations.

–The more general the knowledge about a range of specified phenomena, the fewer details it encompasses; but the reverse is also true: the more detailed the knowledge, the narrower its focus.

–Different kinds of knowledge are not always directly convertible into each other. For example, we have one theory to explain individual behavior and another for the behavior of large groups or institutions. Attempts to link these theories have not, in the majority of cases, been successful. Similarly, the findings of political economy usually do not jibe with those of classical economics, even though there are important points of intersection between them. Beyond these points, the two fields have a different focus, apply different methodologies to different sets of data, and are incapable of being integrated, except at the most general level of theory.

–The larger the number of variables within a single

theoretical (i.e., explanatory) model, the greater is the effect of random occurrences on the results obtained.

–Reality, and consequently knowledge about reality, is literally inexhaustible. The nature and extent of our knowledge depends essentially upon the questions we can formulate concerning different types of behavior. Historical reality is a continuing flow of events that constantly replenishes itself. As our interests shift, so does scientific effort. New questions are raised about entirely different constellations of facts, while older questions are laid aside or forgotten. We never have enough time to exhaust all possibilities for improving our understanding of a given reality. At any one moment, therefore, knowledge of reality is an infinitesimally small constant that does not rise substantially over the "plains of common ignorance" but is tied to the ephemeral and narrow range of phenomena to which our attention has temporarily turned.

The structure of the future presents a number of serious obstacles of its own to the idea that the future will eventually be mastered by the cumulation of knowledge and the creation of a central intelligence function. I have already mentioned the matter of innovations whose nature, time of occurrence, and potential impact on society cannot be predicted with any reasonable precision, regardless of how much information is accumulated. A quite similar phenomenon is the sudden reversal of a previously dominant trend, the result of unforeseeable changes in public attitudes. The elder Henry Ford could never have dreamed that the California State Legislature during 1969/70 would consider a bill to prohibit the use of the automobile. Nor would any scientist or engineer, even five years before it occurred, have dared to predict such an event.

Another obstacle is the basic orientation of scientific endeavor. Most scientific effort is, naturally, devoted to questions currently of interest to the sponsors of the research, either government or private industry, or to problems that are important in theoretical scientific controversies. Over a period of time, these interests undergo major changes; altogether different questions are raised which have little, if any, connection with the previous set. The result is that the starting point for analysis is put back to somewhere close to zero, with most of the work remaining to be done. The future presents the scientist with ever new valuations, emphases, and conditions. Seen in this perspective, the possibilities for the accumulation of scientific knowledge are, at best, not very great.[4] A knowledge of the future is thus not possible in the scientific sense of the word.

Nevertheless, we cannot avoid having some *expectations* of the future. We say, for instance: I don't think Communist China will overtake U.S. economic levels within a generation; I expect the population of the country to grow by 2 per cent next year; I don't think the United States will suffer critical shortages of strategic raw materials in the course of the next decade; I believe that the rate of unemployment will be held to a level below 5 per cent during the next few years.

All these statements have certain characteristics in common. They are, first of all, statements of personal belief. Beliefs may be strengthened by having other people share them, but this does not make them more probable or "true." Being subjective, beliefs are inherently biased in some direction; they may be based on a faith in either the continuity of the present system or its imminent collapse. They are also strongly colored by the most recent pertinent events. Few people believed, for instance, in the recovery of the German economy following its devastation during World War II. So strong was this belief, unduly influenced by the visible destruction of the country's industrial capacity and the moral corruption of the German people in the immediate postwar period, that even the Germans speak of the recovery as a *Wunder*, or miracle. In retrospect, of course, it is easy to understand how the "miracle" occurred. But retrospect is not prospect.

Second, the statements imply a knowledge based on past events, such as the normal growth behavior of economic systems, past trends in demographic growth and its internal structure, the relation of raw material demand to its supply, and normal government policies to hold unemployment at politically tolerable levels. They are, therefore, in some measure projections of the past suitably modified to reflect the most recent relevant information. In every case, the assumption is that future behavior will not be very different from past behavior, that change is incremental, and that the basic relationships will, by and large, remain the same.

The further we try to project into the future, however, the less we are inclined to take such statements seriously and the more *expected* images give way to those of the *preferred* future. The economic prowess of Communist China is not part of the desired future in the United States and *therefore* we believe it will not be achieved; other reasons that may be adduced in support of this belief are really secondary to the main reason of not *wanting* to believe in it. (Think, for example, of appraisals of Russian or even Japanese technology less than a generation ago. They were uniformly more pessimistic than the facts turned out to warrant. Similarly, high levels of unemployment are not part of our desired future; *therefore* we believe that government will be able to hold the line at 5 or 6 per cent: belief in the possibility of an economic collapse in the United States is simply inadmissible.)

Finally, all the predictive statements cited earlier concern isolated elements of future situations—production levels, population changes, raw materials, unemployment. They are not intended as projections of *total* situations, but assume either that these situations are unimportant or that they will vary so that the implied contextual conditions remain appropriate. Either assumption may turn out to be wrong, of course, in which case the prediction would have to be suitably altered.

In slowly changing situations, such behavior would be reasonable; it is not warranted, however, in periods such as the present one in the United States and, indeed, in most countries where planning is being seriously applied to the guidance of political actions. For the need to plan tends to be greatest where the conventional wisdom of "common sense" has arrived at the end of its tether, and more sophisticated kinds of knowledge are required. This situation is an example of the well-known paradox about planning to which I have already alluded: where the need to plan is greatest, because changes have accelerated beyond the levels of past experience, planning tends to be least effective; where the amount of perceptible change is small, so that planning can be carried out on the basis of nearly perfect knowledge, it is not needed.

Planning occurs in a context of societal relations that include, among other things, the rate of change in existing conditions and the logical limitations on historical knowledge. A style of planning must, therefore, be evolved that is adapted to its cognitive environment.

A Note on the Relation between Expectations and Desires

At the beginning of this chapter, I made a passing comment on the relationship between hope and expectation in predictions. I should now like to expand on this idea.

Most predictions may be regarded as a form of action. Statements about the future are normally made, not because we want to know what *will* happen, but because we wish to influence present actions. This appears to be the principal motivation for such exercises in global forecasting as the recent report on the future of the world environment prepared by a group of M.I.T. scientists for The Club of Rome.[5] This book forecasts "doomsday" sometime within the next 100 years, *unless* we "establish a condition of ecological and economic stability that is sustained far into the future. The state of global equilibrium could be designed so that the basic material needs of each person on earth are satisfied and each person has an equal opportunity to realize his individual human potential."[6] The report is quite explicit about its intentions:

> If the world's people decide to strive for this second outcome rather than the first [i.e., a rather sudden and uncontrollable decline in both population and industrial capacity], the sooner they begin working to attain it, the greater will be their chances for success.[7]

It needs to be emphasized, however, that forecasts such as The Club of Rome's cannot *in principle* be verified. They must rather be accepted on faith. If they are agreeable to us, we will be inclined to believe in them; if they are not, we will probably discover reasons to fault them. What should be clear from this is that the forecaster is not a morally neutral agent who simply records what his simulation models tell him, but an *agent of change* who seeks to influence behavior. He wishes to convince us that such-and-such will be the future in order that it might either appear inevitable or induce actions that will help to avoid it. Forecasting, in his hands, becomes an instrument of persuasion.

Yet another type of prediction is made with an eye to its expected self-fulfillment. Here the forecaster appears in the role of prophet. This type is most visible in economic affairs, where a forecast of inflation is expected to produce inflation, a forecast of depression is expected to produce depression, and a forecast of economic growth ("we shall overtake the United States in twenty years") is expected to enhance economic performance. Such forecasts act upon the confidence with which people view the future; they are intended to diminish or increase hopes. Knowing this effect, what does the forecaster do? Does he publish his forecast widely? Does he "adjust" it to influence actions in the desired directions (e.g., exude great confidence about the economy in order to avoid a depression) or does he, perhaps, refrain from making his prediction widely known in order to forestall a public reaction to it? Is there some advantage, perhaps, in ignorance about the future?[8]

In all these cases the forecaster appears as an "actor" who chooses his forecast. This suggests something less than a scientific attitude. It also makes forecasting a very dubious enterprise.

Even apparently neutral projections may become suspect because of certain implications. Some years ago, I prepared a revision of the accepted rate of population growth in South Korea for the U. S. Agency of International Development. I had become suspicious of the extremely low rate that was then in common use as a basis for determining future aid requirements. My calculations suggested that instead of the widely accepted rate of 2.1 per cent a year, the country's population was probably growing at a rate above 3 per cent. Accepting this new rate would have meant major readjustments in long-term programming and might even have put in doubt the adequacy of current aid-levels, which had been pegged to a population estimate for the current years (projected from the last census) that was considerably below my own figures (the difference, as I recall, was on the order of a few million people). I was naïve enough at that time to believe that my revised figure would be accepted as simply "better" or that, at the very least, there would be a complete restudy of the demographic basis on which U.S. economic aid was planned. I was surprised, therefore, to discover that my rather innocent memorandum was met with implacable hostility by the aid administrators. Counter-experts were called in, an official refutation was made, and after six months the whole episode was buried in the files. (The aftermath was personally gratifying: the 1960 census showed that South Korea's population had, in fact, been growing at close to 3 per cent a year and was much larger than the official forecasts had suggested. But by that time I had already returned to the United States.)

Had I been more experienced at the time, I would have known that any forecasts, projections, or predictions which, if taken seriously, would point to changes in behavior, are likely to be treated as intentional statements equivalent to a political pronouncement. They are certainly not regarded as morally neutral. Since there is no empirical way to verify them—in the example above, South Korea had to wait for the results of the 1960 census—the results of a projection can be challenged without much difficulty. Experts can always be found to produce alternate projections, using equally persuasive methodologies, that will bring the outcome within range of almost any value that may be desired.

The role of "hidden persuader" is not one the planner normally associates with his profession. Yet, whether his purpose is simply to "call the shots as he sees them" or intentionally to choose among the variety of plausible forecasts with a view to influencing the results, his statements about the future may be regarded as having a political dimension. Statements about the future—no matter how elaborate the method of forecasting—do not constitute valid scientific knowledge. It would be more to the point to think of them as prophecy, wishful thinking, or willful distortions.

The Future as an Element of Present Action

Let us now look at the future, not with the eyes of the planner, but with those of the man of action. What are his real needs for information about the future, and with what future is he primarily concerned—the near or the far?

I shall venture a judgment here that many people, particularly planners, may initially have difficulty in accepting. Whether as individuals, groups, or organizations, men of action have in fact little interest in the future except for a very short stretch of time beyond the present. The excitement over the systematic study of the future found in some academic circles, philanthropic foundations, and research organizations reflects the predilections of those who are essentially *divorced* from action. Put more pointedly, the futurologists, as they are called, are either unabashed ideologists paid for their labor by those who seek to justify their own actions or escapists fleeing from the very tough and real issues of the day.

Consider, for instance, the needs of the legislator. Elected for only a few years, he is likely to respond to pressures from those he represents in the hope of being re-elected. The laws he makes and the policies he may establish are the result of compromise among contending claims for his attention. Laws may be visionary, and their preambles invocations of a more perfect social order in which justice and equality prevail for everyone. But most of the legislator's time will be spent on the details of the law and on the politics of compromise and negotiation. Who will benefit and who will lose? And how may the losers be compensated or mollified? His temporal concerns will at most extend to what the British novelist John Le Carré has called the recent future.

Or consider the manager and administrator. His interests

in the future are chiefly related to program development
and budgeting. Budgets are usually prepared for one year
in advance; occasionally they may be projected for two or
three years beyond that. Programs are envisioned for about
the same period, though certain agencies have considerably
longer planning horizons. The U. S. Army Corps of Engineers, for instance, makes project studies fifteen years in
advance of possible construction and carries out analyses
of costs and benefits over nothing less than a century!
The results are not damaging in the case of projects, since
fifteen years gives ample time for their review and restudy.
The hundred-year projection of costs and benefits, however,
is simply a form of ritualistic behavior and a rather uninspir-
ing exercise in science fiction. But most of an administrator's time is spent not in pondering the future, but in the
management of his organization's daily affairs. He operates
within extremely narrow horizons, making only limited commitments when he can, proceeding cautiously from step to
step, and digesting an enormous amount of "current" information as a basis for correcting his decisions.

Or consider, finally, the entrepreneur who perceives an
opportunity for innovative action. He will proceed as if
risking is more important to him than knowing the future.
He relishes his ability to solve problems as they arise.
As he sets out upon a course of action, he is *not* interested
in knowing all the obstacles that may lie in his path. The
entrepreneur in business enterprise or social organization
acts largely on the basis of hope (i.e., the pleasure he
finds in realizing something new against the inertia of existing ways and confidence in his abilities to carry through
his project). If he has both the time and the inclination,
he may look at the projected future, but whatever *expectations* he may have about it matter little in comparison with
his strong desire to prevail and by his unusual willingness to
shoulder risks. What impresses one in studying the lives
of the great men of action is the inner assurance—often
bought at enormous personal cost—with which they faced

the risks that made others tremble. They never asked, "What is likely to happen?" but, "What shall I do?"

All three of these prototypical men of action—politicians, managers, innovators—enjoy substantial autonomy over their environments. Their chief interest in the future is motivational. They seek in the future a purpose and direction that will endow their present actions with a transcendent meaning. To *act* is more significant to them than to believe.

The man of action is an explorer of unknown regions: he casts himself into the dark, unstructured spaces of the future, leaving the traces of his route behind him. His presence in the twilight zone between present and future time creates a field of gravitational forces that attracts others to follow. It may be true that the seeds of the future are already planted in the present, but the man of action alters the conditions under which the seeds will sprout and shapes what is to happen in ways that no one can foresee. Alexander the Great joined Eastern and Western civilization. Columbus proved the world was round and discovered a wilderness into which feudal Europe could pour her surplus millions. Martin Luther reformed the Christian Church and established a new relation between Man and God. Lenin and Mao led revolutions that fundamentally altered the future for one third of mankind.

The number of Alexanders and Maos in world history is small. But the principle of action their lives exemplify is available to anyone prepared to use it. As Humpty Dumpty said, it's all a question of who's to be master. We can become the objects of history, passively waiting for things to happen to us, or we can bestir ourselves to become the protagonists of historical action. As such, we are not free, but we can gain a measure of control over the environment so that what happens is, at least in some small part, a reflection of what we want to happen. The motives of an action may remain forever elusive and ambiguous, but the results of action are tangible and real: they show the limits of the possible, they define the true character of the alternatives before us, they lay down new patterns of meaning.

The job of the technical expert and planner acquires a new significance in this context. In complex, rapidly changing situations, the politician, manager, and innovator cannot afford to do without the special knowledge that planners can, in principle, supply. The axiom concerning the primacy of action implies only that knowledge must be fitted to the requirements of action, since actions will, in any case, be undertaken.

In these circumstances, the planner no longer gazes into the distant future. His work is chiefly concerned with a study of the recent past and the near future in terms of the interests and requirements of actor-clients. This study should enlarge the actor's understanding of the context within which he moves; lead him to appreciate the basic structural relations that must be obeyed, together with the rules for their possible transformation; make him aware of the *principia media* that operate within his own environment and of the possible points a system offers for the strategic intervention; provide him with a continuous stream of intelligence about both his environment and the results of his actions, together with evaluations or criteria for evaluation; free him of immediate responsibility for the technical aspects of preparing programs, budgets, and projects; and, in general, expose him to the insights of a trained technical intelligence, a wider perspective on the system in which he operates, and thus provide a different reading of the possibilities for action.

Summary

In Figure 6, I have tried to make graphic the several time relations involved in societal guidance. The graph contains no additional information; in the context of the present chapter, it is self-explanatory.

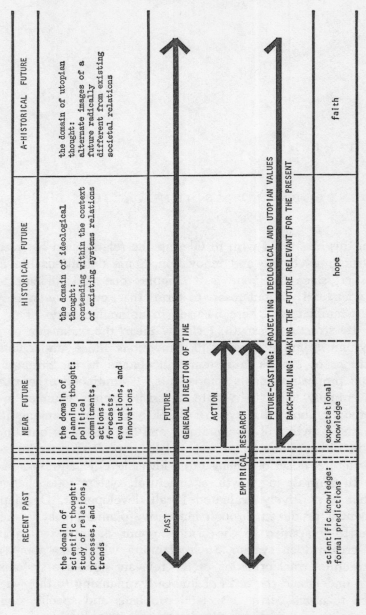

Figure 6. Time Relations in Social Guidance

CHAPTER 6

DEVELOPMENT AS INNOVATION

In this chapter, I wish to take up the relationship between structural change and innovation. Some definitions are in order, since the issue is a complex one and difficult to understand without resort to terms that, even though they are familiar, will here be used in unfamiliar ways.

By structural growth, I simply mean the expansion of a system in one or more of its dimensions. Since, under conditions of growth, a system will change in the strengths and proportions of its components, its continued expansion eventually leads to a state of crisis. Unless changes are brought about that will re-establish a balance among its parts, growth will be contained, and the system in question will either stagnate or experience a prolonged series of structural crises or collapse to a lower level of equilibrium.[1]

In contrast to growth, a structural, system-wide change that is positively evaluated I call development. Development is produced through innovative planning that is successfully applied to the critical points of intervention in a crisis-ridden system. Such planning will bring about a structural transformation of the relevant guidance systems. To understand the tasks of innovative planning in this way, the relations between societal problems and specific deficiencies in guidance systems must be established.

Individual Choice and Collective Phenomena

We are all familiar with the phenomenon of traffic congestion. In behavioral terms, it may be defined as a slow-down of traffic flow associated with an overload of highway capacity. The curious thing about congestion is that none of the motorists caught in a traffic jam have any interest in producing it. They simply chose a particular route to reach their destination. Unfortunately for them, over a certain stretch of road, they found themselves quite unexpectedly and entirely against their will prevented from going on at their accustomed speed. None of them can be held individually responsible for this result, yet together they have produced it.

Traffic congestion is an instance of a class of events that I shall call *collective phenomena*. It is characteristic of these phenomena that they appear as the unintended by-product of many individual decisions. Sometimes, as in the case of traffic congestion, the effect is quite direct: too many cars appear simultaneously in the wrong place. At other times, as with inflation, the lines of causality are more difficult to trace. The point to remember is that collective phenomena are statistical aggregates (the rate of traffic flow, the rate of increase in consumer prices) that behave independently of human volition.

It is useful to think of collective phenomena as the most probable outcome of a set of institutional arrangements that impose constraints on (or provide incentives for) individual decisions. So long as these constraints exist, the outcomes will be roughly the same: congestion and inflation will continue. So will many other collective phenomena, such as the pattern of income distribution, the spatial distribution of a population, and environmental pollution. The institutional arrangements that determine these outcomes constitute their guidance system. For each phenomenon a separate guidance system may be identified. By laying down a network of constraints and incentives for individual actors, this subset of the general guidance system of society generates the phenomenon with which we are concerned.

The verb "generate" in the preceding sentence is used in a rather special sense. The guidance system generates a particular outcome (conceived and measured as a statistical probability distribution) much as a silk-screen template "generates" a certain distribution of shapes and colors on paper for as many times as paint is brushed over it. The exact amount of paint passing through each cutout is indeterminate, but the results from one application to the next will appear to be roughly the same.

Guidance systems may be broken down into separate social institutions and their functions (Table 2). These institutions, their functions, and the network of relations that binds them into a system are not co-ordinated by any central intelligence, and the collective phenomena they generate are not always regarded as beneficial. From what has been said, it is clear that collective phenomena will appear, disappear, or change their character only when the appropriate institutional arrangements are changed in a manner that produces the desired outcome. Traffic congestion and inflation, no less than unemployment, economic underdevelopment, accelerated urbanization, and environmental degradation are collective phenomena that react to changes in the *conditions* that influence individual actions but not to direct controls applied to the actions themselves.

If crime in the streets is a collective phenomenon (as revealed in the statistics of the FBI), adding policemen to the force may reverse the trend in a particular district, but the system of guidance institutions will continue to generate a certain *rate* of criminal behavior, and criminal actions will simply be displaced to other parts of the city. If regional backwardness is a collective phenomenon, the artificial relocation of a few industrial plants may lead to a temporary improvement in the conditions of the recipient

TABLE 2

Guidance Institutions and Their Functions

Institutions	*Functions*
1. Political and legal	a. Interest aggregation
	b. Formulation of purposes and goals
	c. Consensus formation
	d. Conflict resolution
	e. Public resource allocation
	f. External relations to other systems
2. Economic and financial	a. Allocation of material rewards
	b. Production of goods and services
	c. Consumption of goods and services
	d. Savings and investment
	e. Exchange of goods and services
3. Administrative	a. Routine management of programs
4. Cognitive and planning	a. Scientific and technological research
	b. Education and training
	c. Monitoring and information
	d. Analysis and evaluation of systems performance
	e. Idea generation
	f. System design
	g. Strategy design
	h. Resource mobilization and management of innovations

economy, but the guidance system will continue to produce the customary contour lines of regional depression. If traffic congestion is a collective phenomenon, building more highways may provide temporary relief, but the system will continue to generate traffic, at even greater volumes than before, until congestion returns to its earlier level.

The use of direct intervention to alleviate the undesired condition defined as a collective phenomenon is not only costly and cumbersome, but ultimately ineffective. How many police are needed to stamp out crime in our cities? How many industries must be relocated to stem the flow of migrants from economically distressed areas? How many highways must be built to meet potential demand and put an end to traffic congestion? To achieve a definitive solution, their numbers would have to reach astronomical sums. And, having chosen the route of direct intervention and control, we should then discover (and perhaps too late) that we have also chosen, though unwittingly, to live in a state run by police, in an economy run by technocrats, and in a city run by highway engineers. Collective phenomena defined as social problems cannot, in the final analysis, be resolved by suppressing their visible manifestations. They only respond to appropriate changes in the structure of the relevant guidance institutions.

To make this theory of societal controls plausible, I should like to show how specific subsets of society's guidance system are related to particular collective phenomena. We shall then be able to see more clearly, perhaps, what is required if scientific and technical knowledge is to be successfully applied to the processes of societal guidance.

Determinants of Collective Phenomena: Some Examples

The first example deals with centralization of power and its effects on regional development in an industrializing country. The Republic of Chile extends in a narrow band along 2,700 miles of Pacific coastline from Peru to the

Strait of Magellan. In this country of ten million people, decisions affecting even the minutiae of public life are made at the center. The capital city of Santiago houses not only the national government, but the headquarters of practically every important bank and business enterprise as well. The labyrinthine ministries of Santiago decide where to build sidewalks in every city of the country, what should be taught in every school, how much a loaf of bread should weigh and how much bakeries may charge for it, who should be granted a loan and for what project, what hours businesses may keep, what bridges need repairing, what playgrounds may be built and where, who shall receive a house and of what size, how much a pharmacy may charge for aspirin, what highways shall be paved, what power lines are to be built, and how much the fishermen may charge for fish.

The national government is the *Supremo Gobierno* that not only disposes but proposes as well. Provinces are bureaucratic artifices that serve exclusively an administrative convenience: their governors are appointed by the President of the Republic and are responsible to him through the Minister of the Interior. Except in minor emergencies, the governors manage no funds of their own. Although municipalities elect a council and a mayor, city councilmen have very little to decide: 90 per cent of the municipal budget is spent on salaries; the rest may be applied to the beautification of the public square or an addition to the municipal slaughterhouse.[2]

In short, if you want something done for your city, you will be well advised to take the night train to Santiago and try to reach the appropriate minister, his secretary, or a friend of the secretary. The authority of branch offices is carefully controlled by the center. Local banks may give only small loans on their own initiative; the managers of subsidiary business enterprises must check back with Santiago for every non-routine decision; and the decentralized offices of national agencies exist primarily to process documents and start them up through an endless chain of superior offices in the hierarchy only to receive them again, duly stamped and certified, months after the initial request was made.

Bureaucratic tedium is endemic. It results in endless delays, in the diffusion of responsibilities, in problems changing and disappearing while the files are being processed, in a general feeling of helplessness on the part of clients left at the mercy of an implacable and faceless monster.

The judgments that come down from the center, falling like acts of God, inscrutable, without appeal, conform to central wisdom on what should be done. There is a bias built into these judgments that favors large over small projects, and hardware over social programs. If your city is too small to have a large-scale project, the chances are your claims will be ignored. Centralization in decision-making leads to the dominance of large cities.

Under these conditions, Santiago has become an extremely attractive place in which to live. Not only are the probabilities of finding remunerative employment greater there than in the provinces, but the migrant to Santiago can share in the benefits of central wisdom, such as paved streets, good housing, hospitals, and schools, and public playgrounds. And should he need to transact some business with the government authorities, being in Santiago will give him a vast advantage. Contacts are made easily, the daily trip to the ministries takes only a few minutes, one keeps continuously in touch with what is going on, becomes a familiar figure in the corridors of power, invites influential friends to lunch, one's children attend exclusive private schools, and all this might prove helpful in the future.

Those who can, therefore leave the provinces for Santiago. This process of selective migration deprives the provinces of their best talents. Those who choose to stay behind are every day less capable of fending for themselves. The effect is nothing short of tragic. Initiative is drained from local populations. They somehow manage to carry on at a low level of maintenance activity, and a very few prosper. But the great majority live on in the belief that all problems must be taken care of by the central government. With few exceptions, provincial newspapers report primarily on weddings, funerals, and the weather.

This lack of initiative and dwindling competence is not lost on central bureaucrats. They regard it as sufficient reason why they should handle the controls. Local people cannot be trusted; they are likely to waste precious resources; they are not technically prepared. And so the cycle of dependence feeds on itself and becomes total. Santiago is growing, becoming ever more splendid with its skyscrapers, subway, museums, and industries, while the small provincial centers struggle along in the mud.

The second example concerns a different kind of dependency. Countries such as Chile, and indeed most of the Third World, do not devote amounts of their own substantial resources to the development of science and technology. Technological know-how has to be imported. The products in their shops are produced under foreign license. Their industries use machinery designed in England, Germany, the United States, and Japan. The tractors with which they plow their fields carry a Chicago trademark.

A country that remains technologically dependent is at a permanent disadvantage in international markets. By the time it learns to produce a new product, or an old product more cheaply, the inventor country will have had several years in which to introduce the same thing into its own as well as foreign markets. As a result of continued market expansion, the inventor country will be able to achieve production economies and sell at lower prices. The product is backed up by the inventor's guarantee of quality, and "Made in U.S.A." or "Made in France" becomes equated in the mind of the consumer with reliable performance. The technically dependent country, reproducing a product under a licensing agreement, can expect to sell it only in its own internal market which is protected against foreign competition by high tariffs. And its exports continue to be predominantly of primary materials to feed the industries of the inventor nations.

The technology that is imported from abroad may be "advanced," but it is often inappropriate to the conditions of the country. As inventor economies shift increasingly to an emphasis on highly productive and sophisticated services, their equipment and machinery are designed to use less labor. But the dependent country is in precisely the opposite predicament. Its outstanding need is to raise the productivity of low-skilled labor, which is available in plenty, and create massive opportunities for productive employment. Rather than save on labor, it has to save on capital. While in inventor countries the labor displaced through automation may be absorbed into other sectors devoted to the production of cybernetic equipment and related services, the labor that is not employed in automated industry in technologically dependent countries remain part of an underemployed proletariat whose productivity is close to zero. For the capital equipment, and even, in many cases, the specialized maintenance services that go along with it, are not produced at home; they are imported.

As with automation, technologically dependent countries rely on the currently fashionable styles of production engineering. They do not ask how research may help them use their natural wealth to greatest advantage. Chile, for instance, has vast fisheries resources along its coast, but no major research station in marine biology; it relies chiefly on the Japanese for information in this area. Half the country has an extremely dry climate, yet Chile has no important center for arid zone research to study the possibilities of dry land agriculture, water management, and desert ecology. In times of crisis, as in a recent period of drought, foreign (in this case Israeli) scientists and technicians are imported to advise on the appropriate measures. The population of India is never far removed from starvation, but for the de-

DEVELOPMENT AS INNOVATION   151

velopment of drought-resisting strains of rice and wheat, capable of flourishing on Indian soil under Indian conditions, it depends chiefly on studies carried out by American and Japanese geneticists and other specialists, working under the sponsorship of their own nations.

This lack of scientific enterprise, this almost total reliance on foreign inventiveness, is reflected in school systems that teach little science and little love for it. At the universities, the traditional careers of law and medicine have to turn applicants away by the thousands, while departments of physics and chemistry go begging to fill their quotas. The occasional scientific genius who manages to survive this system eventually obtains a fellowship to go abroad, and there he usually remains. There are more Third World scientists working in the United States and Europe than in their own countries. The local interest in what they do does not extend beyond the Sunday supplements of local newspapers.

As a result, the dependent country is unable to adapt imported technology to its own uses; to develop its own products: to compete in export markets; to develop a technology appropriate to its conditions; to exploit its resource base in scientific ways; to develop its own capital goods industry; to reform its educational system in line with the requirements of an industrial age. All these failures may be regarded as collective phenomena that contribute to maintaining the country in a permanent condition of underdevelopment. They can be reversed only by a series of radical reforms in the relevant guidance institutions of the society.

The third example concerns the operation of free market institutions and their effect on environmental degradation. It is an example close to the American experience, though not exclusively confined to the United States. The market works with almost classical simplicity. Its system of prices aggregates the private utilities of buyers and sellers. Under existing arrangements, however, it is incapable of taking into account the values of a community of individuals and families or, indeed, of social collectivities of any sort. Therefore, while transactions in the marketplace may lead to private gains and satisfactions, they may have disastrous consequences for the community and its environment.

Why do motorists continue to foul the air with toxic gases? Because the price of cars and gasoline does not include the costs of damage done to health and to amenities in the community where the poisoned air must be breathed. If these costs could be included, the expense of private motor transportation might become prohibitive for daily use, and air pollution would diminish in proportion. Pollution is a collective phenomenon.

And why do factories continue to pour out noxious effluents into the streams and rivers of the nation? Because this method of waste disposal is free for the factories, though it generates costs for the water treatment plants downstream, taints the recreational amenities of an entire region, and impairs fishery resources. If the true costs of water pollution could be allocated to the contaminators in fair proportion to their contribution to the problem, the industries might find ways of avoiding contamination.

Why does the ecological pattern of land uses often take a form that interferes with the efficient functioning of cities and with their fitness as a habitat for man? Because the price of land does not include a social valuation of its costs and benefits to the community. Land values rise with the unearned increments of improvements made by others and ultimately redound to the benefit of private individuals rather than to that of the community at large. The result is a pattern of land use that has no stable relationship to the community's long-term needs for such things as internal social cohesion and residential amenity. As land values rise, giant office buildings are constructed. They may block out a view and destroy the village character of a community that serves the specialized needs of 40,000 students, professors, and staff at an adjacent university. But the university is not consulted.

Not far from Los Angeles, across the mountains in the Mohave Desert, a new international airport is planned for construction. When completed, it will be able to handle an estimated hundred million passengers a year. In the short time that has elapsed since its location was decided, land values in the area have risen tenfold. Powerful private interests, long conscious of this possibility, successfully lobbied with the state some years ago to divert water from the surplus areas in northern California and carry it through a marvelously engineered system of canals to the south. Within a few decades, the Mohave Desert may become fully urbanized, but the people of Los Angeles were never asked whether they wanted still another million people in their spreading metropolis. Yet the costs imposed on them by this "spontaneous" growth—in further pollution, further congestion, further sprawl, further misgovernment, further outward flow of central populations and the resulting readjustments needed throughout the metropolis—are not absorbed by the developers. No doubt some pocketbooks will bulge, new fortunes will be made. The speculators have already cashed in on the promise of future public improvements. But the growth of Palmdale City will not reflect a public choice. It will come into being as a collective phenomenon and its existence is likely to impose a substantial burden on future generations of Angelenos.

Because the market works this way, laws have been passed from time to time to regulate its effects in the interest of what is called the public good. An outstanding example is provided by zoning ordinances that attempt to limit what can be done with private land and bring its use into closer conformity with public values. But the results have been disappointing. Whenever a substantial difference exists between the private and the public valuation of the land, the public interest tends to give way. The vast majority of requests for zoning variance submitted by private interests are eventually approved by city officials who are unable to muster the necessary political support to defend the community against voracious, profit-maximizing appetites. Zoning practice acts as a brake on the speed with which the city is transformed by the unplanned results of transactions between individual property owners and private developers. But it is unable to resist the pressures generated by the market. So long as the free market operates as it does, unable to incorporate the social valuation of the costs imposed by individuals who seek to maximize their short-term profits, the guidance system will continue to produce environmental degradation.

The fourth and final example deals with the relation of pervasive bureaucratic forms of social organization to widespread social alienation, which manifests itself in such types of collective phenomena as disaffection and dissent, especially on the campuses of the nation's universities. As is typical of most collective phenomena, no one intends that these things should happen. They appear as the outcomes of institutional arrangements that canalize the decisions of individual actors. To a large extent, though not exclusively, social alienation results from individual reactions to forms of governance in both public and private institutions that are hierarchical, authoritarian, rigid, formalistic, non-participative, and distant from the needs perceived by their dependent subjects.

The immediate weight of bureaucratic governance is felt by students who are injected into the system of a large university that seems to pay only passing notice to their major reason for being there—their wish to get an education. Moreover, the bureaucracy of the typical state university with its hundreds of thousands of students dispersed over several gigantic campuses is only the most visible part (to the students) of a much vaster system of bureaucratic organization that extends its influence over all aspects of national life. To a greater or lesser extent, institutions of government and private corporations all exhibit many of the same bureaucratic features. The student rebellion is directly aimed at this system. It represents an attempt to recover a measure of self-direction and personal autonomy from the oppressive weight of bureaucratic controls. But the current forms of student protest may also be regarded as behavior *generated* by the existing system. For the rebelliousness of those dominated by hierarchy is always a latent possibility in bureaucratic organizations. All that is needed are opportunities for it to flourish. When dependent client groups are unable to gain reasonable access to the responsible authorities across the boundary lines of bureaucratic organizations, they may endeavor to force their way through in violent confrontations with authority.

The demands placed upon bureaucratic systems in America—given the enormous scale of our problems, the rapidity of social and technological change, the inability of central authorities to gain a systematic overview of what is happening, and the growing diversity of popular viewpoints—reduce the greater part of bureaucratic work to little more than maintenance activities. As a result of their inability to manage the ongoing processes of change in ways that are reasonably satisfactory, the legitimacy of bureaucratic organizations is coming to be widely challenged. In an effort to meet this challenge, authorities resort to open displays of coercive force. This maneuver diverts attention from the need to adapt organizational structure to the growing demands placed upon it, demands to which the authorities are increasingly unable to respond. So long as bureaucratic structures remain fundamentally unchanged, however, alienation, especially among the young, is likely to continue.

The four examples described in this section—the centralization of power in Chile, technological dependency, free market institutions, and bureaucratic forms of organization in technologically advanced societies—reveal a common

TABLE 3

The Process of Societal Guidance

Examples

Process	I	II	III	IV
(a) Structural Characteristics of Guidance System	A highly centralized system of national government,	A Third World country having a foreign-controlled private sector,	Free market institutions,	Bureaucratic university administration,
(b) Performance Characteristics	frequently ineffective, inefficient, and unresponsive,	politically independent, on the one hand, and technologically dependent, on the other,	unresponsive to social valuations,	unresponsive to the demands of faculty and students and lacking ability to deal creatively with rapidly changing conditions in the university environment,
(c) Networks of Constraints and Incentives on Individual Actors	imposes the condition that all important allocative decisions must be resolved by central authorities,	discourages the development of appropriate scientific and technological research and education within the country,	impose the rule that buyers and sellers should act to maximize their short-run gains on balance,	imposes behavior consistent with its hierarchical and authoritarian structure,

(d) Forms and Patterns of Behavior	thereby inducing a pattern of accelerated and selective migration and a set of attitudes and expectations,	thereby reducing the capacity of national industry to compete in foreign markets,	thereby producing a pattern of market behavior	thereby increasing disaffective forms of individual behavior
(e) Collective Phenomenon (Policy Issue)	that result in the relatively unbalanced growth of the capital city and the stagnation of local economies in the periphery	with the result that the national economy is maintained in a state of permanent underdevelopment	that results in environmental degradation	that result in a condition of widespread social alienation

process in the generation of collective phenomena (Table 3).
A particular set of structural relations in the guidance system (a) displays typical performance characteristics (b)
that impose a network of constraints and incentives on individual actors (c) who, choosing the more probable courses
of action, produce the different forms and patterns of behavior (d) that, seen within the context of a particular society, result in a collective phenomenon (e) having salience
for certain sectors of the population and so becoming an object of concern for public policy.

In none of the cases reviewed were the actual results intended: urban primacy and regional underdevelopment in
Chile; continued economic backwardness of technologically
dependent countries; large-scale environmental pollution in
a market economy; and widespread alienation of populations subject to pervasive but inept control by bureaucratic
institutions. But these results did not occur by accident.
Properly considered, they represent the *most probable* outcomes of the specific guidance systems described. So long
as the relevant structural characteristics of these systems
remain unchanged, they can be expected to continue producing similar results, even where point interventions in
particular situations are, for a short while, able to reverse
the general trend. Changes in the structure of guidance systems that might significantly alter these results would include, in the first example, selective decentralization in resource allocation for regional development; in the second
example, an effort to increase national autonomy in development decisions by creating institutions that would promote
scientific and technical research; in the third, changes in the
mechanism of the competitive market to make it reflect
more accurately the social costs and benefits of individual
and collective choices; and in the fourth, the substitution of
non-bureaucratic forms of governance in major national institutions. Devising and implementing such changes may be
considered acts of innovative planning.

Evaluating the Performance of Guidance Systems

The variety of individual guidance systems is immense and their complexity is great. It is appropriate to ask whether criteria do not exist by which their performance may be evaluated. Provided we can give a positive answer to this question, these criteria might then be used in a normative, prescriptive sense. Where performance fails to live up to the standards we have set, we could expect the corresponding collective phenomena to be perceived as social problems.

Tentatively, I should like to propose that guidance systems be judged by their *autonomy, responsiveness, innovative ability, effectiveness, efficiency,* and *legitimacy.*

A guidance system is *autonomous* to the extent that it has the capacity to set its own objectives and pursue them effectively. This capacity may be restricted in two ways: first, by a condition of relative dependence on powers external to the system, and, second, by a condition in which the rate of internal change in the society is so precipitous that the responses of the guidance system are, in large measure, merely reactions to the "turbulence" produced.

Many Third World countries, for instance, are, as I have shown, almost completely dependent on imported technology for their industrialization; their central guidance institutions, therefore, rank very low on a potential scale of autonomous behavior. On the other hand, the guidance system of American society is gradually losing its capacity to act autonomously, as the pace of internally generated change exceeds its abilities for positive guidance. As a result, the change processes in the society are increasingly experienced as random events, giving an impression of rising disorder and unpredictability.

A guidance system is *responsive* to the extent that it is able to take into account the variety of particularized interests, needs, and values of population groups affected by its actions. Where actions are initiated far from their ultimate points of impact, system responses are slow and selective. Where communication channels to the relevant action levels are clogged, many potential demands are filtered out and fail to be considered. Where interests are not expressed for want of coherent social organization, the guidance system ignores them. Where mechanisms are not established for resolving competing and conflictive interests in mutually acceptable ways, the guidance system is relatively unresponsive, imposing either an arbitrary will of its own or the will of the most powerful of the competing groups. Bureaucratic forms of organization, as described in the preceding section, are typically unresponsive to the needs of their clients. Access through their multiple hierarchical levels is difficult; the information upon which they act is fragmented and distorted; the possibilities for negotiating conflicting client interests are exceedingly restricted. Bureaucratic systems, therefore, encourage a politics of confrontation. Only the threat of violence seems capable of inducing bureaucratic elites to heed the needs of clients whose grievances have been systematically neglected. Only the threat of violence will keep the clients docile.

A guidance system is *innovative* to the extent that it is able to respond creatively to new problem situations. Many guidance institutions are unable to break out of their traditional routines, to conceive of programs substantially different from their taped repertoires, much less to bring such new programs to life. In Chapter 3, I suggested an Environmental Conservation Corps as a means for dealing with a serious problem of unemployment among young people. None of the established federal departments is likely to have the ability to manage such a program; it would have to be organized as an independent, semi-autonomous government agency.

A guidance system is *effective* to the extent that its actions are both timely and accurate with respect to the problems to which they are addressed. System responses that consistently lag behind permit the problems to continue, spread, and multiply, until a major crisis is produced. Equally serious consequences may follow from acting too soon. The accuracy of a response, on the other hand, is in some ways independent of its timing. A doctor may prescribe the correct medicine, but the patient may have consulted him when the illness was already too far advanced for the medicine to arrest it. Accuracy of response depends chiefly on the accuracy of the preceding diagnosis. The right questions must be asked, and the information obtained filtered through the system without major distortion. At the same time, the information must be complete and pertinent, and correctly interpreted. Yet timing and accuracy frequently go hand in hand. Urban zoning practices, for example, are unable to shape the city in accordance with social needs, partly because the zoning map projects a pattern of future land uses long before anyone, except city planners, has any real interest in the matter, and partly because the map and its related zoning ordinance are based on faulty diagnosis. The stream of land use decisions generated by a competitive market of buyers and sellers cannot be effectively controlled by legal instruments.

A guidance system is *efficient* to the extent that its work is accomplished at a cost that is reasonably low compared to alternative employments of the resources required. The relevant measure here is social costs. To illustrate: A paper mill may find that, from the standpoint of its private calculus of benefits and costs, the most efficient method for disposing of its noxious effluents is discharging them untreated into a nearby stream. But in a social perspective, the resultant destruction of downstream fisheries and recreational resources must be taken into consideration. Social costs require a comprehensive system of accounting.

A guidance system, finally, is *legitimate* when it inspires loyalty and is capable of mobilizing popular support for its actions. Where the guidance system performs well on all five of the preceding criteria, it will probably be considered legitimate, since it is likely to satisfy the basic needs and aspirations of the population. But where it fails with respect to some or all of the criteria mentioned, public support for its legitimacy is apt to be withdrawn. In this case, the guidance system must either undergo a major structural change or rely increasingly on coercive force to maintain its authority.

The several performance criteria discussed are not completely independent of each other. Effectiveness is related to innovative capacity, for example, while legitimacy is related to the responsiveness of a system. Nevertheless, each characteristic sheds light on an important dimension of institutional performance.

One of the important aspects of performance analysis is that it leads us to study the organizational characteristics of a guidance system in detail. For the organization of a system has a great deal to do with the way it performs, and its degree of success or failure in the terms outlined above. In a complex guidance system, for example, innovative capacity would seem to require some mixture of hierarchical and non-hierarchical features of organization. Although the latter would increase the probability of innovative ideas arising in response to concrete situations, the former are needed to overcome resistance to innovative action. No less conducive to successful innovation is a relatively high level of information. But care must be taken not to overload the system, with information, for in the extreme case, this would only turn its performance into ritual adherence to formal rules. In general, linkages among systems are helpful in permitting the rapid diffusion of innovations, but face-to-face contacts are needed if innovations are to be adopted. A large organizational memory (together with a fast and competent retrieval system) facilitates search processes that are part of the more comprehensive innovative process, providing the answer to such questions as: What has been tried already? What successes and failures were scored, and why? What answers were proposed but rejected, and why? But in addition to memory, an innovative system requires special instruments for searching out alternatives and generating innovative responses. This suggests linkages to knowledge systems outside the organization, which may be less restrained in the search for and sifting of innovative solutions. Finally, innovative systems require a benevolent internal climate that tolerates ambiguity, contradiction, challenge, and unconventional approaches; demonstrates a willingness to assume organizational risks; and offers rewards for behavior that departs from customary responses.

A study that subjects a given set of guidance institutions to this type of structural analysis will lead to the discovery of ways to reorganize the system so that it will produce more desirable types of collective behavior.

Studies of this type are a good part of the task of innovative planning. The total effort involves the series of interrelated steps shown below (Table 4).

This methodology differs considerably from that currently applied in planning practice. To explain this difference, I return to an earlier example. In Chile, there are many poor and backward regions that have been of concern to government. From time to time the National Development Corporation (CORFO), which is located in Santiago and is staffed by highly competent and dedicated engineers, decides to establish new industries in these areas—a paper mill, an anchovy processing plant, a tomato packing plant, a series of sugar beet mills, or a shipyard for small coastal vessels. The job occupies a good part of the corporation's staff for a number of years. Projects are studied and prepared, private capital is invited to participate, and finally the plants are built and inaugurated by the President of the Republic. But what has really happened?

TABLE 4

The Tasks of Innovative Planning

1. Identify and describe the problem situation as a collective phenomenon.

2. Identify and analyze the relevant forms and patterns of collective behavior.

3. Identify the institutions of the guidance system that are thought to be primarily responsible for this behavior.

4. Analyze the specific performance characteristics of these institutions as they relate to the collective behavior identified in (2) above in terms of their degree of autonomy, responsiveness, innovativeness, effectiveness, efficiency, and legitimacy.

5. Relate these performance characteristics to particular organizational features of the guidance system, such as hierarchy, centralization, participation, information processing, and organizational linkages.

6. On the basis of this analysis, formulate specific proposals for structural innovation in the guidance system that are expected, if carried out, to change the relevant performance, produce a different outcome in terms of collective behavior, and result in significant improvements in the initial problem situation; and propose a strategy for innovative action.

7. Take part in the realization of this strategy, making the adjustments that are necessary in the course of the action.

A small industrial enclave employing several hundred workers has been set down in a region with an essentially passive local population. The plants are managed privately by a professional staff imported from Santiago, under virtual guarantees against economic failure. The gross profits eventually return to company headquarters in Santiago, where they are rechanneled, in part to liquidate the debt to CORFO, in part to raise the living standards of the original investors, purchase Santiago real estate, or occasionally complement a CORFO investment in some other part of the country. A regional development process has not been set in motion, and the guidance system continues to generate a stream of collective behavior that further consolidates the pattern of regional economic depression.

In contrast with the widespread technique of responding to collective phenomena, such as regional underdevelopment, with specific projects, innovative planning might point to the inability of the existing guidance system to generate innovative, entrepreneurial responses in the region concerned. Thus, instead of proposing a project intended to raise local production, the innovative planner might recommend measures to alter the structure of the guidance system in the direction of increased regional autonomy in development decisions. The question of what specific projects might ultimately be undertaken under this new arrangement is a secondary matter. All that can be said is that increased autonomy would be expected to raise the probability of pushing the region's long-term rate of economic growth above previous levels.

Similar examples could be found in the United States. Job retraining programs for the poor have enjoyed a certain vogue in recent years. They have also been notably unsuccessful. But no serious effort has gone into a study of the guidance system, which consistently generates a stream of people who become redundant in an economy geared to rapid technological obsolescence and the maximization of private gain. A lasting solution to the problems of structural unemployment and poverty will be found only when we are prepared to make the changes that will cut off this stream at the source.

The Need for Structural Change

A term such as structural change can easily become a fashionable slogan. Why, we may ask, should we not simply muddle through, adjust in incremental ways that keep the system running at an even keel? But the conflict between structuralists and incrementalists poses the issues involved in a wrong way. The structuralists have in mind a dramatic historical moment in which some cataclysmic transformation is accomplished. Yet, except for rare periods of violent, accelerated change, structural modifications in the guidance systems pertaining to particular collective phenomena succeed one another as partial improvements in the society's guidance system as a whole. In a superficial view, these changes may indeed appear as tinkering, reform-mongering, and muddling through.[3] The more precise term, however, is structural change. It refers to a process that is a necessary condition for the successful, long-term development of social systems.

Societies that are internally expanding—increasing their populations or the volume of their economies—inevitably become subject to severe internal stresses. A successful response to these stresses requires a continuing series of innovative adaptations in the relevant guidance systems. If sustained development implies an ability to generate and absorb such changes indefinitely, the majority of national societies today is confronted with the challenge of development. The United States is no exception to this. We are accustomed to think of our country as "developed," but this is a conceit that we can ill afford. The growth of our remarkably productive economy, rapid urbanization, and a population that has increased to over two hundred million, have produced a series of interconnected crises that pose an issue of development for us no less severe than that of countries only recently embarked on industrialization.

Growth in social systems generates conditions of structural disequilibrium for at least four reasons. Their growth processes are (1) *asynchronic,* that is, different parts of the system grow at different rates. The relative ease with which mortality rates could be reduced in many of the newly industrializing countries, for instance, threatened to produce a doubling of the population every twenty years. This incredibly rapid growth put enormous pressures on the ability of the society to adjust its institutions to the new requirements of food production, urbanization, export expansion, educational services, and internal savings. Housing had to be built on a massive scale. New information systems had to be created. Economic growth had to be accelerated. The political institutions of the country had to become oriented to continuing and super-heated change. The lagging elements of the system had to be adjusted merely to stay abreast of population growth.

In the United States, the same thing seems to be occurring with respect to cultural change. The emerging culture requires a vast reorganization of the rest of society to bring it into harmony with the new values.

Growth also leads to (2) an *enlargement of scale,* so that institutions that served the society well when it was small have to be adjusted to the requirements of increased size. Small organizations can conduct most of their business through face-to-face contacts, but certain threshold sizes may be reached that will render the old structures unworkable. An apartment building of twenty stories cannot be built with the same features (or even the same materials) as a single-story residence. At the very minimum, its ratio of service to residential space has to be increased by a substantial amount. A small denominational college whose president knows every faculty member by his first name can function with a relatively "flat" organizational structure. A major state university with thirty thousand students, on the other hand, devises increasingly complex and multi-leveled hierarchical structures to manage its affairs. As information requirements increase, computers are installed that impose their own forms of discipline on the suppliers and users of the information. But as information continues to grow, the power to make effective decisions may have to be decentralized in order to maintain even a modicum of effective performance.

In a growing social system, stresses are also produced by changes in (3) its *external relations*. New resource demands may be imposed on potential external suppliers; growth in power may lead to conflict with those on the outside who are already powerful; the system may grow not only in an inward but also an outward direction, threatening its immediate neighbors. New institutional arrangements become necessary to deal with the resulting problems. External relations may become a dominant preoccupation in the society. Coercive powers, such as an army, may have to be built up. New trade arrangements may have to be invented. Intelligence and counter-intelligence systems may have to be devised to keep the government informed about potential competitors and enemies.

Finally, growth tends to produce changes in (4) *public demands*. These may come about as the result of an accelerated "demonstration effect," as innovative ideas spread more rapidly throughout the system. Or they may happen as a reaction to bureaucratization and the leveling effects of a mass society. Or, yet again, they may arise in response to what are felt to be growing injustices in the relations among social groups that are favored differentially by asynchronic growth. Whatever the reason, these new demands will require substantial changes in a responsive guidance system.

In summary, growing systems produce a need for structural change. The phenomena of stress are collective phenomena. But there is no assurance that the system will inevitably choose the path of development by undertaking the necessary changes. The failure to change at the right time or a choice of the wrong responses will lead to a number of alternate outcomes. Growth may be de-escalated, resulting in stagnation, as in Argentina or Portugal. Changes, such as certain kinds of social legislation, may give a superficial impression of development, even though the structural relationships remain unaltered. The inability of stagnant societies to control all the growing elements within themselves, however, may lead to explosive political situations, as in Chile, where past increases in population have virtually wiped out improvements in the popular standard of living. In this case, the society may eventually be "pushed" into development; other systems, under similar pressures, may respond with violent repressions of the presumptively innovative forces, or sink into chaos and societal breakdown.

Politically conservative and repressive regimes, for instance, were imposed during the 1930s in Austria, where a semi-fascistic government all but destroyed the socialist labor movement centered in Vienna, and more recently in Brazil and Greece, where military governments have come to power and proceeded systematically to suppress political actions that are interpreted as threatening the *status quo*.

Dissolution and breakdown is yet another possibility. It comes about when the society is so torn apart by internal changes that it can no longer govern itself successfully. In this case, the country may either be conquered by a stronger foreign power, as was Republican China during the period of Japanese occupation, or fall into the hands of a revolutionary government that promises to carry out the necessary transformations. This happened after World War I in Turkey under the leadership of Kemal Atatürk, in Egypt under Gamal Abdul Nasser, and in Cuba under Fidel Castro. Their subsequent successes and failures are not at issue here. All three men were revolutionary leaders who eliminated systems of government that were no longer capable of managing the processes of change which had been generated in their respective countries and that had therefore ceased to be regarded as legitimate. In every instance, it was the hope and expectation of the revolutionary leader to initiate and guide a process of development that would combine economic growth with the appropriate structural changes in the society.

The choice of development is thus a crucial one. It can only be avoided at great cost. Facing the 1970s, America confronts just such a challenge. The country is caught up in one of its worst national crises. A similar crisis during the Great Depression brought in its wake the structural reforms of the New Deal, but what will be our answer for today? A major and, indeed, frightening part of the present situation is our growing inability to bring the relevant scientific and technical knowledge to bear on political action. The crisis is one in the guidance processes of the society. Unless we are able to devise new ways of fitting planning into the context of American society, making it consistent with the new values of person-centeredness, authenticity, existential commitment, and communal life, but also with the conditions of knowing, we are in danger of following one of the roads that lead to repression, stagnation, or breakdown. We have gone beyond the point where changes can be introduced in homeopathic doses. The kinds of changes that are needed now are likely to affect our entire way of life. To link knowledge successfully with action means to reorganize society according to entirely new principles.

In the following three chapters, I shall propose specific ways by which the ascending spiral of crisis might be brought under control. Actions unmoored from reason can only engulf us in a national disaster. The great challenge before us is to make reason an active element in our history.

CHAPTER 7

THE TRANSACTIVE STYLE OF PLANNING

Bridging the Communications Gap

Transactive planning changes knowledge into action through an unbroken sequence of interpersonal relations. As a particular style of planning, it can be applied to both allocation and innovation. This chapter states the principal conditions for transactive planning and explores its major implications.

Transactive planning is a response to the widening gulf in communication between technical planners and their clients. To simplify the discussion, let us assume that planners as well as clients are individual persons rather than institutions, and that clients generate streams of action on which they wish to be advised.[1]

This assumption is not altogether unrealistic. Institutions do not relate to each other as wholes, but through a complex series of exchanges among individuals. Although these individuals behave primarily according to their formal role prescriptions, each role masks a singular personality. Roles are defined by a set of abstract behavior patterns, but the person assuming a particular role may be straightforward or devious, disposed to be tranquil or angry, approachable or remote, eager for power or reluctant to assume responsibility. The planner steeped in the practice of the transactive style will try to reach out to the person who stands behind the formal role.

The difficulties planners and clients experience in communicating valid meanings to each other have already been discussed (Chapter 4). The barriers to effective communication between those who have access primarily to processed knowledge and those whose knowledge rests chiefly on personal experience are rising. We have seen that this problem is not unique to America; it is found to some extent in all societies that seek the help of technical experts. Messages may be exchanged, but the relevant meanings are not effectively communicated. As a result, the linkage of knowledge with action is often weak or nonexistent. This is true even where planning forms part of the client system itself; even there, actions tend to proceed largely on the basis of acquired routines and the personal knowledge of the decision makers. Planners talk primarily to other planners, and their counsel falls on unresponsive ears. As we shall see, however, the establishment of a more satisfactory form of communication is not simply a matter of translating the abstract and highly symbolic language of the planner into the simpler and more experience-related vocabulary of the client. The real solution involves a restructuring of the basic relationship between planner and client.

Each has a different method of knowing: the planner works chiefly with processed knowledge abstracted from the world and manipulated according to certain postulates of theory and scientific method; his client works primarily from the personal knowledge he draws directly from experience. Although personal knowledge is much richer in content and in its ability to differentiate among the minutiae of daily life, it is less systematized and orderly than processed knowledge. It is also less capable of being generalized and, therefore, is applicable only to situations where the environment has not been subject to substantial change. The "rule of thumb" by which practical people orient their actions is useful only so long as the context of action remains the same. Processed knowledge, on the other hand, implies a theory about some aspect of the world. Limited in scope, it offers a general explanation for the behavior of a small number of variables operating under a specified set of constraints.

The difficulties of relating these two methods of knowing to each other reside not only in their different foci of attention and degrees of practical relevance (processed knowledge suppresses the operational detail that may be of critical importance to clients), but also in language. The planner's language is conceptual and mathematical, consciously drained of the lifeblood of human intercourse in its striving for scientific objectivity. It is intended to present the results of his research in ways that will enable others, chiefly other planners, to verify each statement in terms of its logic, consistency with empirical observation, and theoretical coherence. Most planners prefer communicating their ideas in documents complete with charts, tables, graphs, and maps, as well as long appendices containing complex mathematical derivations and statistical analyses. The concepts, models, and theories to which these documents refer are often unfamiliar to the clients to whom they are supposedly addressed.

The language of clients lacks the formal restrictions that hedge in planning documents. It, too, employs a jargon to speed communications, but the jargon will be experience- rather than concept-related. Client language is less precise than the language of planners, and it may encompass congeries of facts and events that, even though they form a meaningful whole in terms of practice, are unrelated at the level of theory. Planners may therefore seize upon a favorite term from their client's specialized vocabulary and subject it to such rigorous analysis that what originally might have been a meaningful expression to the client is given back to him as a series of different but theoretically related concepts that reflect a processed reality.

Housing administrators, for example, have long been accustomed to derive quantitative program targets from what they call the housing deficit, which is calculated on the basis of new household formations, a physical index of housing quality, and an estimated rate of housing obsolescence. Planners have recently replaced this concept with what they believe to be a theoretically more valid model for establishing the housing needs of a population. They postulate an *effective housing demand* that arises in the context of particular submarkets organized according to major income levels and locality. Each submarket has unique characteristics with respect to the type of housing offered, the credit available, and the degree to which it is able to satisfy the social—as distinct from the economic—demand of each population group. Aggregate housing demand, therefore, is seen to evolve not only in accord with the differential growth rates of the affected population groups but also in relation to changes in the growth and distribution of personal income and in the structural characteristics of each submarket.

I do not know how housing administrators will react to this conceptually more satisfying model for calculating housing requirements, but I suspect that they will not be overly pleased. They may even accuse the planner of purposefully misconstruing the "real" (i.e., experiential) meaning contained in the traditional and administratively more convenient term of housing deficit.

The language of clients—so difficult to incorporate into the formalized vocabulary of the planner—is tied to specific operational contexts. Its meanings shift with changes in the context, and its manner of expression is frequently as important as the actual words employed. This is probably the reason why planners prefer written to verbal communications, and why the latter tend to be in the form of highly stylized presentations. Tone of voice, emphasis, subtle changes in grammatical structure and word sequence, so important in the face-to-face communications of action-oriented persons, are consistently de-emphasized by planners. Whereas planners' formal communications could be translated by a computer into a foreign language without substantial loss of meaning, a tape-recorded conversation among clients could not.

Planners relate primarily to other members of their profession and to the university departments responsible for the transmission and advancement of professional knowledge. Clients, on the other hand, relate chiefly to organizations of their own kind. The reference group of each acts as a cultural matrix that helps to confirm and strengthen differences of approach and behavior.

Reference groups are powerful institutions for molding behavior. This is especially true for the planner, whose situation tends to be less secure than that of his clients. His professional association not only keeps him continuously informed through newsletters, specialized journals, and conferences, but also confers on him the dignity and status of formal membership in a profession. The association reassures him when his competence is being challenged by outsiders and provides support when it is needed. In order to receive these benefits, the planner must conform to the norms of professional conduct. There are countless planning documents whose content is not primarily addressed to clients but to other planning professionals. For a planner's reputation is made more by impressing his fellow practitioners than by successfully serving his clients.

The reference systems of clients work in similar ways to enhance (or destroy) individual reputations. To the extent that clients also become professionalized—a trend that is very strong in American society—differences between planners and clients diminish, but the impediments to effective communication remain.

The mutual dependence of planner and client, coupled with a relative inability to exchange meaningful messages, leads to ambiguous and stereotyped attitudes that do little to resolve the basic problem. Speaking among themselves, planners say: "Ours is clearly a superior form of knowledge that enables us to gain incisive insights into conditions of structured complexity. As members of a professional elite, we are able to achieve a greater rationality than our clients. Effective problem-solving lies in the widespread use of processed knowledge." But they also admire the practical successes of their clients and secretly deplore their own inability to score in the same game.

The clients, on the other hand, in the sheltering environment of their own groups, counter the planners' claims: "Experience clearly counts most. Ours is a superior kind of knowledge, tested under fire. Planners are impractical dreamers who know more and more about less and less. Nothing of what they know can be applied. Problems get solved because we are in charge." But they also admire the planners' knowledge of things that are not visible to the unaided eye and so transcend the possibilities of knowledge grounded in experience.

What can be done to overcome these barriers to effective communication between planners and clients? The traditional means, an exchange of formal documents, has not proved spectacularly successful in the past. Strangely enough, most planners are probably still unaware of this.

A few years ago, I served as an advisor to the government of Chile on questions of urban and regional development. Several foreign experts working with me were connected with a number of central institutions, such as the National Planning Office and the Ministry of Housing. My own office, however, was independent and not formally associated with any agency of the government.

After a few months of initial reconnaissance, I thought that I had obtained a sufficient grasp of the situation to make a series of far-reaching recommendations. I set forth these recommendations very carefully in a lengthy memorandum, which, translated into Spanish, was carried by messenger to a number of leading government figures. A covering letter explained the general purpose of my effort. After letting two weeks go by, I arranged for an interview with each person who had received a copy. During the interviews, formal courtesies were exchanged, and some noncommittal references were made to the memorandum on which I had labored for several months. Afterwards I returned to my office to wait for a formal reply, but none ever came.

What had gone wrong? A good part of the answer can be found in my failure to establish, long before I ever set to work on the memorandum, a transactive relationship with the people whose encouragement I wanted. There was, indeed, no compelling reason why the government of Chile should have adopted any part of my recommendations. Who was I, after all, except an expert with a vague professional reputation abroad? Was it not presumptuous, not to say arrogant, for me, a foreigner who had spent only a few months in Chile, to suggest a whole series of sweeping reforms to responsible people who had been working for a good part of their political lives on problems of which I myself had only recently become aware?[2]

All these questions converge upon a single answer. If the communication gap between planner and client is to be closed, a continuing series of personal and primarily verbal transactions between them is needed, through which processed knowledge is fused with personal knowledge and both are fused with action.

Transactive Planning as the Life of Dialogue

In transactive planning, two levels of communication have to be distinguished. The first is the level of person-centered communication. It presumes a relationship that is applica-

ble to all forms of human intercourse. This I shall call
the life of dialogue. The second is the level of subject-
matter-related communication, which is sustained by the
primary relation of dialogue and cannot be understood
independently of it. Both levels are indispensable to planning. Where they become dissociated, thought is reduced
to theorems and action to pure energy.

The life of dialogue always occurs as a relationship between two persons, a You and an I. Its characteristic features
may be briefly stated:

1. *Dialogue presumes a relationship that is grounded in
the authenticity of the person and accepts his "otherness"
as a basis for meaningful communication.* In the life of
dialogue, each person seeks to address the other directly.
To be authentic means to discover yourself through dialogue
with many others. And therefore we can say: The life of
dialogue engenders a process of mutual self-discovery. At
each stage in the process, you attempt to integrate discoveries about yourself into the already existing structure of
your personality, thereby changing and expanding it. To do
this well, you must have found an inner security based on a
consciousness of what you have become and are yet capable
of becoming; a basic confidence in your ability to integrate
new learning; and, finally, a willingness to open yourself
to others.

Opening yourself to another implies an acceptance of the
other in his radical difference from yourself. The life of dialogue is not possible between two persons who hide behind
their many masks and are therefore incapable of growing
and extending their knowledge about themselves. It requires an openness that confirms the other in all the differences of his being. It is precisely this that makes changes
in self possible. Through dialogue, you accept the freedom
of the other to choose himself.

2. *Dialogue presumes a relation in which thinking, moral*

judgment, feeling, and empathy are fused in authentic acts of being. The authentic person is an indivisible whole. Nevertheless, four states of his being can be distinguished. The permanent dissociation of these may lead to a warping and even to the destruction of the person. Intellect alone is barren; moral judgment alone is self-righteous; feeling alone is destructive; and empathy alone is unresponsive. These four states of being must be held in mutual tension so that each may regulate the others. The point of intersection among them may be called the center of the fully integrated person, whose thought is tempered by moral judgment, whose judgment is tempered by feeling, and whose feeling is tempered by empathy.

Where these four states are brought into conjunction, speech becomes simply an extension of being, and the meanings of speech are backed up by the person as a whole: they can be taken on good faith. This does not always make them right, however. The learning person in the life of dialogue can make mistakes, he may be torn by inner doubts and conflicts, and he may be incapable of expressing himself integrally, leaving his meanings ambiguous and only partially articulated. Nevertheless, the standards of his speech are based not upon the extremes of truth, morality, feeling, and empathy taken each alone, but on the values that result from the conjunction of these states.

3. *Dialogue presumes a relation in which conflict is accepted.* The acceptance of the other in the plenitude of his being as a person different from yourself implies that the relationship cannot always be harmonious. Conflict arises out of your different ways of looking at the world, your different feelings about the world, and your different ways of judging the world. It may also arise from a failure to make your meanings clear within the context of the other's perceptions and feelings. But conflict can be over-

come by a mutual desire to continue in the life of dialogue. This is the basis for resolving conflict at the level of interpersonal relations.

4. *Dialogue presumes a relationship of total communication in which gestures and other modes of expression are as vital to meaning as the substance of what is being said.* Everything you say and everything you do—or fail to do—carries a message to the perceptive other. Dialogue is a web of meanings from which not a single strand can be separated. Where gesture and speech convey contradictory meanings, the authenticity of dialogue is put in doubt. Such contradictory behavior is, by itself, no proof of lack of authenticity, but it gives rise to a suspicion of bad faith.

5. *Dialogue presumes a relation of shared interests and commitments.* The life of dialogue cannot be sustained unless there is a sense of partaking in the interests of the other. Mutual participation in a matter of common concern is not a precondition of authentic dialogue; it may evolve through dialogue. Where it fails to evolve, the dialogue is interrupted.

We sometimes use one another to advance different interests. To the extent that this occurs, dialogue becomes an instrument to subordinate the other to your will. Presenting yourself to the other according to the demands of the situation is an inescapable part of dialogue, but "using" the other for interests that are not shared destroys any possibility of sustaining it. The life of dialogue is a relation of equality between two persons. It must not be perverted into an instrumental relationship.

6. *Dialogue presumes a relationship of reciprocity and mutual obligation.* Though dialogue is possible only between two persons who are free to choose themselves, this freedom is by no means unlimited. Dialogue is a contractual relationship. In accepting the other in his radical difference, you also assume responsibility for the consequences of

this relationship. The act of "accepting" implies an act of "giving." The other "gives" or "entrusts" himself to you as a person, as you entrust yourself in turn. This exchange need not be balanced equally: no records are or can be kept. Nevertheless, a one-sided giving cannot continue for long. To the extent that you are willing to "accept" the other, your obligations to him will increase, and you must be willing to give at least a part of yourself in return.

7. *Dialogue presumes a relationship that unfolds in real time.* Dialogue takes place in the "here and now" even as it relates what has gone before to what is yet to come. It is therefore a time-binding relationship capable of infinite evolution. Nevertheless, it cannot escape the constraints of a given situation and must ultimately become relevant to the particular conditions of each participant's life. Storytelling is not dialogue; dreams are not dialogue. You cannot crawl out of time; dialogue is not a route of escape. Dialogue brings you back into time and into the conditions of your being here.

As described, the life of dialogue suggests an intimacy that most people associate with the relationship between husband and wife, parents and children, and close friends. In the circle of this extended family, non-utilitarian, person-centered relationships predominate. Outside its magic circle, relationships are expected to rest on a working, professional basis, to be centered on specific roles rather than persons—a form of behavior that carefully isolates intellectual and technical contributions from their matrix of moral judgments and feelings and presumes purely utilitarian transactions, in which no sharing need occur.

But this conception is basically wrong. The world of planning need not be qualitatively set apart from the world of non-utilitarian relationships. On the contrary, the impersonal, professional style of communication has been notoriously unsuccessful in joining knowledge to action.

It is true, of course, that one cannot maintain deep personal relationships with everyone one meets. But a person-centered relationship can be sustained at varying degrees of intensity and over periods of time that extend from only a few minutes to an entire life. Looking back at the requirements of dialogue, we see that the conditions are applicable to any relationship. We can be open and alert to the other, whoever he may be. We can accept him as a person different from ourselves without being threatening or feeling threatened in turn. We can try to hold our intellectual, moral, affective, and empathetic states of being in mutual tension. We can accept conflict as an inevitable part of dialogue and not its termination. We can look for the patterns of shared interests. And we can concentrate the life of dialogue on the here and now.

An attitude favorable to dialogue tends to call forth on the part of the other a desire to engage in it. Some persons are more difficult to reach than others, but in most cases, the response to an attempted dialogue is dialogue.

Transactive planning is carried on the ground swell of dialogue. When I prepared the memorandum for the Chilean Government, the basis for dialogue had not yet been established. Later, all this changed. In recruiting the advisory staff, emphasis was given to the personal qualities of each advisor—his ability to be a person (not a role-playing professional alone), to establish direct relations with others that would not be perceived as threatening, to be sensitive to the needs of others, and to learn quickly from complex, novel situations. Technical qualifications were also considered important, but they carried less weight.

At the start, the newly recruited advisor spent from six months to a year learning about the multi-faceted situation in which he had been placed and establishing relations of dialogue with a few key persons in the offices to which he was assigned. Although his formal role was not eliminated, it was so loosely structured that the advisor was able to emerge as a person. And once a relationship of this kind had been established, transactive planning could begin in earnest.

The Process of Mutual Learning

Planners are forever coming up against new situations, but they confront them with knowledge that is little more than an aid to rapid and effective learning. Their theories, hypotheses, conceptual schemes, and analytical methods are useful only for converting the raw data of observation into general statements about reality. The validity of these statements is limited to a set of specified conditions. But the problems on which planners work—whether the design for a new town, a program for harnessing the waters of a river, or a policy for the development of scientific capabilities—must be studied in the fullness of historical circumstances. The number of variables that must be considered is substantially greater than those included in the analytical models of scientific work.

The planner's special skill, therefore, lies in his ability to be a rapid learner. His is an intelligence that is trained in the uses of processed knowledge for the purpose of acquiring new knowledge about reality. He comes equipped to bring order into a seemingly chaotic universe of data and sense impressions, to reduce this to a structure of relative simplicity, to isolate the processes responsible for the emergence and maintenance of the structure, to probe its propensities for change, and to locate the points of potentially effective intervention. Regardless of his specific procedure, the planner makes substantial use of analytical techniques in his work. The greater his virtuosity in this regard, the greater his pride in the results obtained. As I have said, his interests as a professional often get the better of his interest in serving his client. The following story serves to illustrate the point.

Some time ago, the U. S. Department of Transportation

sought the advice of a major research corporation on a proposal to decentralize its services. The corporation contracted with a group of professors at a number of different universities to prepare scholarly papers on the subject. The professors dug into their files, prepared the papers on schedule, and collected their fees. The papers were subsequently edited, and the completed set was forwarded to Washington, together with a summary of findings and recommendations. But neither the corporation nor the professors knew the exact reasons for the original request; nor were they aware of what factions pulled in what directions, what arguments had been already made, who were the figures in the unfolding drama of departmental politics. How could work done in ignorance of these things have been relevant to their client except by chance?

In this as in so many other situations, planning was carried out with no regard for the processes of goal clarification and policy formation. The research corporation and the professors conceived of their task exclusively in technical terms. They had no stake in the results of their studies. They failed to take their client on a learning trip.

What might have been done? Assuming that the original request for technical assistance was a serious one, an office might have been established in Washington for as long as necessary. Personal contacts might have been established with the originators of the request in the department, flesh-and-blood people with passions of their own. A review of the department's activities might have been jointly undertaken to see which might be decentralized and why. In problems such as these, the outside technical expert can be of greatest help by structuring the questions in a useful way and supplying concepts to help clarify the basic issues involved. The experts in this case might have served a catalytic role in organizing such a study, mediating among the different factions, proposing hypotheses, and summarizing the current state of theoretical knowledge. In doing all these things, they would have had to be in daily contact with the client staff. Personal relationships would gradually have developed. And in the end, the solution would have appeared as a discovery of the client himself.

In mutual learning, planner and client each learn from the other—the planner from the client's personal knowledge, the client from the planner's technical expertise. In this process, the knowledge of both undergoes a major change. A common image of the situation evolves through dialogue; a new understanding of the possibilities for change is discovered. And in accord with this new knowledge, the client will be predisposed to act.[3]

The Tao of Transactive Planning

Planners are often inspired by a wish to change existing reality. This almost compulsive desire stands in direct relationship to their inability to influence the requisite behavior to produce a change. The head of a large technical assistance operation once exclaimed in my presence, pounding his fist on the table: "We have to show controlled impatience." It was not clear to me then, nor is it clear to me now, why impatience was called for. He had neither the power nor the responsibility to act. His job was simply to advise the government, not to replace it.

This incident has remained with me over the years. It reflects, I think, a complete lack of understanding of the essential tasks of planning. Clearly, the man was eager to step into the driver's seat. Lack of sufficient progress, according to his lights, was due entirely to the laziness, corruption, recalcitrance, decadence, cupidity, political irresponsibility, and irrationality of the guidance institutions of the country to which he had been called. He knew what needed to be done, and he had told his clients how to do it. Why did they not follow his advice?

His model of the planning process was exceedingly simplistic. The planner plans; the client buys the plans and uses all the means at his disposal to see them carried out. If planning follows a transactive style, however, a different, more complex model has to be considered (Figure 7). The Taoist philosophy of *wu-wei*—doing nothing—would seem to be more appropriate to this model than controlled impatience.

The Tao says: *All things go through their own transformations.* —All systems obey their own laws of internal change. These laws cannot be arbitrarily reversed without causing substantial harm to the system. Both the maintenance and the change of a system are the result of processes that relate the system's elements to one another. A good deal of system behavior is regulated automatically, but sometimes there is insufficient change, or the change is not the kind we would like, or changes are too rapid, causing the system to fall into disorder. If the planner wants to rectify any of these conditions, he must concentrate upon the processes of maintenance and transformation in order to see how to accelerate, decelerate, or contain them; occasionally a new process should be introduced or a process that has lost its vital functions should be discarded. To change a process means to act upon the sources that generate the lawful behavior of the system. But both planner and client must respect the laws of transformation and be mindful of their limited abilities to control the flow of events.

The same principle applies to mutual learning. Learning cannot be imposed; it obeys the laws by which a structure of thinking, feeling, and valuing is changed. The planner may learn rapidly. But the more he assimilates his client's knowledge, the greater the complexity of which he is aware. To change the reasons why people act the way they do and produce the results they do, one must respect the processes by which they learn. Anxieties have little influence upon the outcome. Students do not learn because their teachers want them to. They learn only when they are ready to ac-

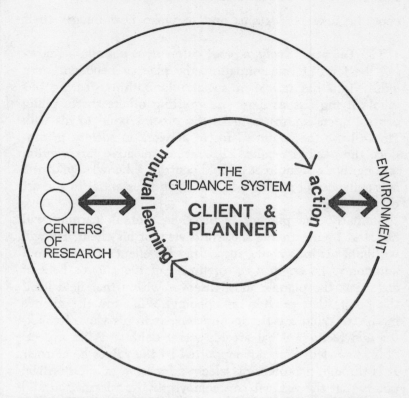

PLANNERS CONTRIBUTE

* concepts
* theory
* analysis
* processed knowledge
* new perspectives
* systematic search
  procedures

CLIENTS CONTRIBUTE

* intimate knowledge
  of context
* realistic alternatives
* norms
* priorities
* feasibility judgments
* operational details

Figure 7. A Model of Transactive Planning

cept the new perceptions and to make new images their own.

The Tao says: *Truly, a great cutter does not cut.* —Knowing the laws of transformation, the planner need not slash wildly into the tangle of social relationships, tearing out whole living tissues here and grafting others there, piling control upon control to make the process bend to his will. He will use the "natural" forces at work in society to produce the desired results. This means selective intervention and methods of indirect or field control. A knowledge of the consequences of strategic intervention is essential to the art of planning.

Similarly, the planner involved in mutual learning will not start by destroying the world view of his client. He will withhold his judgments, respecting his client's freedom and autonomy. To begin a restructuring of the client's field of cognition, the planner must discover within that field itself the points that provide an opening. What are the client's interests? What are the inconsistencies in his way of thinking and feeling? What are his secret doubts? What aspects of his knowledge are not supported by the values he affirms? It is through a process of selective focusing at such critical points that the planner can achieve the transformation and expansion of his client's learning.

The Tao says: *Tao invariably does nothing, yet there is nothing that is not done.* —Under conditions of mutual learning, the planner appears to be doing nothing: he learns, and, learning, he imparts new knowledge. As perceptions and images are changed, so is the behavior that flows from them. Time is necessary for changes in behavior to occur. In the natural course of things, little appears to happen, yet everything happens in due time. Persons change, institutions change, the environment for action changes. The ideas of the learner take root, are themselves transformed, and pass into action, affecting the behavior of society.

The Tao says: *The most yielding of things outruns the most unyielding.* —Mutual learning cannot be compelled; the planner cannot accelerate the processes of understanding and behavior change. Time is needed; listening is needed. If the planner listens carefully and long enough, his own thoughts may eventually be given back to him as the ideas of others. Only then can the planner truly be said to have succeeded in his task.

The future cannot be conquered by the present; compulsion destroys the generative forces in society. The planner must learn to yield when necessary, but also to persuade. Dialogue is essential to learning. Through dialogue, mutual learning occurs; and through mutual learning changes are brought about in the collective behavior of society.

The Tao says: *To give life, but not to own, to achieve but not to cherish, to lead but not to be master—that is the mystic virtue.* —This is the most important, and also the most difficult of the five teachings of the Tao. It says: let everyone be free to choose himself, do not desire what is not your own, do not hold back on what you know. As a teacher, fade into the background and let the student speak; as a student, take new learning and use it to advantage. But when there are neither teachers nor students, as in mutual learning, the property of learning is held in common trust: no one is master, each has something to give and something to receive. From period to period, you pass to higher levels of understanding. Do not cherish them. Keep your mind open to what is yet to come.

If the processed knowledge of planners is serviceable only insofar as it is used as an instrument for learning; if learning cannot be imparted to others except through dialogue; and if dialogue creates a process in which each partner has as much to give as to receive, then the Tao provides good counsel.

Transactive Planning in the Context of Society

American society needs a heightened capacity for learning about itself and, to make what it learns effective in guiding its own development, a way to transform learning into appropriate actions. This implies that we must find a way to join scientific and technical intelligence with personal knowledge at the critical points for social intervention. I have argued that transactive planning is the most appropriate method for achieving this linkage.

The transactive style is not, admittedly, applicable to every situation where expert knowledge is joined to action. It is inappropriate, for instance, *where expertise carries sufficient authority to act without the benefit of mutual learning*. The mechanic, the airplane pilot, or the surgeon is each prepared to do his job without elaborate discussion with his clients. There is no need for dialogue. Few questions will be asked and fewer answered. Nor are situations of mutual learning between expert and client common in highly stratified societies, where technical expertise enjoys high social esteem and clients unhesitatingly accept its judgments simply because they are offered under a prestigious professional label. In all other situations, however, the transactive style is essential to the ultimate success of planning. And this holds true with particular force in American society today.

Transactive planning is a style that humanizes the acquisition and uses of scientific and technical knowledge. But how can humanization in this sense occur at the level of society? Is it possible to extend the processes of mutual learning to society as a whole? Is societal learning possible?

Before answering these questions, we must define the nature of the problem with greater precision. What are the principal performance characteristics of the guidance system in American society today?

The most critical aspect is perhaps its increasing incapacity to respond effectively to the demands that processes of change within society are generating. Throughout American society, there is an extraordinarily high degree of centralization in the power to make effective decisions; actions are initiated far from their ultimate points of impact. A system so structured experiences great difficulties in responding to the needs of the people. Because of the many levels through which information must be filtered, decisions tend to be made too slowly in the face of accelerating changes all about. Problems stand in line, waiting to be resolved, but nothing happens. Only those that seem urgent to those who occupy positions of power are advanced up the queue. As the line of unattended problems grows, dissatisfaction rises among the population. Because of its agonizing slowness, but also because its diagnoses are often incorrect, being made on the basis of highly aggregated but often incomplete and misleading information, the system frequently responds with the wrong answers. As a result, problems compound. Finally, some of the demands are simply filtered out and never receive a hearing, unless they are made in violent and screaming protest and so move up the scale of institutional priorities.

All these problems are aggravated by the fact that there is relatively little feedback of meaningful information to the centers of action. Feedback is generally slow, especially where actions have not yet been routinized. In addition, much that is relevant is eventually filtered out as information moves from its points of origin up through the hierarchy of action levels; subject to all manner of distortions on the way, it arrives at the top lacking the context that would permit a reasonable interpretation of its meaning.

The other aspect of a progressively unresponsive guidance system is a population that is progressively less and less the master of its destiny, whose lives are subject to random impersonal forces that no longer seem to be intended or controlled by anyone. Despite the official rhetoric to the contrary, America is becoming a non-participant society. Its people have little understanding of their own environment. They are fed ready-made explanations by the media, but none of these seems to account for what is happening. Being so remote from control over events, the non-participant subject finally ceases even to care. He does not read the annual reports of the business in which he works but concentrates instead on the small world of his job. His view of politics is cynical. He skims the news about his city, hurrying on to the sports and entertainment pages, and he is mesmerized by evening prime-time television. From time to time, some spectacles, such as the landings on the moon, are arranged for his diversion.

The non-participant society is stirred up by its troubles, because they affect the lives of individuals within it: the war swallows its children, automation eliminates its jobs, the reeking air destroys its lungs, the poor make claims upon its pocketbooks. But no one really understands how all this comes about. The world seems alive with mysterious and evil forces. Conspiracy is suspected everywhere.

The system we have engendered is approaching the breaking point. The combination of growing unresponsiveness and non-participation is tearing the society apart. The guidance system is becoming increasingly reactive, moved by the unexpected turbulence of events, frantically putting out fires without ever seriously approaching the structural sources of a conflagration that seems to be gaining on what is left of the inherited order. These palliative measures are only partially effective, and their costs to the society are rising vertiginously. As a result, a small but growing segment of the population is beginning to withdraw its allegiance from the society.

The basic structural problem of the American guidance system is its rising level of ignorance. Reason has become unhinged from action, leading knowledge to take refuge in the cloistered irrelevancies of esoteric language, and actions to lag farther and farther behind the events they seek so desperately to control. To re-establish the essential linkage, society needs a heightened learning capacity. This will never be achieved by creating some sort of super-brain that is plugged into a nationwide monitoring system of social indicators and whose repository of quantitative models spews out appropriate answers. The realization of this current dream, so dear to technocrats, would only widen the existing breach between knowledge and action with truly tragic consequences for the society.

CHAPTER 8

DESIGN FOR GUIDANCE: A LEARNING
SOCIETY

It may be useful here to review the argument up to this
point.

1. Societal guidance is concerned with directing collective phenomena in ways that will improve the overall condition of society or some sub-sector within it.

2. Societal guidance is achieved through a set of institutional arrangements (political, legal, economic, financial,
administrative, cognitive, and planning) that generates a
stream of collective phenomena and produces salient outcomes. Some of these outcomes are intended; others are not
and present themselves to policy makers as problems to be
solved.

3. The present system of societal guidance in America is
producing outcomes that are causing widespread social concern. I have tried to show that this precarious level of
performance is, to a large extent, the result of a structural in-
compatibility between the guidance system and its environment.

4. To improve its overall level of performance, the guidance system must be reorganized to make it structurally
compatible with the conditions of a post-industrial society.

5. The general solution to this problem would seem to lie in the design for a "learning society" in which the structural conditions for a transactive style of planning will be maximized. Transactive planning integrates processes of mutual learning with an organized capacity and willingness to act. It is applicable to both allocative and innovative forms of planning.

In Chapter 3, I concluded with a series of questions about the connections between command, policies, corporate, and participant styles of planning, the relative importance of these styles and their related processes in the overall design of guidance systems, and the ways by which a scientific-technical intelligence might be effectively related to action. In the present chapter, I shall endeavor to answer these questions and, in so doing, to outline the structural conditions likely to favor a learning society in the context of post-industrial America.

1. What Institutional Arrangements Will Establish Effective Connections among the Different Styles of Allocative Planning?

Styles of allocative planning were seen to depend, in part, on the methods of implementing decisions and, more broadly, on the distribution of power in society. Four styles of allocative planning were accordingly described, though it was pointed out that none is likely to exist in unadulterated form. Historically, different mixes of these styles are found, with one or the other predominating. It was further suggested that a complete guidance system would have to link the four styles of participant, corporate, policy, and command planning into a sequence. Despite limited attempts in recent years to develop such a guidance system and, in particular, to establish conditions for participant planning in urban communities, we have yet to evolve a structural principle that would permit us to build up a complete guidance system adapted to present conditions. As a nation, we seem to flounder from one extreme position to another, from rejecting the principle of hierarchy (and embracing the idea of a completely atomized society that somehow manages to hold its million fragments together through mutual adjustments among them) to rejecting the principle of participation (and embracing the idea of a completely hierarchical society, with a universally accepted authority as the legitimizing basis for social interaction). Neither of these mutually exclusive systems of social order is, in fact, a viable one for contemporary America. The search must rather be for a principle of organization capable of relating participant to command structures by connecting the corporate and policy-making components of the guidance system.

Such a principle may be found in *cellular structure*.[1] A society organized according to this principle would have as its smallest effective unit the *task-oriented working group*. Such groups exist already in abundance (though they are not yet organized into a cellular structure), and it is relatively easy to describe them. Task-oriented working groups may be characterized as:

—*temporary:* existing only as long as the problems with which they are meant to deal remain under active consideration. Once a given problem has been solved, or ceases to be socially important, the group that has been working on it disbands, its members joining other groups that are still active elsewhere or are in process of being formed;

—*small scale:* effective working groups rarely exceed twelve members, and many are smaller. Their size is limited by the members' ability to meet in face-to-face encounters as frequently as the nature of their task requires;

—*interpersonal:* working groups operate primarily on the basis of verbal communication among their members;

they provide an optimal setting for the life of dialogue. A working group may be thought of as simply a gathering of individuals who are joined by their interest in dealing effectively with a given problem. In the course of their work, specialized roles are minimized and facets of the whole personality of each member of the group become engaged;

—*having a self-appointed and/or representative, inclusive, and cross-tied membership:* working group members either join on a voluntary basis or are sent as representatives of other organizational units; their membership, in any event, is as inclusive as the nature of the problem requires. Individual members, however, may simultaneously belong to several working groups, thus establishing informal communications among them;

—*self-guiding:* working groups generally enjoy a high degree of autonomy. They can devise their own rules of procedure, redefine the original task or problem set, and may be given wide scope for initiating actions related to their mission;

—*responsible:* working groups are generally given their charge by parent organizations to which they are ultimately accountable. In a society having cellular structure, these parent organizations would be *assemblies of working groups* (see below). The legitimacy and formal authority of working groups would derive from these assemblies.

Two major traits of cellular structure deserve special consideration: its organization into clustered networks of working groups and its permeability. *Networks* of communication links relate clusters of working groups in ways that respond solely to their needs to be in contact with one another: cellular structure is an impermanent form of organization. It is evident that the intensity and direction of communication lines will change with the character of the tasks that must be carried out. The communications network of working group clusters will thus be in a state of flux. Where certain tasks must be continued over extended periods, the working groups involved may well establish more formal relationships among themselves. Since the turnover in their membership is likely to be great, however, further modifications in the pattern of communications will probably occur, as new members "import" group relations from their own earlier associations. In general, network organization, though more permanent than any of its individual components, will be a relatively fluid organizational arrangement.

A second major trait of cellular structure is its *permeability*. This has a double aspect. The membership of individual working groups is open and can be easily augmented or contracted as individuals drift in and out, participating in the group's activities for only limited periods of time. But the entire network of working groups is also open, as new working groups are started and others disbanded. Both individual working groups and the networks into which they are organized are essentially without boundaries or closure. This permeability of structure is, of course, a matter of degree. Certain relations are more intense and of longer duration than others, and the size of working groups is limited to the possibilities of face-to-face relationships. The absorptive capacity of networks is greater than that of individual working groups. Where a participating working group is in danger of growing too large for effective collaboration, new groups can easily be formed around subdivisions of the original problem.

This description of cellular structure has so far avoided the concept of hierarchy, leaving unanswered the question of how the activities of working groups are to be accumulated over larger areas of shared concern. It is possible to imagine entire industries, universities, hospitals, and other service institutions, as well as ecologically patterned communities, dissolving into clustered networks of working groups. But unless some integrative structure can be created to define the nature of their tasks, the priorities, and the basis for resolving competing claims against the same set of resources, working groups will remain essentially atomistic, mutually antagonistic, and without effective power. The principle of hierarchy must therefore be wedded to the cellular principle. This can be done by establishing *working group assemblies* at both corporate and supra-corporate levels of organization.

The assembly of working groups is hierarchically superior to the individual working groups that compose it and provides both a stable point of reference and a legitimate base for their activities. All working group members participate in assembly meetings. It is important to restrict the size of meetings, however, in order to enable members actively to engage in the proceedings. Each assembly is able, therefore, to aggregate only a limited number of working groups, corresponding to a total membership of probably less than fifty, a size equivalent to about eight average-sized working groups. Each assembly would delegate a limited number of members, say ten, to still higher-level assemblies, and so on, until the entire corporate structure is exhausted. Delegates from corporate assemblies would then participate in the activities of supra-corporate assemblies that would tie into policy-making bodies at central government levels. *It is, therefore, through a network of permanent assemblies that the social system is integrated and societal guidance occurs.*

The major functions of working group assemblies include (1) the exchange of information between members from different working groups (or lower-level assemblies) and (2) determination of system-wide policies, including the identification of tasks for new working groups. In cellular structures, information tends to flow upwards from the direct encounters of working groups with problem situations, though a reverse flow of information also takes place, having its point of origin in the deliberations of higher-level assemblies.

Cellular structure creates an environment conducive to mutual learning. Working groups proceed largely on the basis of personal knowledge. This, as I have argued, is essential but inadequate knowledge for societal guidance. For this reason, *technical secretariats,* whose business is to process information and make it available to the appropriate working groups, must be established at the level of assemblies.[2] This transfer of knowledge, facilitated by an environment that favors dialogue, requires that mutual learning extend in a web of interpersonal transactions, downwards to individual working groups and upwards to higher-level assemblies. Representatives from the technical secretariats must take an active part in the deliberations of assemblies as well as in the activities of individual working groups. Through this process of close collaboration, the calculations of the technical secretariats can be made operationally more relevant, as technical experts draw on the personal knowledge of working group members. At the same time, experts will find it easier to communicate the relevant processed knowledge they possess.

The role of leadership in cellular structure deserves special comment. The temptation to ignore leadership is strong: cellular structure may appear to be self-motivating, self-regulating, and self-guiding. This is to a large extent true, but it would be wrong to suppose that leadership is, therefore, rendered superfluous. Within small working groups, leadership may arise spontaneously and change with the task performed; each working group member may rise to leadership in his turn. In any event, the contribution of each member to the accomplishment of the collective task is far more important than hierarchical relations of leaders and followers. In most working groups, it would be difficult to tell just who the leader is.

But assemblies of working groups cannot conduct their day-to-day business without vesting formal leadership authority in one person or a small group of persons. Properly conceived, these leaders serve with the consent of the assembly. Their terms of office may be relatively brief, and a system of rotating leadership may be evolved. In this respect, assembly leaders within a system having cellular structure appear to occupy positions analogous to those of leadership in bureaucratic organizations. But in most other respects, they will differ.

Assembly leaders must orchestrate the work of the assemblies at each level in the hierarchy. Rather than exercise a prerogative of command, assembly leaders are responsible for maintaining a holistic and balanced perspective despite the fragmentation of decision-making powers. They must see to it that the larger tasks get done, that stalemates among evenly matched working groups do not occur, or, where they do occur, are amicably resolved. In highly decentralized organizations governed by adherence to the principle of consensus, one group or a small number of groups is capable of imposing an effective veto on the efforts of all others. But too many such instances cannot be permitted if cellular structure is to remain viable. It is the job of the assembly leader to ensure that every voice is heard, but also that suitable compromises among conflicting groups are reached.

Another important leadership role is that of serving as a clearing center for information. By virtue of their position and visibility, assembly leaders will have information that is not readily available to everyone. There is no question but that the handling of "privileged" information will enhance the power of the leader. The abuse of this power, however, can be minimized by the assembly acting to replace its leadership. The wise leader, on the other hand, will play his game with open cards. Although this seems contrary to much experience, it is probably true that candor with working groups and the individual membership of the assembly will tend to accrue to the long-run benefit of everyone. In fact, the rapid dissemination of information as it becomes available will not only prevent possible resentments from building up among assembly members, it will greatly enhance the quality of the decisions made. An open information policy is, by all odds, the best.

Finally, it falls upon the leadership to provide for the moral integration of working group assemblies. Unless a sense of common purpose informs everyone's efforts, cellular structure falls apart. The collaborative spirit of individuals and working groups will remain high so long as everyone believes in the transcending importance of his work. By deeply involving many individual persons in collective tasks, and by permitting relations of dialogue to flourish, cellular structure will generate its own moral climate. It is nevertheless true that the larger purposes of the assembly must be articulated and adequately symbolized. From time to time, individual commitments must be rededicated to the overarching purposes of the assembly. This is all the more important as neither utilitarian nor coercive means for achieving and maintaining group cohesion are permissible. Upholding and perfecting a mythical belief in the intrinsic importance of the collective enterprise is one of the chief responsibilities of the assembly leadership. Not the least of these beliefs is a devotion to continuous learning through an active engagement with the world.

A learning society has cellular structure. Being cellular, and therefore involving a significant portion of the total membership of the society in guidance activities, it is also an *activated* society. Cellular structure is capable of infinite expansion both horizontally and vertically. Where participant planning is tied to corporate levels, corporate planning to policy levels, and policy planning to command levels, assemblies and technical secretariats provide for the integration of partial interests and the establishment of guidelines for action. Some of these will be self-executing, others will require implementation through command structures. In general, however, what is left to command planning will be relatively little, since only those problems that cannot be successfully resolved at lower levels are filtered upwards.

2. Should Any Particular Planning Style Have Preference in the Overall Guidance System of Society?

In cellular structure, the participant style of planning clearly predominates, infusing the entire process of societal guidance with its distinctive qualities. In principle, it might be thought to involve every grown member of society in significant guidance activities. This is not likely to occur, however, since many people prefer to "freeload" on society, leaving the business of guidance to others, so long as they themselves are able to carry on their activities without unusual hindrance. A more realistic estimate, therefore, would put the number of active participants at between one fifth and one third of the entire adult population. Even so, compared to current levels of participation, the numbers would be staggering. For an adult population of more than 130 million, the successful introduction of cellular structure into the life of the nation would imply an "activated" population of between twenty-five and forty million people, or roughly one participant for every two families. Since many among the activated population would take part in more than one working group and assembly at a time (e.g., in their residential communities and their places of work), considerable overlap in interests and activities would occur.

It is difficult to imagine the changes that would come about as a result of shifting from the present system of societal guidance—which is largely bureaucratic in its organization and involves only small numbers of the population—to one in which nearly everyone would have a neighbor or working colleague somewhere engaged in "steering" the course of societal development. The idea is, in fact, revolutionary in its implications, and critics may object that (a) the majority of mankind is intellectually unfit to engage in guidance activities (an essentially elitist argument, which ascribes to a small minority the exclusive capacity to govern) and/or (b) such widespread participation can result only in chaos and could never be properly co-ordinated around the central tasks of a society. Both these arguments can be turned aside so long as it is realized that an active society is also a society engaged in learning; that mutual learning can penetrate to any level of society, involving even persons of limited intellectual attainments; and that the structure of assemblies is able to co-ordinate and integrate the efforts of individual working groups far more effectively than the traditional means of central planning and bureaucratic control.

Moreover, it is simply false to assert that the expression of a diversity of interests and value positions will inevitably result in chaos. A large and wealthy society like America's is quite capable of accommodating a multiplicity of life styles and the simultaneous pursuit of many different interests. The single-common-denominator approach to societal guidance is more appropriate to small, culturally homogeneous, poor societies that are obliged to concentrate their efforts on a limited number of overriding objectives. Present-day America is perhaps the only national society that can afford to be experimental in the exploration of its future. Original ideas can arise at any point within the network of a cellular structure and can often be acted upon without infringing upon the central interests of others. From a society-wide point of view, innovations may therefore be regarded primarily as experiments that bear watching for any possible value they might have for other sectors of society.

A learning society cannot afford to give doctrinaire answers, especially where the knowledge to lend assurance to any given reply probably does not exist. In addition, it may be worth recalling that, in America, even a very small percentage of the total population implies large absolute numbers, and that the interests of large numbers cannot very well be ignored without endangering the peace of the nation. Two million people may represent less than one tenth of 1 percent of the national population, but where the vital interests of two million citizens converge, it may be altogether advantageous to let them determine their own future within the larger framework of the polity. And the possibility that something of general value might be learned from their particular experience should not be lightly dismissed.

The participant style of cellular structure is, therefore, hospitable to the expression of minority interests and accommodating to styles of life that depart from that of the majority. This permissive quality will tend to reduce the overall amount of friction in society. A learning society must be extremely reluctant to say "no" to any new design for living without full knowledge of its expected consequences. Since such knowledge is usually unobtainable in advance of actual implementation, an experimental "pilot project" approach is far more advisable than an uninformed, and therefore useless conflict over "right" and "wrong." The only way to discover the facts of the particular case is to sink "live probes" into the system and carefully observe the results.

One very important aspect of the participant style of planning is its ability to overcome the specter of partial truth that was of such concern to Karl Mannheim. Perspectivism, related to the social position occupied by an observer, undoubtedly exists and could, indeed, lead to a decline in social order in the event that a particular perspective were to succeed in becoming the sole basis for societal guidance. Mannheim's answer to this problem was incorrect, however. Trusting in the capacity of intellectuals-turned-planners to obtain an all-embracing view of society, he was wrong on the grounds both of sociology and of the theory of knowledge. Sociology should have taught him that planners, regardless of their class position (or lack of it), must operate from particular centers of power in society, a condition that necessarily blinds them to many existing phenomena and distorts their vision with regard to all the rest. And the theory of knowledge should have taught him that an integral vision is, in principle, unobtainable, since the possibilities of knowing are infinitely large, and no one can embrace infinity. What we know is always a transitory speck out of the oceanic infinities of what is knowable. Mannheim's claim that any group of men, however wise, has the ability to reach beyond a partial understanding of the world is little short of folly.

But the participant planning style comes close to this embracing view—or as close as any human organization can—though it, too, is unable to exhaust the possibilities inherent in potential knowledge. Its effect is best described as kaleidoscopic, or as the peaceful coexistence of many fragments of known reality. Fragmented images of problem situations are brought together in the assemblies of working groups, where they are "assembled" into larger compositions, not necessarily according to some classical standard of aesthetic appeal but perhaps following the seemingly "irrational" criteria of contemporary art, where the unthinkable is thought and, being thought, is often discovered to be a valid expression of artistic sensibility.

It may be difficult for us to accept the fact of the temporary quality of social experience, when the Platonic ideals of truth, goodness, and beauty are still thought to be cast in immutable forms possessed of a higher reality than are the impermanent shadows of "mere" appearances. Yet accept it we must as a condition of collective survival. Strange as it may seem, because it is contradictory to inherited beliefs, a society "composed" of many superficially irreconcilable elements may be stronger and more resistant to both internal and external shocks than one that is shaped according to the monistic ideals of classical design.

This generally hopeful view leaves out of account the ancient human desire to impose one's own view of the world upon the rest of humanity. The Germans call it *Gleichschaltung*, plugging everyone into the same current of thinking and acting. The personal truth of one is seen as threatening the personal truths of others. People believe, more widely than one would like to admit, that the world cannot contain more than a single truth or ideology. Neither cellular structure nor a transactive style of planning will banish a motivation so deeply rooted in the human personality. To the extent that contending truths are at the root of social conflict, a learning society will not be without conflict. Whether man can be re-educated to desist from this inherent drive for domination is a question to which I shall return in the final chapter.

A participant style of planning, finally, makes an enormous volume of information available for the guidance of societal development. Each of the twenty-five to forty million participants acts both as receiver and sender of information to be processed and used in the deliberations of both working groups and assemblies. The amount of information so internalized is many times that which is currently available. If participant planning mobilizes ten times the number of active contributors to the process of societal guidance, the increase in the volume of information that becomes available will be many times greater. In addition, the network of working groups generates its own new insights into problems and permits the rapid verification of reality images at any level of the system.

Of great importance here is the reaction time of the entire system to new information. The stress placed on verbal and informally written communication and the possibility of direct contact between any two participants *regardless of their location in the network* (i.e., the elimination of formal channels), makes it possible to bring together the relevant information on short notice, to make it count in group deliberations, and to take appropriate action. Although the informal nature of network communications introduces a good deal of redundancy into the system, this is desirable, since the system will also generate much random information or "noise." Redundancy is needed so that the critical information may "get through" and not be lost.

The bulk of information processing will take place at the level of working groups. These elemental units may therefore be regarded as reasonably efficient "filters" of information, leaving the hierarchy of assemblies to deal with progressively more comprehensive problems. This upward, but filtered, drift of information assures a close environmental fit of problem solutions at any given level, at the same time that it relieves assemblies of having to cope with information that should more properly be scrutinized at lower levels.

The participant planning style creates an information-saturated environment. This brings with it two sets of consequences. The emphasis placed on verbal communication means that guidance activities in a context of cellular structure are extremely time-consuming. It also means that participant members will be asked to absorb more information than they are able to process efficiently.

The first of these problems can be overcome by erasing what appears to be an increasingly artificial distinction between "normal" activities (system outputs) and activities related to guidance (system inputs). This distinction is a carry-over from bureaucratic organizations, where management is clearly separated from the activities to be managed. In cellular structure, where a participant style of planning predominates, such a division of roles (and tasks) is no longer defensible. Where the "activities to be managed" are themselves subject to frequent redirection and reorganization (because of rapid changes in environmental conditions and the quick response times of the system), *work* and *guidance* can no longer be conceptually distinguished. The high percentage of the population participating in groups, in fact, requires that members be drawn from both work and client situations, so that the process of guidance becomes truly a process of *self*-guidance in which each member helps to design the conditions under which he will perform his work. This expanded concept of work (expanded to include guidance activities) is equally applicable to community situations, where the parallel concept would be residential activities. Societal guidance is, therefore, something that must be done during the hours of "normal" activity and not as a part-time pursuit for one's hours of "leisure." The practical effect of this radical reinterpretation of work, residential activity, and leisure is to increase the total amount of time devoted to societal guidance. This is a step essential to correct a situation where the increasingly "blind" performance of regular activities leads to the unsatisfactory performance of the system as a whole. The existing guidance system is not only inappropriate in its structure but insufficient in the total amount of guidance it makes available.

The problem of communication overload is not solved quite so easily. There is a widespread popular belief that overload can be readily dealt with by the increased use of high-speed electronic computers. This belief is often coupled with the assertion that, in the future, we shall all be able to devote our time to the pursuits of leisure while computers, quietly humming away in their crystal enclosures, will do the work. This is wrong. Verbal communication may be inefficient from some points of view (though very efficient and, indeed, irreplaceable for certain tasks), but it will not be reduced by increased computation capacity; it will merely be redirected to focus on other issues. Where the demand for information is infinitely greater than the system's capacity to process it, the introduction of computers provides no relief whatever; *it merely permits more information to be taken into account*. The same conclusion applies to any other method intended to relieve the individual of his burden as an information processor. All it will eventually accomplish—allowing for a relatively brief period of adjustment—is to make more information available.[3]

If this is so, the problem is not how to reduce the amount of overload in the system—since this will, in any event, remain at fairly constant levels, the potential demand for information in societal guidance being practically inexhaustible—*but how to decide at what level of total information an overload should occur.* Participant planning greatly increases the guidance system's capacity for information processing. It is more likely, therefore, to generate "fitting" problem solutions than a guidance system operating in the same environment but at lower levels of information-processing capacity.

The participant style of planning obviously cannot exist without its complement of corporate, policy, and command styles. These will become increasingly important at higher assembly levels, where temporary policy agreements are negotiated and where, in the final instance, commands must be used to deal with hypercritical issues of societal guidance that cannot be left to the looser, more permissive framework of field controls and voluntary compliance. At all these levels, however, the preponderant influence of the participant style will be felt.

3. How May a Scientific-Technical Intelligence Be Linked Effectively to Each Style in the Guidance System?

A network of working groups and their assemblies is capable of mobilizing an immense amount of personal, pragmatic knowledge and putting it to immediate use. At the same time, network organization is a tremendous device for societal learning. And the network of assemblies is so arranged that opportunities for transactive planning—mutual learning related to action—are maximized.

Within this general context, mutual learning takes place primarily in two ways. It occurs, first, through the frequent exchange of specialized, personal knowledge between members. Personal knowledge is "purified" in assembly meetings, where it comes under scrutiny and must prove itself in open contention with the equally personal knowledge of others. The limits of its validity in a particular action context are thus established, and its tendency to subjective bias is controlled. Out of these discussions emerges a collective image of reality that, because it takes into account a wide variety of perspectives, is more comprehensive than any of the individual contributions from which it is synthesized. Once these images are internalized by individual assembly members, they form the basis for subsequent decisions and actions, as well as for still further learning.

The second process through which mutual learning occurs involves the technical secretariats. Secretariats are the principal centers for the generation of the processed knowledge that is pertinent to guidance. In addition to the specific services they perform for working group assemblies, such as the preparation of agendas, follow-up actions, the provision of information, and formal reporting, they also engage in policy analysis, program monitoring, the measurement of system states, program evaluation, short-term forecasting, experimental system design and testing, and technical assistance.[4] In order to make the results of this work available to the assemblies, frequent personal contacts must be established, setting in motion a learning process that will facilitate the flow of communications between planner and client in both directions.

Technical secretariats carry out activities that lie beyond the competence of individual working group members. But their functions exceed the merely technical; they must be concerned with problems of system-wide integration, the balancing of working group efforts, pulling into the discussions of working groups and their assemblies information that would otherwise not be available to them, and a variety of activities that require a full-time, professional effort and are best performed from a central position.

Assemblies will exist at critical nodes in network organization for the purpose of mediating transactions between major planning levels (see Figure 8). One such assembly

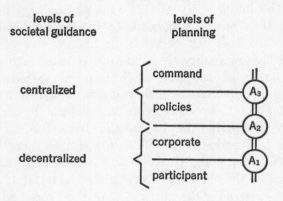

Figure 8. A Hierarchy of Working Group Assemblies

(A_1) will be found at the level of corporate planning, where it will mediate between participant and corporate structures; another (A_2) will be found at the level of system-wide policy formation, mediating between decentralized and centralized guidance structures; yet a third (A_3) will mediate between policy-making and command structures at centralized levels of societal guidance. This hierarchy of assemblies must perform tasks that are crucial to successful system guidance. Each is likely to operate from distinct perspectives and be concerned with different sets of questions. These admittedly partial perspectives must eventually be integrated not only through successive negotiations between planning levels but also, and fundamentally, through frequent transactions up and down the hierarchy through the corresponding technical secretariats. The personal participation of secretariat members in assembly meetings will facilitate this contact and allow for at least some mutual learning between experts working at different levels in the guidance system.

It might be argued that the loss of competitive knowledge will increase the risk of error in societal guidance, since the widespread acceptance of certain premises and information as a foundation for practical reasoning removes the possibility of internal checks on their accuracy. Errors committed because the collective image of reality is distorted might thus turn out to have disastrous consequences.

This critique must be rejected, because it fails to take into account the processes by which collective images are generated and ultimately revised. The organization of working groups and assemblies into networks provides security against the commission of major errors to the extent that it permits the confrontation and synthesis of multiple perspectives and, at the same time, provides for their quick verification at any point within the system. In short, network organization steps up the amount of potential intelligence available for societal guidance.

4. How May the Learning Capabilities of the Entire Guidance System Be Enhanced with Respect to Its Environment?

Learning has many connotations. One of its basic meanings is conveyed by the concept of "feedback." A man observing an environment continuously studies its changing character and pattern, evaluates what he finds against pre-existing standards of guidance, and takes corrective action on the basis of what he has just learned, possibly even revising the standards themselves. What is true for the individual is equally true for society, except that the process in this case is infinitely more complex. In multiplex societies, such as America, learning must pass through an "intelligence" that is dispersed among the population and can become truly effective only if it is closely related to the means for acting on new knowledge. In both cases, however, learning requires the devices and skills of *environmental sensing* and *evaluation*.

To "sense" means to detect, observe, and correctly report on changes in the states of the relevant environment; to "evaluate" means to interpret the significance of what is found for the purpose of correcting and redirecting action. The two activities are closely related; evaluation not only requires the presence of a device for environmental sensing but also provides the necessary motivation to engage in certain types of sensing. Ships use radar to scan the horizon for possible obstacles. The ship's measured ability to move out of the path of a dangerous object determines the use of radar equipment, its design, its degree of sensitivity, and its specific mode of operation. More generally, the repertoire of possible actions determines what is to be sensed, establishes criteria of significance, and helps establish the "grain" and frequency of the sensing operation.

The most serious drawback of this relation is that the sensing operation relies on a *prior assumption concerning the range of actions that are possible* (e.g., the maneuverability of the ship), so that the system is relatively insensitive to environmental changes that might require heretofore "unthinkable" responses. This helps explain why major crises often descend without forewarning and only then, when crisis is already apparent, give rise to innovative behavior that falls outside the normal range of available actions. Although a few "eccentric" thinkers may actually foresee the crisis by using sensing devices tuned to a wider spectrum of conceivable responses, their warnings, lacking credibility, go usually unheeded.

Another drawback is that evaluation is commonly thought to involve *a comparison between sense data and expected standards of performance.* This explains the frequent insistence on the definition of goals and performance standards *prior* to acting and, consequently, the belief that *all* actions are directed at the achievement of specific goals.

There may, however, be a set of actions that does *not* require the prior formulation of a goal. What matters in the process of societal guidance is not only "performance," in the limited meaning of program results, but also changes in the total configuration and behavior of a system, where the criteria for evaluating change are not known in advance.

The concept of evaluation must, therefore, be expanded to mean *a journey of exploration into the potential value field of a society.* Rather than presetting a number of specific values (objectives) for a measured comparison with the data of sense experience, we may *activate* entire value regions and use them in judging the significance of the data collected. What is to be observed can thus be decided independently of the potential values for judging it.

Essential to this formulation is the recognition and acceptance of a class of actions that, rather than being goal-oriented, is *exploratory* in nature and recalls the Zen-like dialogue between a mother and child:

"Where did you go?"
"Out."
"What did you do?"
"Nothing."

I shall argue that this class of non-directed actions is becoming increasingly important in a society where we can know relatively little about the probable consequences of actions, except in certain restricted areas of behavior.

Can organizations having cellular structure provide a solution to these problems? Specifically, can they increase the probability of surprise-free sensing? And can they, at the same time, increase the probability of exploratory evaluations and the use of the resultant learning in redirecting actions? The answer to both questions is a tentative yes.

A. *Surprise-free sensing.* This depends, essentially, on our ability and willingness to "think the unthinkable" in terms of future action-responses. In line with this requirement, organizations having a cellular structure:

—provide a fluid and experimentally inclined medium for communication that encourages the rapid diffusion of ideas and information from any location within the network;

—contain a very large number of points for environmental sensing at which information enters the system, as well as many points for its review, verification, and evaluation; network organizations engender an information-saturated environment that increases the likelihood of novel action-responses;

—thrive on the concatenation of multiple perspectives, which permits new information, viewpoints, and beliefs to be expressed more frequently than in bureaucratic organizations; working group assemblies in which the life of dialogue flourishes are respectful of minority opinions and are prone to consider them in their overall assessment of a situation.

B. *Exploratory evaluation.* Organizations having cellular structure:

—have no overall ends except for the survival, social peace, and physical and moral well-being of the population, but are dedicated to an exploration of the future in the context of a generally "turbulent" social environment[5];

—tolerate the coexistence of many different values and viewpoints; although some of the subsystems of network organization may have quite specific, concrete ends in view, the system as a whole does not;

–are more ready than bureaucratic organizations to withhold judgments until the full context of a situation is widely understood; prefer to use "live probes" as a method of exploring consequences rather than prior moralistic arguments of "right" and "wrong"; and

–facilitate the wider penetration of potential value-fields and hence also the activation of wider "regions" for the evaluation of sense data.

5. How May the Guidance System's Stability Be Assured under Conditions of Multiple Internal and External Stresses?

Within reason, the guidance system of a society works successfully so long as it is able to hold the level of stress in its environment to tolerable levels. If societal development is to occur, conflicts produced by both internal and external changes must be contained within "optimal" bounds for the generation of creative responses by the system. A certain amount of stress is not only inevitable in societal relations; it is desirable to the extent that it stimulates a search for new solutions. A threshold limit is reached whenever a society begins to behave defensively, hoarding what it has instead of continuing its exploration of the future. A society that permits the level of stress to rise above this level of "creative tension" will start to disintegrate and witness a gradual but cumulative withdrawal of loyalty from its established but now impotent guidance institutions.

The current crisis in the guidance system of America can in large measure be traced to failures in the society's capacity for learning. We learn too little and too late; events are happening faster than we can gain information about them. And despite the feverish pitch of their activities, the managers of America's resources are unable to meet the challenges of today as, contrary to their best intentions, they labor to solve yesterday's problems with yesterday's routines.

These failures have their origin in certain structural features of American society—the predominant forms of bureaucratic organization, the hyperspecialization of roles within the bureaucracy, the nearly exclusive reliance on efficiency as a criterion for making major social decisions, and the prevalence of conditions uncongenial to the life of dialogue and, consequently, to a true sense of mutual involvement in community.

As Harold Wilensky has pointed out, these features eventually lead to a failure of intelligence concerning the conditions of society's environment and signal an impending breakdown in the social order.[6] Although the conditions for societal breakdown have so far been studied extensively only for traditional societies embarked on large-scale modernization, breakdown must also be considered a distinct possibility for Western societies as they enter the era of post-industrialism and are faced with the challenge of a major social transition.[7]

The reasons for breakdown in these two contrasting cases are quite different. The path to industrialism requires a greater amount of impersonality in public dealings, an increased measure of functional rationality and greater centralization of control. The virtues of "rudimentary learning" in industrially backward societies cease to be productive when a certain pattern and scale of complexity is reached. Forms of organized social life that are better adapted to the new conditions and will commensurably enlarge society's capacity for learning must then evolve.

I have suggested that cellular structure is the best adapted form of organization for post-industrial societies. The cellular principle yields a flexible, resilient organization that is able to contain, like Heraclitus' river, an immense amount of internal change without losing its basic form. Its outstanding feature, however, is its capacity for nourishing the life of dialogue and cementing interpersonal bonds among its members. Where the power of modern technology can be linked to the psychic energy of a participatory social order, the survival and good health of the society is assured even under conditions of great stress.

Appendix: *The Elementary Republics of the Wards*

In 1816, Thomas Jefferson summarized his views on political organization in a letter to Joseph C. Cabell. These views were an extension of the belief on which the Union had been established that the power to govern themselves is an inalienable right of the people. Hence power is delegated *upward*, in distinction to the practice of monarchies and, one might add, bureaucracies, where power originates at the top and is reluctantly released to lower units.

For Jefferson, the elementary unit of "good and safe" government is the "republic of the ward," a subunit of the county. The criterion of how much effective power is to be internalized at each level of government is *competence*. Jefferson believed that the majority of public issues could be competently resolved at lower levels. By letting decisions filter upwards, as in cellular structure, he hoped to achieve the widest possible mobilization of citizens in the affairs of their communities and so prevent the usurpation of people's power by a dictator—a Caesar or a Bonaparte.

Jefferson's ward-republics were to be more permanently constituted than the task-oriented working groups of a learning society that I have attempted to describe. But this difference merely reflects, I think, the difference between a small agrarian society and the post-industrial super-power we have become. The basic principle is very much the same.

It is easy to criticize Jefferson's conception. Since he wrote his letter to Cabell, power has become highly centralized in bureaucratic organizations; a corporate structure has replaced the simple symmetry of Jefferson's model for self-governance. Public issues have become vaster in

scope and more complex, interdependencies greater, the desire to get things done expediently more urgent. For a long
time, we thought that progress required the centralization
of powers. But of late we have come to realize that we
have allowed central power to become too important and
that the guidance system we have evolved is in a state
of crisis. Cellular structure—composed of "wards" or "working groups" and rising through a series of permanent assemblies to higher and higher levels of governance—is a radical
answer to this crisis.[8]

The Elementary Republics of the Wards:
Thomas Jefferson to Joseph C. Cabell

The way to have good and safe government, is
not to trust it all to one but to divide it among the
many, distributing to every one exactly the functions he is competent to. Let the national government be entrusted with the defence of the nation,
and its foreign and federal relations; the State
governments with the civil rights, laws, police, and
administration of what concerns the State generally;
the counties with the local concerns of the counties, and each ward direct the interests within
itself. It is by dividing and subdividing these republics from the great national one down through
all its subordinations, until it ends in the administration of every man's farm by himself; by placing
under every one what his own eye may superin-
tend, that all will be done for the best. What has
destroyed liberty and the rights of man in every
government which has ever existed under the sun?
The generalizing and concentrating all cares and
powers into one body, no matter whether of the
autocrats of Russia or France, or of the aristocrats
of a Venetian Senate. And I do believe that if the
Almighty has not decreed that man shall never be
free (and it is a blasphemy to believe it), that the
secret will be found to be in the making himself

the depository of the powers respecting himself, so far as he is competent to them, and delegating only what is beyond his competence by a synthetical process, to higher and higher orders of functionaries, so as to trust fewer and fewer powers in proportion as the trustees become more and more oligarchical. The elementary republics of the wards, the county republics, the State republics, and the republic of the Union, would form a gradation of authorities, standing each on the basis of law, holding every one its delegated share of powers, and constituting truly a system of fundamental balances and checks for the government. Where every man is a sharer in the direction of his ward-republic, or of some of the higher ones and feels that he is a participator in the government of affairs, not merely at an election one day in the year, but every day; when there shall not be a man in the State who will not be a member of some one of its councils great or small, he will let the heart be torn out of his body sooner than his power be wrested from him by a Caesar or a Bonaparte. How powerfully did we feel the energy of this organization in the case of embargo? I felt the foundations of the government shaken under my feet by the New England townships. There was not an individual in their States whose body was not thrown with all its momentum into action; and although the whole of the other States were known to be in favor of the measure, yet the organization of this little selfish minority enabled it to overrule the Union. What would the unwieldy counties of the Middle, the South, and the West do? Call a county meeting, and the drunken loungers at and about the courthouses would have collected, the distances being too great for the good people and the industrious generally to attend. The character of those who really met would have been the measure of the weight they would have had in the scale of public opinion. As Cato, then, concluded every speech with the words, "*Carthago delenda est*," so do I every opinion, with the injunction, "divide the counties into wards." Begin them only for a single purpose; they will soon show for what others they are the best instruments.[9]

CHAPTER 9

ON RE-EDUCATING MAN

A friend has read the foregoing chapter on the learning society. She is deeply dissatisfied. "It does not tell me how to do it. The language is abstract and formalistic." I have to agree. The structural design for a learning society shows but the contours of a state of future possibilities. To bring it to life, living experiments must be carried on. But in the course of social experimentation, new and different ideas will be generated, adding to and altering the original design. Little purpose would be served by painting possible scenarios. The real scenario will almost certainly be different.

The learning society is an ideal; it is also in growing measure a necessity. A trillion-dollar society cannot survive its central management. Learning must be more widely diffused throughout the social body, each cell becoming a vital element in the whole configuration. But where and how is one to start transforming a centrally managed society into one that is learning from its experience? Little help can be expected from the center; the impulses for change and wholesale transformation must come from below. The social revolutionary seizes opportunities wherever he is: he starts a learning cell!

The Stages of Man's Relation to Environment

The design for a learning society posits a change in the relationship between man and his environment. Broadly speaking, we have passed through two stages in this relationship. I shall call them the stages of subservience and imperial domination. We are now entering upon a third stage, one of development.

In the beginning, man was a creature of the environment. It imposed severe constraints on his capacities for growth. His energies were chiefly human strengths; he had yet to learn to control the potent energies locked up in the environment. Densities were low and vast stretches of uninhabited land separated human communities. By carefully observing the rules set forth by priests and soothsayers who knew about such things, he succeeded in wresting a modest living from the earth, but natural disasters held his numbers in check. There was no question of who was ultimately master. Man had either to obey the sacred laws or to perish. Belief in supernatural forces was his chief protection against ill fortune.

The stage of subservience began to fade with the first stirrings of modern science in the seventeenth century; its final demise came with the industrial revolution less than two hundred years ago, when, for the first time, science was applied on a large scale to the processes of production. In Siegfried Giedion's triumphant phrase, "mechanization took command,"[1] and man's relation to environment was turned around. Trusting in what he thought was his infinite capacity for changing the environment to suit his needs and tastes, man took hold of the controls. He saw himself as the unchallenged ruler of an environment that he regarded simply as raw material, food for his insatiable appetite for power. Environment had been stripped of its myths. Reduced to its elementary particles, it no longer seemed to impose external limits on man's ability to turn it to some use. The relation, as we have slowly come to realize, was an exploitative and ultimately self-destructive one.

Concurrently there arose a conviction that, properly applied, environmental controls were capable of inducing fundamental changes in human behavior. The origins of all problems, it was believed, were either social or physical; reorganizing society and the methods by which environment was harnessed to human purposes would help to solve them. Henceforward, environment would be controlled, liberating man from whatever remained of his former condition of bondage. In due course, all mystery would be revealed; functionally rational thought would reign over the whole of creation.

We are now entering upon a new stage, that of development. By the measure of history, the duration of the imperial stage was brief. Its premises were shattered by the cybernetic revolution, which taught us that man's relation to environment has to be based on reciprocity, involving both control and adaptation.

The cybernetic revolution forced us to see ourselves as an organic part of the environment. The doctors of the new science spoke of man-environment *systems*, in which man invariably produces reciprocal effects on the environment that run through intricate chains of consequences back to himself. Not all these consequences, it turned out, are beneficial. Some appear to endanger the very basis of life itself. The limits of man's abilities to control his environment are being rediscovered. His acquisitive drive for power has been slowed down; in places it has even been brought to a halt. Environment can no longer be subordinate to man; it has to be accepted as a partner.

The developmental stage of man's relation to environment requires at its core a learning process reflecting the fundamental relationship of reciprocity. This process has four major phases: *observation, experimentation, evaluation,* and *redirection of effort.* This new understanding, based on the key concepts of feedback and control, changes human evolution into a frankly experimental process that tests the validity of ideas by an intensive probing of reality.[2] No longer confined to the carefully arranged conditions of the laboratory, experiments are now applied to life itself. The process might also be described as one of discovery; the emerging image is that of man in search of his historical self within an environment that only to a limited degree is capable of being modified without incurring major harm. Integrally a part of this environment, man is capable of producing some measure of autonomous change within himself.

For well over two thousand years, the Chinese have called this insight "The Great Learning" or *Ta hsüeh.*

The ancients who wished clearly to exemplify illustrious virtue throughout the world would first set up good government in their states. Wishing to govern well their states, they would first regulate their families. Wishing to regulate their families, they would first cultivate their persons. Wishing to cultivate their person, they would first rectify their minds. Wishing to rectify their minds, they would first seek sincerity in their thoughts. Wishing for sincerity in their thoughts, they would first extend their knowledge. The extension of knowledge lay in the investigation of things. For only when thoughts are sincere are minds rectified; only when minds are rectified are our persons cultivated; only when our persons are cultivated are our families regulated; only when families are regulated are states well governed; and only when states are well governed is there peace in the world.

From the emperor down to the common people, all, without exception, must consider cultivation of the individual character as the root. If the root is in disorder, it is impossible for the branches to be in order. To treat the important as unimportant and to treat the unimportant as important—

this should never be. This is called knowing the root; this is called the perfection of knowledge. . . .[3]

The reconstruction of society must thus begin with man's re-education. Its starting place is in "the extension of knowledge . . . the investigation of things," in insight, study, and learning. In this concluding chapter, therefore, which is also a kind of beginning, I turn to the question of re-educating man. What changes in individual men are required so that a transactive style of planning may flourish in society?

Before attempting to answer this question, however, it might be appropriate to examine the underlying assumption that the transition to a learning society requires concurrent and even prior changes in man himself.

Explanations of Social Change

The problem of how change in society is brought about has not, so far, been satisfactorily explained.[4] If society grows out of the interaction among individuals, groups, and institutions, it also *socializes* individuals into conformity with its prevailing norms of conduct. This is the source of its great power. To assume a perfect fit between man and society, however, would mean to deny the possibility of any change whatever; the man-environment system would rest in perfect equilibrium forever.

This theoretical possibility is contradicted by observable facts. Even primitive societies, where one might expect to find a very close fit between individual conduct and social norms, are subject to quite substantial changes over time. In American society, changes seem virtually ubiquitous. Nevertheless, the theoretical assumption of an underlying condition of social equilibrium is supported by a good deal of empirical evidence. How, then, given the great socializing powers of society, does social change occur? Varieties of explanations have been offered. With their help, we may be able to determine in what ways change in man is a condition of further changes in the larger patterns of society.

1. *The Great Man theory.* This theory is reminiscent of biological mutation. Every so often, it is claimed, an individual is born with endowments greatly superior to those of his fellow men. Rising to a position of power among them, the Great Man is able to see beyond the confining horizons of his fellow citizens. He alone is able to glimpse as yet unrealized forms of future history. By charismatic leadership he succeeds in wrenching society loose from its anchoring place in present equilibrium and turning it into the uncharted seas beyond the known and familiar lands. "As I take it," wrote Thomas Carlyle, "the history of what man has accomplished in this world is at bottom the history of the great men who have worked here."[5] The Great Man, by little virtue of his own, has seemingly escaped the socializing powers of his environment. Although generally regarded now as somewhat outmoded, this theory has been resurrected in contemporary models of elites in social transformation.[6]

2. *The theory of insufficient socialization.* This theory argues that the processes of socialization do not achieve completely homogeneous results. Although the majority of individuals will, indeed, be so thoroughly acculturated to their environment that they are unable to conceive, much less produce, significant changes within it, certain small numbers will always remain to a degree *marginal* to the dominant cultural pattern. They may be immigrants, temporary sojourners, members of specific subcultures, individuals partially alienated from the traditional matrix of their society, and others. It is within these groups of marginal individuals that social change originates; it then fans out through the society, until the main body of the population adopts the new patterns of behavior and brings its values into some rough conformity with them.[7] According to this

theory, impulses of change originate among creative minorities at the periphery of a society and spread from there towards its center.

3. *The dialectical theory*. This is a variant of the preceding theory. It finds that society is structured vertically into a finite number of social classes, which stand in a superior-inferior relationship to one another with regard to the management of social power. The relation is charged with tension and potential conflict, as the "inferior" classes seek to improve their condition in life against the resistance of the "superior" classes. Each social class, moreover, has a distinctive style of life, mode of behavior, world view, and set of cultural characteristics. As the "inferior" classes successfully press their claims against the dominant or ruling class, profound changes arising from below push upwards, until formerly "inferior" modes of behavior and accompanying values become accepted as the new standard.[8]

4. *The diffusion theory*. This theory, recognizing the cultural diversity of mankind and its grouping into different societies, argues that ideas, customs, artifacts, and social organizations spread across existing boundaries, introducing changes into receptive host societies, often at great distances from their places of origin.[9] When diffusion theory is linked with the theory of insufficient socialization, it is argued that the sectors of society most receptive to *outside* innovations will frequently be marginal to the mainstream of the indigenous culture. Innovations, therefore, are said to travel from extra-societal points of origin, via the insufficiently integrated sectors of society, to its very heart, transforming basic social relationships in the process.

5. *The idealistic theory*. Some theorists believe that although socialization is capable of adequately controlling individual behavior to maintain given patterns of social order, its powers to compel conformity do not extend to ideas, which constitute the only realm of human life that is com-

pletely free. As dictatorships throughout history have recognized, this freedom—centered in the autonomy of the human mind—is dangerous to the existing order. Yet every effort at rigid control over ideas has ultimately failed. Since ideas that are carried into practice have material consequences, this theory asserts that social change may be "explained" by the essential autonomy of ideas.[10] In contemporary society, one would add, this power of ideas to change society further extends to the free inquiry into the nature of physical and social relationships, in other words, to the practice of modern science.[11]

6. *The theory of the hiding hand.*[12] Those who hold to this theory, although accepting the basic premise of equilibrium as a limiting relation between man and environment, stress the fact that all actions produce consequences that are, in principle, unforeseeable. Even though an action may be undertaken with the full sanction of society behind it, in the belief that it will maintain or re-establish basic equilibrium, consequences will be generated that go considerably beyond original intentions, introducing disequilibrating changes into the system of social relations. Social change is thus traced back to man's unavoidable ignorance about the future and to the hidden dynamics of his actions.

7. *The theory of experimental evolution.* This is basically a learning theory. It claims that man escapes the equilibrium trap of complete socialization by his ability to learn from experience, to make new discoveries, to evaluate the results of his actions, to set new objectives, and to incorporate into society what he finds useful while rejecting what he considers harmful or useless.[13] In this theory, history appears as a process of social learning in which old knowledge yields to new as it emerges from the interplay of theory and practice.

It may be best to regard these several theories as complementary to one another. None is capable of fully accounting for the varieties of social change. From the standpoint of *guided* social change, however, all but the last are useless. The "great man" of history cannot be planned at will. Insufficient socialization is considered dysfunctional by most societies to the point where greater cultural homogeneity in the population is encouraged, while "creative minorities" whose actions may be dangerous to the established order are excluded from the exercise of power. The dialectical theory is offered as an explanation of the historical process as though this process worked independently of human volition. The revolution in which, from time to time, class conflict culminates may be accelerated through revolutionary actions. In its propensity to cataclysm, however, it fails to offer a basis for continuously guiding the processes of social change. Diffusion theory is rather more concerned with the mechanisms of innovation transfer than with the roots of social change. The idealistic theory is completely non-deterministic. It simply asserts that the mind is essentially free, not subject to the otherwise great powers of society to mold man in its image. The theory of the hiding hand posits social ignorance of the future as the mainspring of change in society. But ignorance cannot serve as a major principle of societal guidance.

The only theory capable of providing such a principle is the theory of experimental evolution. Central to its concerns is the principle of learning. The *Ta hsüeh* says: "From the emperor on down to the common people, all, without exception, must consider the cultivation of the individual character as the root." In the context of a learning society, this means the cultivation of individual faculties for taking active part in the mutual learning experiences of transactive planning, specifically, a heightened capacity for effective learning and for the life of dialogue. A guided transformation of society is possible only insofar as it begins with a transformation in man. Just as a democratic society needs to be sustained by democratic man and socialist society by socialist man, so a learning society requires a learning man for its existence.

A Heightened Capacity for Effective Learning

If man is to learn effectively, four of his abilities must be strengthened: the ability to question existing reality, the ability to draw general lessons from concrete experience, the ability to test these lessons in practice, and the ability sincerely to examine the results.

1. *The ability to question existing reality.* Children are born without prejudice; their minds have yet to be imprinted with a special way of seeing the world and to accept the appearance of things unquestioningly. Young children are still innocent enough to ask that most disturbing of all questions, *Why?* Indeed, this line of questioning is generally encouraged among children. But, as we grow older, childish naïveté is for the most part lost. We fall into a mental stupor and start to take the world for granted.

This ability to question the world as we find it, to cease taking it for granted, lies, for adults just as it does for children, at the root of all effective learning. Why are the poor poor? Why are our cities ugly and polluted? Why are we in Vietnam? Why are there no black people in my neighborhood? Why is the scholastic performance of children in ghetto schools consistently lower, on the average, than that of children attending schools in middle-class suburbs? Why are we trying to colonize the moon? Why do people in America sue each other over even small imagined wrongs? Why do women receive less pay than men for essentially the same type of work? Why is one third of urban real estate in America exempt from taxation? Why is a freeway being built through my neighborhood? Why is there unemployment in America when Western

European nations have to import workers from abroad?
Why are traffic fatalities on our highways greater than our
casualties in foreign wars? Why are grade school teachers
predominantly women? Why do certain kinds of fish, such
as tuna, suddenly become dangerous to eat? Why do children start each day in school with the pledge of allegiance
to the flag? Why are we afraid?

Pages might be filled with questions such as these. They
are radical questions, because to ask *why* implies that
things could possibly be different from what they are.
During the last few years, many Americans have learned
to ask these questions and have as a result learned much
about their own country. Many more have still to acquire
the new habit and to shake themselves loose from their
accustomed complacency. They might well ponder the words
of Mao Tse-tung: "Complacency is the enemy of study.
We cannot really learn anything until we rid ourselves of
complacency. Our attitude towards ourselves should be
'to be insatiable in learning' and towards others 'to be
tireless in teaching.'"[14] This is the principle not only of
the questioning mind but of mutual learning as well.

2. *The ability to draw general lessons from concrete experience.* Many people still confuse effective learning with
what they learn at school. Their image of learning is that
of a schoolmaster placing solid nuggets of knowledge in the
vessel of the mind until it is filled up. When it is full, the
student receives a diploma attesting to the amount of
knowledge he has received.

This image is grossly misleading. It portrays processed
knowledge as a finite stock that, like gold, is valued primarily
for its own sake. It separates knowledge from life. There
is another kind of learning, however, that is not confined
to school. Far from being separated from life, it is directly
drawn from it. Personal knowledge comes from encounters
with practical realities. Many things we know because we
have lived through them. Such knowledge is confined to

particular situations, beyond which it ceases to be valid as a guide to action.

Effective learning requires that we reflect on personal experience, pulling away from the particular and concrete to the more general, from personal to processed knowledge. In this way, we shall succeed in liberating ourselves from the overwhelming power that experience has over our thinking. We shall be able to examine the lessons of experience critically in terms of logic, to test the consistency of concepts and their relationships, to manipulate the knowledge so obtained according to accepted rules of transformation, to correct perceptual errors, and to generalize what has been learned to other situations.

This is inductive learning, leading to sharpened observation, as a naturalist might observe a corner of the forest, advancing tentative conceptualizations to cover the primary data he collects. To some degree, we all learn in this sense. But most of us lack the intellectual discipline and background to extend and deepen our observations and build from them into theory. The study of theory is, therefore, a precondition for effective learning. But in effective learning, theory itself will be transformed. "Those experienced in work must take up the study of theory and must read seriously; only then will they be able to systematize and synthesize their experience and raise it to the level of theory, only then will they not mistake their partial experience for universal truth and not commit empiricist errors."[15]

To learn from experience and to impart what has been learned to others—on the job, on the playground, in the community—are two facets of the same process. *Everybody can learn to learn effectively;* but also: *everybody can learn to teach.* In this way, the total amount of learning available to society will increase manifold.

3. *The ability to test theory in practice.* To become truly effective, theory drawn from and enriched by experience must eventually be reinjected into experience. In this way,

actions will benefit from the new learning; in this way, learning will be tested under the exacting conditions of living reality.

Proving themselves in action, theories acquire an historically limited validity. By contributing to the achievement of stated purposes, they become useful theories in a particular context. Such "proof" as might be adduced has nothing to do with the method of scientific validation, which seeks to arrange critical tests whose results will contradict the predictions made on the basis of theory. The return of theory to practice in the fullness of historical situations, with none of the variables held constant as in a laboratory, will either confirm or deny the theory's practical value in these specific situations. It will not say anything about the potential applicability of the theory in other situations that, however similar in some respects, will have different overall contexts. The theory will have been shown to be historically, not scientifically valid. Whether it is also the latter is a question that must be left to scientific study. "Knowledge begins with practice, and theoretical knowledge which is acquired through practice must then return to practice. The active function of knowledge manifests itself not only in the active leap from perceptual to rational knowledge, but—and this is more important—it must manifest itself in the leap from rational knowledge to revolutionary practice."[16] Whether revolutionary or not, practice here is the crucible for testing the value of new learning.

This principle clearly implies a form of social experimentation that is closely joined to the processes of formulating theories. Practice not only provides a springboard for new conceptualizations, it is also the condition for their ultimate test under fire. The professions—from medicine to engineering—have long proclaimed this view of learning. Otherwise, patients would not be cured, nor bridges built. Scientists, on the other hand, have always disdained pragmatic learning, preferring more deductive modes of theorizing. The majority of men, finally, trained neither in the professions nor in the sciences, instinctively suspect any form of theorizing, trusting instead in personal knowledge, popular wisdom, and intuition as guides to action.

The third principle of effective learning argues for the joint evolution of practice with theory. Rather than being applied only to the trained professions, however, the principle must be extended as the ground for *all* effective learning, "from the emperor on down to the common people." The dizzying abstractions of positive science, particularly as applied to social phenomena, would then stand out as the extraordinary departures from the immediately life-sustaining processes of normal reasoning that they, in fact, represent.

In the formal structure of a learning society, described in the preceding chapter, the encounter of theory with practice would occur in task-oriented working groups, or learning cells. There, "planners" would meet with "clients" and both with the palpable reality of their environment. The dialectic of mutual learning takes place in closest possible contact with the immediate problems to be solved. As working groups link up with each other, larger social experiments become possible.[17]

4. *The ability sincerely to examine the results.* The final step in the process of effective learning involves an honest probing of the results of action and their immediate causes. This step is often difficult to take. Critical evaluation and the open admission of error are inextricably a part of learning through action. If mistakes are either not perceived or, being perceived, are not admitted, action cannot be corrected, nor can learning take place.

The wish to deceive oneself and to discount, if not ignore, some inconvenient fact is strong. The ego is easily wounded; we dread the possible loss of face in the eyes of others. To look at the outcome of one's work with honesty, to judge it severely, and to seek out the causes of any imperfections within oneself requires overcoming a deep-seated inclination to hide behind one's pride and to defend what one has done.

Even if no apparent error has been committed, the results of action should be critically examined. Complacency is the worst enemy of learning. "We must not become complacent over any success. We should check our complacency and constantly criticize our shortcomings, just as we should wash our faces or sweep the floor every day to remove the dirt and keep them clean."[18] In self-criticism lies the ultimate power for self-renewal.

Members of working groups, sustained by dialogue, must adopt an attitude of permissiveness towards self-criticism and collective evaluation; indeed, they must encourage it. This is made easier by the underlying trust of the members in one another. No member, nor the group as a whole, can shipwreck in any ultimate sense, except by failing to hold the other in trust. This is the basic morality of dialogue. Inability to grasp this fact will break the bonds of dialogue that hold the group together. But trustingly to accept another and to give oneself in return will sustain the dialogue, even when it involves a critical assessment of one's work. It is the moral foundation of a learning society.

A Heightened Capacity for Dialogue

Dialogue is central to mutual learning, yet modern man's capacity for dialogue is stunted. Split up into the fragments of his roles, relations among which are determined almost solely by a criterion of utility, he hears without listening and talks without responding. Extremely skillful in exchanging functional bits of information, he fails in assessing the underlying meanings because he assumes, incorrectly, that information has a reality independent of the persons through whom it becomes available and to whom it is addressed.

Most of us are afraid to become truly authentic as human beings, to join our feelings to reason, to turn completely to the other in all of his particularity, listening to what he says beyond the logic of semantics and responding with care to his essential needs as a person caught up in a concrete situation. Most of us are either unable or unwilling to sustain such dialogue, especially when we feel threatened. We withdraw defensively inside our shells, closing the doors to our innermost selves, and leave the protective "space between" ourselves and others to be filled with programmed messages unable to convey essential meaning.

There are those who believe that the relation between teacher and student can be exhaustively described as one of exchanging information. This may be an adequate description of traditional learning, but it completely mistakes the character of mutual learning in transactive planning. Unless teaching can be placed on the firm ground of a trusting personal relationship, mutual learning will be reduced to a mere trickle of disconnected facts from teacher to student and expert to client. No amount of facts will come to life, except as facts are filtered and arranged through a dialogic process between two persons who address each other out of the fullness of their lives. "If we are serious about thinking between *I* and *Thou*," writes Martin Buber, "then it is not enough to cast our thoughts towards the other subject of thought framed by thought. We should also . . . live towards the other man, who is not framed by thought but who is bodily present before us; *we should live towards his concrete life*."[19] Thus thought (ideas, learning, knowledge) comes towards us in the concreteness of the life of the other person through whom it is communicated. Abstracting thought from life destroys the possibilities of rendering thought meaningful. Such meaning can grow only out of the living relationships of dialogue.

All this sounds very difficult, couched as it is in imprecise and unaccustomed language. But that to which it speaks is an experience familiar to each of us. How often do we pay attention not only to *what* a person says but also to his reasons for saying it, reasons which, on the surface of things, have no apparent connection with his words? Nothing will change normal conversation into dialogue as quickly as the question that speaks directly to the heart. And once a relation of dialogue has been established, it will continue for as long as there exists a mutual determination to sustain it. The dialogic relation values what is being said not because it is either true or false according to some absolute standard, but precisely because it is important to the person saying it. Often unbeknown to himself, he is, in fact, turning to you for confirmation, denial, encouragement, or redirection of his thought and often of his life as well. He is addressing a question to you. In a relation of dialogue you, who are being addressed, are asked to respond precisely to this question. This is what dialogue is all about.

The life of dialogue is within reach of everyone, but to increase our capacity for it, we must practice dialogue from earliest childhood onward. Its best chance for growth lies in the intimate setting of the task-related group that endures for a period of time, permitting interpersonal relations to be established at a level deeper than mere surface interaction. Its basic movement involves speaking towards another person's life.

To the extent that transactive planning is upheld by dialogue, this basic movement must be mastered by all who wish to take a part in it, regardless of their rank or station. It presumes neither an underlying harmony of interests and concerns nor a mystical fusion of the self with a larger metaphysical whole. It does presume accepting the other in his radical difference from everyone else. Dialogue springs from the face-to-face encounter of two persons in which neither is afraid to endure the physical presence of the other. If pursued, it will lead to the discovery of what unites them, but also of the real differences that separate their lives.

What Is To Be Done

A fundamental lesson we may draw from the preceding discussion is that learning is at its most effective when it occurs in interaction with environment. If transactive planning skills are to be learned, therefore, what better way is there than to establish task-related working groups in which transactive planning naturally will take place because it is essential to the group's performance? In other words, the requisite cognitive and interpersonal skills will be developed in individuals because they are engaged in transactive planning.

The small, irreducible cell of a learning society can easily be formed anywhere at any time. It requires neither central permission nor central allocation of resources. Indeed, it requires no central direction of any sort. All that is needed is a few people willing to band together and a manageable problem on which to test the group's abilities and to provide the necessary discipline. As the complexity of the task increases, new cells may be started. After a while, assemblies having a more permanent character may be established to integrate and guide the overall activity of working groups. Thus structure will be shaped by constantly evolving needs. Yet even as it changes, the basic cellular unit of a learning society—temporary, yet indestructible—remains intact.

Task-oriented working groups may be spontaneously created in a variety of environments—in factories, offices, neighborhoods, clubs, schools, and universities. Their actions will have an experimental character; the ingenuity of working group members will lead to innovations and discoveries. The life of dialogue will be encouraged, simply because it

is the most natural way to approach a problem solution
that asks of every member a commitment to the total
effort and, above all, to the group's continued existence
so long as the challenge of a task remains. The group
has no means of survival but for the strength of its internal
dialogue.

Beyond dialogue lies the cognitive effort itself. Theories
formulated in the course of the work will come to be tested
in practice; a critical review must follow. Experts may be
asked to join in group deliberations and in the formulation
of a course of action. But mutual learning is not confined
to the dialogue between members and experts. Each member,
himself possessing special knowledge, will of necessity impart his learning to others, just as he will learn in turn.

But in the longer view, all this may not suffice. If new
capacities and skills are to be learned, and if re-educating
man is basic to the reconstruction of society, the requisite
skills must be internalized at an age when individual
character is yet sufficiently flexible to be shaped into new
forms. Careful studies have shown that most effective learning takes place in early childhood.[20]

If we accept this finding, together with its corollary
that the normal learning curve declines with age, the teaching of transactive planning skills should begin in the first
few grades of school. The task-oriented working group would
thus be introduced as the basic unit for learning from the
primary grades onward. This suggestion finds support in
the writings of Jean Piaget, who, on the basis of experimental evidence, argues that knowledge is based on the
co-ordination of actions and is, therefore, evolutionary, rising
from primitive intuitions through a variety of novel constructs to complex understandings of reality.[21] Although
not every subject can be taught using the framework of
task-oriented working groups, a number of experiments
could be tried. Within it, the teacher would guide the
effort of the group, particularly with regard to developing

the appropriate cognitive and interpersonal skills among its members. Special projects could be undertaken that would take the child outside his classroom for substantial amounts of time, leading to an active exploration of community resources, environmental quality, the functioning of public service systems, low-income housing, and the like. In approaching these problems, rather than being indoctrinated with traditionally approved ways of thinking, the children might be encouraged to ask the radical question "Why?", find answers, and test their validity in real or simulated situations. Along with this, they would be taught the arts of evaluation and criticism, including self-criticism, without fear of embarrassment, while their capacities for dialogue would be enhanced by the establishment of a respectful yet personal relationship between teacher and student.

If all these things are done, and if the basic assumptions turn out to be correct, a learning society will stand an even chance to come into existence in America. The apparent simplicity of the approach, with its emphasis on development from below, hides the enormous complexities that will have to be faced when we begin to link up the individual elements of cellular structure into a larger system. As we proceed to do this, we shall need to make social innovations on a scale unheard of until now. But so long as the root remains healthy, the "investigation of things" exerts its formative influence on individual character, and life is celebrated in dialogue, even the topmost branches will be vigorous and bear new shoots.

GLOSSARY

ACTION
An intentional mobilization and use of resources to produce a given effect. Actions can be either individual or organized. Where actions are undertaken by the political institutions of a society, they are called political actions.

ALLOCATIVE PLANNING
One of the basic *forms of planning*, concerned with actions that affect the distribution of limited resources among competing users.

ASSEMBLY OF WORKING GROUPS
A deliberative and executive body hierarchically superior to individual *working groups* and the exclusive basis for their legitimacy. It is through the network of permanent assemblies that the social system is integrated and *societal guidance* occurs.

BUREAUCRATIC STRUCTURE
An hierarchical, non-adaptive form of organization whose internal relations are characterized by the authority of superior positions over all dependent inferior positions.

CELLULAR STRUCTURE
An adaptive form of organization built up from small task-oriented *working groups* into larger *assem-*

blies. Cellular structure combines both hierarchical and non-hierarchical elements and is capable of infinite expansion.

COLLECTIVE
PHENOMENA

Statistical aggregates, such as the rate of traffic flow, that appear as the unintended by-product of individual decisions. They are produced by particular configurations of the relevant *guidance system*.

COMMAND PLANNING

A *style of allocative planning* occurring under conditions of power that is strongly centralized and whose predominant method of control is by way of sanctions that are attached to the fulfillment of compulsory targets.

CORPORATE PLANNING

A *style of allocative planning* occurring under conditions of power that is decentralized among a relatively small number of corporate actors and whose predominant method of control is by way of normative compliance with the agreements reached through bargaining and negotiation.

DEVELOPMENT

Structural changes in an expanding system of societal relations. Development is a condition of continued *structural growth* in social systems.

DIALOGUE

A form of person-centered communication, generally requiring face-to-face interaction and essential to *transactive planning*.

FORMS OF PLANNING

Two forms of *planning* are distinguished: *allocative* and *innovative*.

GUIDANCE SYSTEM

The pattern of institutional arrangements (political, legal, administrative, economic, cognitive, and planning) that guides the processes of change in society. A "complete" guidance system involves elements of *command*, *policies*, *corporate*, and *participant* planning.

INNOVATION

The successful introduction of structural changes into the *guidance system* of society.

INNOVATIVE PLANNING

One of the basic forms of planning, concerned with actions that produce structural changes in the *guidance system* of society. Innovative planning is essential to the continued *structural growth* of a social system and consequently to *development*.

MUTUAL LEARNING

A process in which the *processed knowledge* of the planning expert is related to the *personal knowledge* of his client in the joint exploration of problems and possible solutions to them.

PARTICIPANT PLANNING

A *style of allocative planning* occurring under conditions of power that is dispersed among a large number of actors and whose predominant method of control is the voluntary compliance of participants with the results of group deliberations.

PERSONAL KNOWLEDGE

Knowledge based on the direct experience of the knower with the facts at hand. Personal knowledge is neither formally codified nor subject to a process of systematic verification. Rich in detailed observation, it is incapable of being generalized beyond the specific case from which it has been drawn.

PLANNING

The process by which a scientific and technical knowledge is joined to organized *action*. Planning forms a critical subprocess of *societal guidance*. Two forms of planning may be distinguished: *allocative* and *innovative*.

POLICIES PLANNING

A *style of allocative planning* occurring under conditions of power that is weakly centralized and whose predominant method of control is a restructuring of the decision environment for others.

PROCESSED KNOWLEDGE

Another term for scientific-technical knowledge and expressed in statements that can be formally communicated, critically examined, and revised on the basis of both new observations and the critique received.

SOCIETAL GUIDANCE

The processes by which the incidence, rate, and direction of change in society are controlled. The exercise of societal guidance may be intentional or not, and its results may be both favorable and unfavorable.

SOCIETAL LEARNING

The processes by which society gathers and internalizes knowledge about the changing conditions of both its internal and external environment.

STRUCTURAL GROWTH

Expansion of a system of societal relations in one or more of its dimensions. Structural growth without *development* is self-limiting.

STYLES OF ALLOCATIVE PLANNING

Characteristic behavior of *allocative planning* processes that result from adaptations to the conditions of power, valuing, and knowing in society. With reference to the distribution of power, four styles may be distinguished: *command, policies, corporate,* and *participant.*

TECHNICAL SECRETARIAT

Permanent planning body attached to *assembly of working groups.*

TRANSACTIVE PLANNING

A style applicable to both *allocative* and *innovative planning* in which processes of *mutual learning* are closely integrated with an organized capacity and willingness to act.

WORKING GROUPS

Elemental units of *cellular structure* that are task-oriented, temporary in composition, small in scale, based on interpersonal relationships, inclusive and cross-related in their membership, self-guiding in their actions, and responsible to *assemblies.* Clusters of working groups are organized into networks whose connecting links crisscross each other in a manner brought about solely by the need for particular working groups to be in contact with one another.

NOTES

Preface

1. R. G. Tugwell and E. C. Banfield, "Governmental Planning at Mid-Century," *The Journal of Politics*, Vol. 13 (1951), pp. 133–63.

2. James G. March and Herbert A. Simon, *Organizations* (New York: Wiley, 1958), Chapters 6 and 7.

3. P. J. D. Wiles, *The Political Economy of Communism* (Cambridge, Mass.: Harvard Univ. Press, 1962).

4. Alexander Ehrlich, "Development Strategy and Planning: the Soviet Experience," in Max F. Millikan, ed., *National Economic Planning* (New York: Columbia Univ. Press, 1967), pp. 233–72, with "Comment" by Abram Bergson, pp. 272–78.

1. Encounters

1. The Chicago Planning Program is described in Harvey S. Perloff, *Education for Planning: City, State, and Regional* (Baltimore: Johns Hopkins Press, 1957), Part III (in collaboration with John Friedmann).

2. Rexford G. Tugwell, "The Superpolitical," *Journal of Social Philosophy*, Vol. V, No. 2 (1940), p. 97.

3. Ibid., p. 113. For views critical of the public interest view of planning, see Carl J. Friedrich, ed., *The Public Interest*. Yearbook of the American Society for Political and Legal Philosophy, Vol. V (New York: Atherton, 1962).

4. Herbert A. Simon, *Administrative Behavior: A Study of Decision-Making Processes in Administrative Organization*, 2d ed. (New York: Free Press, 1965). Banfield laid out the model with even greater clarity in Martin Meyerson and Edward C. Banfield, *Politics*,

Planning, and the Public Interest: The Case of Public Housing in Chicago (Glencoe, Ill.: Free Press, 1955), "Note on Conceptual Scheme," pp. 303–30.

5. Edward C. Banfield, *Political Influence* (New York: Free Press of Glencoe, 1961).

6. Edward C. Banfield, *The Unheavenly City: The Nature and the Future of Our Urban Crisis* (Boston: Little, 1970). See also his earlier book, *The Moral Basis of a Backward Society* (Glencoe, Ill.: Free Press, 1958), which begins with a quotation from Hobbes: "In such condition there is . . . continual fear, and danger of violent death; and the life of man, solitary, poor, nasty, brutish, and short."

7. Harvey S. Perloff, *Puerto Rico's Economic Future: A Study in Planned Development* (Chicago: Univ. of Chicago Press, 1950).

8. "Planning, Progress, and Social Values," *Diogenes*, No. 17 (Spring 1957), pp. 98–111. Written in 1954.

9. Ibid., p. 99.

10. Ibid., pp. 108–9.

11. Ibid., p. 112.

12. "Introduction to the Study and Practice of Planning," *International Social Science Journal*, Vol. XI, No. 3 (1959), pp. 327–39.

13. Ibid., p. 327.

14. Ibid., pp. 329–30.

15. Ibid., pp. 327–28.

16. Ibid., p. 330.

17. Ibid., pp. 330–32.

18. Ibid., p. 332.

19. Ibid., p. 333.

20. "Planning as a Vocation," Part I, *Plan* (Canada), Vol. 6, No. 3 (1966), pp. 99–124.

21. Ibid., 112.

22. Ibid., pp. 118–20.

23. Ibid., pp. 122–23.

24. "Planning as a Vocation," Part II, *Plan* (Canada), Vol. 7, No. 1 (1966), pp. 21 and 25.

25. Bertram M. Gross, "The Managers of National Economic Change," in Roscoe C. Martin, ed., *Public Administration and Democracy*, Essays in Honor of Paul H. Appleby (Syracuse, New York: Syracuse Univ. Press, 1965), Chapter 6; "National Planning: Findings and Fallacies," *Public Administration Review*, Vol. 25, No. 4 (1965), pp. 263–73; and Bertram M. Gross, ed., *Action Under Planning: The Guidance of Economic Development* (New York: McGraw, 1967).

26. *Venezuela: From Doctrine to Dialogue.* National Planning Series, Vol. I (Syracuse, New York: Syracuse Univ. Press, 1965).

27. Ibid., pp. 28–30.

28. "The Institutional Context," in Gross, ed., *Action Under Planning*, Chapter 2. Written 1964.

29. "Planning as Innovation: The Chilean Case," *Journal of the American Institute of Planners*, Vol. 32, No. 4 (1966), pp. 194–203.

30. "A Conceptual Model for the Analysis of Planning Behavior," *Administrative Sciences Quarterly*, Vol. 21, No. 2 (1967), pp. 225–52.

31. Ibid., p. 250.

32. Amitai Etzioni, *The Active Society: A Theory of Societal and Political Processes.* (New York: Free Press, 1968).

33. "Notes on Societal Action," *Journal of the American Institute of Planners*, Vol. 35, No. 5 (1969), pp. 311–18.

34. Ibid., p. 312.

35. Ibid., p. 314.

36. Etzioni's article "Toward a Theory of Societal Guidance," in Sarajane Heidt and Amitai Etzioni, eds., *Societal Guidance: A New Approach to Social Problems* (New York: Crowell, 1969), came to my attention only recently. It is generally supportive of the view of societal guidance which I came to evolve independently.

37. "Notes on Societal Action," p. 317.

38. *Urban and Regional Development in Chile: A Case Study of Innovative Planning* (Santiago, Chile: The Ford Foundation, 1969).

39. "The Future of Comprehensive Urban Planning: A Critique," *Public Administration Review*, Vol. 31, No. 3 (1971), pp. 320–21. This article was written in 1969.

40. Shortly before I finished the final draft of this book, Edgar Dunn's important book *Economic and Social Development: A Process of Social Learning* (Baltimore and London: Johns Hopkins Press, 1971) was published. To my amazement, I found in Dunn's work many parallels to my own thinking, down to such particulars as mutual learning, dialogue, and cellular social structure. This was all the more astonishing and, at the same time, gratifying, as we had worked in complete independence of each other and, indeed, had arrived at substantially similar conclusions by very diverse routes. Then, as I began to look further, kindred spirits turned up elsewhere, such as Manfred Halpern, "A Redefinition of the Revolutionary Situation," *Journal of International Affairs*, Vol. XXIII, No. 1 (1969), pp. 54–75; Eric Trist, "Urban North America—The Challenge of the Next Thirty Years: A Social Psychological Viewpoint," *Plan* (Canada), Vol. 10, No. 3 (1970); Richard Bolan, "The Social Relations of the Planner," *Journal of the American Institute of Planners*, Vol. XXXVII, No. 6 (November 1971), pp. 387–96; Denis Goulet's *The Cruel Choice: A New Concept in the Theory of Development* (New York: Atheneum, 1971); and Charles Hampden-Turner, *Radical Man: The Process of Psycho-Social Development* (New York: Anchor Bks., 1971).

2. Precursor: Karl Mannheim

1. A brief account of Mannheim's influence on sociological thinking is given in the appendix to this chapter.

2. This chapter is based chiefly on the following works by Karl Mannheim: *Ideology and Utopia* (New York: Harcourt, 1949); *Man and Society in an Age of Reconstruction* (New York: Harcourt, 1949); *Diagnosis of Our Time* (London: Routledge, 1943); and *Freedom, Power, and Democratic Planning* (New York: Oxford, 1950).

3. Mannheim referred to planning indiscriminately, sometimes in its narrower connotation of the application of a scientific-technical intelligence to the problems of society and sometimes in its broader meaning of an instrument for guiding processes of social change. Throughout this chapter, I shall follow his usage, and the meaning will be clear from the context.

4. Jay W. Forrester, *Urban Dynamics* (Cambridge, Mass.: M.I.T. Press, 1969), pp. 110–11.

5. Material balances is a method for determining the physical inputs required to achieve specific production targets.

6. The evidence for this statement is neatly brought together by P. J. D. Wiles, *The Political Economy of Communism.*

7. John Friedmann, "The Future of Comprehensive Urban Planning: A Critique," *Public Administration Review* (June 1971).

8. See, for example, Robert K. Merton, *Social Theory and Social Structure.* Rev. ed. (New York: Free Press, 1957), Chapters VIII and IX.

9. For one of the leading contributions to this approach, see J. Tinbergen, *Economic Policy: Principles and Design* (Amsterdam: North-Holland Pub. Co., 1964).

10. Robert A. Dahl and Charles E. Lindblom, *Politics, Economics, and Welfare* (New York: Harper, 1953).

11. Rexford G. Tugwell, "The Fourth Power," *Planning and Civic Comment* (American Institute of Planners and Civic Association, April–June 1939), Part II; "The Superpolitical," *Journal of Social Philosophy*, "Implementing the General Interest," *Public Administration Review*, Vol. I, No. 1 (Autumn 1940), pp. 32–49; "The Study of Planning as Scientific Endeavor," Michigan Academy of Science, *Report for 1948*, pp. 34–48; and *The Place of Planning in Society*, Puerto Rican Planning Board, Technical Paper No. 7 (San Juan, Puerto Rico, 1954).

12. Amitai Etzioni, *The Active Society* (New York: Free Press, 1968).

13. Irving Louis Horowitz, ed., *The New Sociology: Essays in Honor of C. Wright Mills* (New York: Oxford, 1964).

14. Herbert A. Simon, *Administrative Behavior*, 2d ed. (New York: Free Press, 1957); Charles E. Lindblom, *The Intelligence of Democracy* (New York: Free Press, 1965).

15. Kurt Lewin, *Field Theory in Social Science* (New York: Harper, 1951).

16. Warren G. Bennis, Kenneth D. Benne, and Robert Chin, eds., *The Planning of Change*, 2d. ed. (New York: Holt, 1969).

17. Daniel Lerner and Harold D. Lasswell, eds., *The Policy Sciences* (Stanford: Stanford Univ. Press, 1951).

18. Yehezkel Dror, *Public Policymaking Reexamined* (San Francisco: Chandler Pub., 1968); Raymond A. Bauer and Kenneth J. Gergen, eds., *The Study of Policy Formation* (New York: Free Press, 1968); Warren F. Ilchman and Norman Thomas Uphoff, *The Political Economy of Change* (Berkeley and Los Angeles: Univ. of Calif. Press, 1969), and Charles E. Lindblom, *The Policy-Making Process* (Englewood Cliffs, N.J.: Prentice-Hall, 1968).

3. The Forms and Styles of Planning

1. Benjamin Higgins, "An Economist's View," in H. M. Phillips, ed., *Social Aspects of Economic Development in Latin America* (Paris: UNESCO, 1963), p. 247.

2. Neil W. Chamberlain, *Private and Public Planning* (New York: McGraw, 1965), p. 175.

3. Bertram M. Gross, "The Dynamics of Competitive Planning," preface to Robert J. Shafer, *Mexico: Mutual Adjustment Planning* (Syracuse: Syracuse Univ. Press, 1966), p. xix.

4. Bertram M. Gross in the preface to Benjamin Akzin and Yehezkel Dror, *Israel: High Pressure Planning* (Syracuse: Syracuse Univ. Press, 1966), pp. xxvi–xxvii.

5. The distribution of power (i.e., of the capacity to influence the behavior of others) will vary with the issue being considered. For the purpose of this discussion, however, I shall assume that the distribution of power is uniform with respect to all issues.

6. In contrast to the growing literature on allocative planning, there are no significant studies describing systematic variations in the styles of innovative planning. Although it is quite likely that such styles exist as adaptations to the social environments of particular institutions, I am unable to describe them at this time. Chapter 6, which is devoted to a discussion of innovative planning in a context of societal development, includes some methodological suggestions for a relevant procedure of analysis. Since a relevant theory based on empirical findings is still lacking, however, operational aspects of innovative planning have had to be set aside. For a summary of current studies of institutional development, see Joseph W. Eaton,

A *Review of Phase I: 1964–1968*, The Inter-University Research Program in Institution Building (University of Pittsburgh, December 1, 1968).

5. The Uses of the Future

1. Pierre Teilhard de Chardin, *The Future of Man* (New York: Harper, 1964); and *The Phenomenon of Man* (New York: Harper, 1965).

2. Utopian thinking is shown to rise vertically along the ordinate axis to suggest its essentially timeless character. Nevertheless, each successive utopian construct is believed to be superior to the one preceding it. In the absence of a neutral standard of evaluation, however, no preference can be given to the advocates of either u_1 or u_2.

3. Thomas S. Kuhn, *The Structure of Scientific Revolutions* (Chicago: Univ. of Chicago Press, 1962), Chapter II.

4. As Thomas Kuhn points out in the work cited earlier, the idea that scientific knowledge is cumulative is largely an illusion. Following each revolutionary upheaval, during which old assumptions are overthrown, a massive rewriting of scientific texts occurs which makes it appear as though the current situation is the logical consequence of earlier efforts. The fact of the matter, however, is that the revolution in scientific thinking flew into the face of traditional opinion and probably owed only small, and negative debts to previous work.

5. Donella H. Meadows, Dennis L. Meadows, Jørgen Randers, and William W. Behrens III, *The Limits to Growth*, A Report for The Club of Rome Project on the Predicament of Mankind (New York: Universe Bks., Inc., 1972).

6. Ibid., p. 24.

7. Ibid.

8. Wilbert E. Moore and Melvin M. Tumin, "Some Social Functions of Ignorance," in Bernard Rosenberg, Israel Gerver, and F. William Horton, eds., *Mass Society in Crisis* (New York: Macmillan, 1964).

6. Development as Innovation

1. K. E. Boulding, "Toward a General Theory of Growth," in Joseph J. Spengler and Otis Dudley Duncan, eds., *Population Theory and Policy: Selected Readings* (New York: Free Press, 1956), pp. 109–124.

2. This description of the Chilean bureaucratic system refers to the situation as it existed prior to the recent change in government, which

brought an alliance of Marxist parties to power. It is unlikely, however, that the centralist principle of government, which is so much a part of the political culture of Chile, will be abandoned by the new government. On the contrary, President Allende may well decide to follow out this principle to its logical perfection.

3. Albert O. Hirschman, *Journeys Toward Progress: Studies of Economic Policy-Making in Latin America* (New York: The Twentieth Century Fund, 1963), Chapter 5, "The Contriving of Reform."

7. The Transactive Style of Planning

1. The institutional setting for transactive planning will be taken up in Chapter 8.

2. The language in which the memorandum was written was reasonably straightforward and non-technical, so that the failure to understand the quantitative manipulations and conceptual refinements contained in many planning reports was not a point at issue here.

3. There are problems so technical that the authority of experts will be accepted at face value. These problems are usually close to the operational level, such as the design specifications of a bridge. Mutual learning is not applicable to these cases. It is useful only where the personal knowledge of the client is an important component of any solution that my be offered.

8. Design for Guidance: A Learning Society

1. The principle of cellular structure is not a new invention. An early reference to it is found in the writings of Thomas Jefferson, who, in his "elementary republics of the wards" conceived of a structure of governance for the United States quite similar in form to the one I am proposing here. A more complete account of Jefferson's thinking is given in the appendix to this chapter.

2. Technical secretariats may themselves by organized into working groups. The role of these secretariats in the guidance process is discussed in more detail in Section 3.

3. There is good reason to believe that this is a very common phenomenon. Highway engineers have known for a long time that improving transportation facilities will only increase the total volume of traffic that must ultimately be accommodated, leaving congestion about the same as before. Development economists, in turn, have discovered that intensive efforts at industrialization in labor-surplus economies tend to increase the rate of visible unemployment. And telephone engineers are barely able to cope with the increasing demand for machine-mediated communication, despite their truly re-

markable ability to increase channel capacities. The law to which these three examples seem to conform may be formulated by saying that, under conditions of potential surplus demand, any system will tend to generate a service load that is beyond its capacity for efficient handling up to the point where the marginal costs to the individual user of the service are equal to his expected benefits. As a result, it is permissible to speak of an equilibrium rate with reference to traffic congestion and unemployment as well as communications overload.

4. Each of these functions would tie into specialized counterpart agencies operating independently of working group assemblies as part of the overall guidance system of society. Though themselves organized according to the principles of cellular structure, and therefore permeable, they would be independent of the control of external assemblies and able to concentrate their efforts on fundamental research, especially into the techniques of planning analysis. The staffs of these research organizations would include many former members of secretariats and prepare future planning analysts for work in the assemblies. Mutual learning can also take place among "experts" across institutional boundaries!

5. This and the following attributes of cellular organizations hold true only for societies such as ours, where affluence has replaced a widespread condition of scarcity, and where the margin for experimental behavior is consequently greater than before.

6. *Organizational Intelligence: Knowledge and Policy in Industry and Government* (New York: Basic Bks., Inc., 1967).

7. S. N. Eisenstadt, *Modernization: Protest and Change* (Englewood Cliffs, N.J.: Prentice-Hall, 1966), Chapters 6 and 7.

7. For a discussion of Jefferson's views on the organization of governmental powers in society, see Samuel P. Huntington, "The Founding Fathers and the Division of Powers," in Arthur Maass, ed., *Area and Power: A Theory of Local Government* (Glencoe, Ill.: Free Press, 1959). Because Madison's views prevailed historically, Huntington treats Jefferson's theories as one would those of a loser: an interesting contribution, but obviously second best. A contemporary reinterpretation of Jefferson in a more positive light would seem to be in order.

9. Reprinted from Leonard Dalton Abbott, ed., *Masterworks of Government* (New York: Doubleday, 1947), pp. 570–71.

9. *On Re-educating Man*

1. *Mechanization Takes Command* (New York: Oxford, 1948).

2. George W. Fairweather, *Methods for Experimental Social Innovation* (New York: Wiley, 1968).

3. William Theodore de Bary, Wing-tsit Chan, Burton Watson,

eds., *Sources of Chinese Tradition,* Vol. I (New York and London: Columbia Univ. Press, 1960), p. 115.

4. For an interesting, if not exhaustive, survey of existing theories of social change, see J. A. Ponsioen, *The Analysis of Social Change Reconsidered,* revised and enlarged edition (The Hague: Mouton, 1969).

5. Quoted from Ernest Scott, *History and Historical Problems* (Melbourne: Oxford, 1925), p. 70.

6. A recent interpretation of this theory is Suzanne Keller's excellent book *Beyond the Ruling Class: Strategic Elites in Modern Society* (New York: Random House, 1963).

7. Everett E. Hagen, *On the Theory of Social Change: How Economic Growth Begins* (Homewood, Ill.: The Dorsey Press, 1962).

8. This theory, usually formulated in more sophisticated versions than this brief summary permits, underlies Marxian and neo-Marxian thinking. For the best modern restatement of this theory in the context of social change, see Ralf Dahrendorf, *Class and Class Conflict in Industrial Society* (Stanford: Stanford Univ. Press, 1959).

9. The most complete statement of this theory is found in anthropological writings, specifically in A. L. Kroeber, *Anthropology* (New York: Harcourt, 1948). An equally important statement of its basic principles is found in H. G. Barnett, *Innovation: The Basis of Cultural Change* (New York: McGraw, 1953).

10. R. G. Collingwood, *The Idea of History* (Oxford: Clarendon Press, 1946).

11. Lewis Mumford, *The Pentagon of Power* (New York: Harcourt, 1970).

12. The expression "hiding hand" is borrowed from Albert Hirschman's brilliant essay "The Principle of the Hiding Hand," in his book, *Development Projects Observed* (Washington, D.C.: Brookings, 1967), Chapter 1.

13. The concept of experimental evolution is central to Edgard S. Dunn's analysis in *Economic and Social Development.* Closely related to Dunn's work is John H. Kunkel, *Society and Economic Growth: A Behavioral Perspective of Social Change* (New York: Oxford, 1970); and Denis Goulet, *The Cruel Choice.*

14. *Quotations from Chairman Mao Tse-tung* (Peking: Foreign Language Press, 1966), pp. 310–11.

15. Ibid., p. 308.

16. Ibid., pp. 208–9.

17. This description comes very close to the "participation survey" advanced by Robert Caillot. See Robert Caillot, "Une Connaissance Engagée: L'Enquête-Participation," in *Options Humanistes* (Paris: Les Éditions Ouvrières, 1968). Caillot's proposals are summarized in Denis Goulet, op. cit., pp. 161–64.

18. Mao, op. cit., p. 266.

19. Martin Buber, *Between Man and Man* (Boston: Beacon Press, 1955. Emphasis supplied.

20. Benjamin S. Bloom, *Stability and Change in Human Characteristics* (New York: Wiley, 1964).

21. Jean Piaget, *Genetic Epistemology* (New York: Columbia Univ. Press, 1970).

ANNOTATED BIBLIOGRAPHY:

SOCIETAL GUIDANCE AND PLANNING

BIBLIOGRAPHY

GENERAL WORKS

Bauer, Raymond A., ed. *Social Indicators*. Cambridge, Mass.: M.I.T. Press, 1966.

The first major contribution to what has come to be known as the social indicators movement, whose purpose is to devise a methodology for introducing a broader range of issues into discussions of national policy than has been possible with the traditional Keynesian models of counter-cyclical economic planning. One of the best essays in this volume is Albert D. Biderman's critical view of "Social Indicators and Goals."

——, and Gergen, Kenneth J., eds. *The Study of Policy Formation* New York: Free Press, 1968.

Concentrating on planning as a decision-making process, this series of essays, written especially for this volume, provides an excellent and critical overview of earlier work as well as a number of case studies. Should be read in conjunction with Kahn and Ilchman-Uphoff.

Bennis, Warren G.; Benne, Kenneth D.; and Chin, Robert, eds. *The Planning of Change*. 2d ed. New York: Holt, 1969.

A major book of readings concerned with innovative approaches to planning at the level of business management. From a societal standpoint, this book acquires new significance in the context of a transactive model of planning processes.

Chamberlain, Neil W. *Private and Public Planning*. New York: McGraw, 1965.

Finding important parallels between planning for the business firm and for society, Chamberlain provides a systematic treatment of some important issues based on a close knowledge of management problems.

Dahl, Robert A., and Lindblom, Charles E. *Politics, Economics, and Welfare.* New York: Harper, 1953.
Although it belongs to an older generation of writings on the theory of societal guidance, Dahl and Lindblom can still be read with profit. Its major contribution lies in the analysis of social processes for rational calculation and control.

Deutsch, Karl W. *The Nerves of Government: Models of Political Communication and Control.* New York: Free Press, 1963.
One of the early efforts to reinterpret social science theories in terms of a cybernetic control model. Extraordinarily rich in insights and ideas, this book is badly in need of further and more systematic extension into a general theory of societal guidance.

Dunn, Edgar S., Jr. *Economic and Social Development: A Process of Social Learning.* Baltimore and London: Johns Hopkins Press, 1971.
A major breakthrough in the theory of societal guidance, closely paralleling my own analysis. One of a growing number of books published within the last two years that interpret social change in terms of learning processes. Common to all these interpretations is an emphasis on the small learning cell.

Etzioni, Amitai. *The Active Society: A Theory of Societal and Political Processes.* New York: Free Press, 1968.
Difficult but rewarding reading. A major statement in the theory of societal guidance, somewhat marred by a rather narrow and inappropriate view of planning processes.

Ilchman, Warren F., and Uphoff, Norman Thomas. *The Political Economy of Change.* Berkeley and Los Angeles: Univ. of Calif. Press, 1969.
Like Dahl and Lindblom's work, this book is the result of collaboration between an economist and a political scientist. It represents an attempt to resurrect the ancient study of political economy.

Kahn, Alfred J. *Theory and Practice of Social Planning.* New York: Russell Sage Foundation, 1969.
Narrower in scope than either Etzioni or Dunn, this book is the most sophisticated recent statement of the traditional view of planning as rational decision-making. Social learning approaches

to planning are beginning to render works such as Kahn's obsolete.

Kunkel, John H. *Society and Economic Growth: A Behavioral Perspective of Social Change.* New York: Oxford, 1970.

Antecedent to Dunn's work, Kunkel's approach is rather too narrowly based on a conditioning theory of the learning process. Kunkel appears to be less aware than others of the complexities of planning and societal guidance, particularly as they arise in the developing countries.

Miller, George A.; Galanter, Eugene; and Pribam, Karl H. *Plans and the Structure of Behavior.* New York: Henry Holt, 1960.

Planning as a learning process. Essential reading.

Quade, E. S., and Boucher, W. I., eds. *Systems Analysis and Policy Planning: Applications in Defense.* New York: Am. Elsevier Pub. Co., 1968.

A Rand Corporation study, introducing the reader to the mystifications of scientific policies planning. Diametrically opposed to Goulet and Dunn, its philosophical foundations are found in the writings of Herbert Simon.

Simon, Herbert A. *The Sciences of the Artificial.* Cambridge, Mass.: M.I.T. Press, 1969.

The "sciences of the artificial" include, but are not limited to, the engineering-design sciences. Concerned with the interface between inner and outer environments, Simon is attempting to work out the logical basis of processes linking scientific knowledge to organized actions. An intellectual *tour de force*.

Vickers, Geoffrey. *The Art of Judgment: A Study of Policy Making.* New York: Basic Bks., Inc., 1965.

Sir Geoffrey writes from his own experiences as a policy maker. One of the best of the new writers on public policy, Vickers fails in explicating the critical relationship of policy to action. Nevertheless, a valuable contribution. See especially his brief chapter on "Decision as learning."

CASE STUDIES OF PLANNING

Akzin, Benjamin, and Dror, Yehezkel. *Israel: High-Pressure Planning.* National Planning Series, Vol. 5. Syracuse: Syracuse Univ. Press, 1966.

264   ANNOTATED BIBLIOGRAPHY

A provocative study of a planning style not yet legitimized in theory. See Preface by B. Gross.

Altshuler, Alan A. *The City Planning Process*. Ithaca: Cornell Univ. Press, 1965.
A political scientist's view of city planning in Minneapolis-St. Paul. Part II contains important theoretical chapters.

Banfield, Edward C. *Political Influence*. New York: Free Press, 1961.
A theoretical landmark in the study of urban politics, based on Chicago in the 1950s. Aggressively behavioral, Banfield despairs of central planning and, for that matter, of all forms of policy intervention.

Beneviste, Guy. *Bureaucracy and National Planning: A Sociological Case Study*. New York: Praeger, 1970.
A brilliant study of educational planning in Mexico.

Brown, W. H., Jr., and Gilbert, C. E. *Planning Municipal Investment: A Case Study of Philadelphia*. Philadelphia: Univ. of Pa. Press, 1961.
A thoughtful and richly documented study of the politics of budgeting in a major American city. Now unfortunately out of print.

Cohen, Stephen. *Modern Capitalist Planning: The French Model*. Cambridge, Mass.: Harvard Univ. Press, 1969.
A critical, insightful study of the French corporate style of national planning. Reveals some of the difficulties of assessing the results of planning.

Franks, Oliver. *Central Planning and Control in War and Peace*. Cambridge, Mass.: Harvard Univ. Press, 1947.
Describes central planning as it "really is" based on Britain's wartime and immediate post-war experience. Rexford Tugwell wrote a penetrating critique in the *Public Administration Review*, Vol. VII, No. 1 (Winter 1948), pp. 48–59. Compare Franks's analysis with Peter Wiles's of planning under communism.

Friedmann, John. *Venezuela: From Doctrine to Dialogue*. National Planning Series, Vol. 1. Syracuse: Syracuse Univ. Press, 1965.
A brief, but theoretically relevant analysis of national planning in Venezuela.

Gross, Bertram M., ed. *Action Under Planning: The Guidance of Economic Development*. New York: McGraw, 1967.

Proceedings of an international conference on national planning, the first that managed to look at the subject from a behavioral perspective. It marks a turning point in theorizing about planning, by abandoning the rational decision-making model in favor of an inductive model.

Hagen, Everett E., ed. *Planning Economic Development*. Homewood, Ill.: Irwin, 1963.
A series of case studies of national planning, with theoretical chapters by Professor Hagen.

——, and White, Stephanie T. *Great Britain: Quiet Revolution in Planning*. National Planning Series, Vol. 6. Syracuse: Syracuse Univ. Press, 1966.

Hirschman, Albert O. *Development Projects Observed*. Washington, D.C.: Brookings, 1967.
A classic.

——. *Journeys Toward Progress: Studies of Economic Policy-Making in Latin America*. New York: The Twentieth Century Fund, 1963.
This volume gave rise to Hirschman's well-known theory of "reform-mongering." Planning is viewed as a political process of incremental decision-making, and the study provides empirical evidence for Charles Lindblom's *The Intelligence of Democracy*.

LaPalombara, Joseph. *Italy: The Politics of Planning*. National Planning Series, Vol. 7. Syracuse: Syracuse Univ. Press, 1966.

Meyerson, Martin, and Banfield, Edward C. *Politics, Planning, and the Public Interest: The Case of Public Housing in Chicago*. Glencoe, Ill.: Free Press, 1955.
The first major empirical study of American city planning practice, dealing with public housing in Chicago. Banfield's theoretical appendix is especially useful as a formal statement of the decision-making schema.

Rabinovitz, Francine. *City Politics and Planning*. New York: Atherton, 1969.
In the Banfield-Altshuler tradition of urban politics, but more sympathetic to planning. Case studies of five New Jersey cities.

Selznick, Philip. *TVA and the Grass Roots*. Berkeley: Univ. of Calif. Press, 1949.
A major case study and theoretical analysis of America's out-

standing venture into regional development planning. See review by Rexford G. Tugwell and Edward C. Banfield, "Grass Roots Democracy—Myth or Reality," *Public Administration Review* (Winter 1950), pp. 47–55.

Shafer, Robert J. *Mexico: Mutual Adjustment Planning*. National Planning Series, Vol. 4. Syracuse: Syracuse Univ. Press, 1966.
The best of the National Planning Series edited by Bertram M. Gross. See especially Gross's preface.

United Nations. "Planning in Latin America," and "Planning and Plan Implementation in Latin America," in *Economic Bulletin for Latin America*, Vol. XII, No. 2 (October 1967), pp. 1–32.
The first non-ideological look at planning practice to emerge from the work of the U. N. Economic Commission for Latin America.

Waterston, Albert. *Development Planning: Lessons of Experience*. Baltimore: Johns Hopkins Press, 1965.
A monumental work, based on first-hand studies of national planning by a World Bank economist. Lacks a theoretical framework.

Wildavsky, Aaron. *The Politics of the Budgetary Process*. Boston: Little, 1964.
Central planning for resource allocation involves budgeting. This is an important and early contribution to the political elements in this process. Behavioral description is passed off as normatively valid prescription. Compare to Brown and Gilbert's study of capital programming in Philadelphia.

Wiles, P. J. D. *The Political Economy of Communism*. Cambridge, Mass.: Harvard Univ. Press, 1962.
A brilliantly provocative study of command planning, principally based on Soviet experience.

PLANNING FOR SYSTEM MAINTENANCE: ALLOCATION

Arrow, Kenneth J. *Social Choice and Individual Values*. New York: Wiley, 1951.
Demonstrates, by the use of symbolic logic, the impossibility of deriving a community welfare function from the welfare maximizing choices of individuals. By implication, Arrow demonstrates the intellectual bankruptcy of welfare economics as a scientific field of study.

Dorfman, Robert, ed. *Measuring Benefits of Government Investments*. Washington, D.C.: Brookings, 1965.

Welfare economics continued on the more mundane but practically more important level of cost-benefit analysis. Concrete applications to a number of major policy areas.

Dyckman, John W. "Planning and Decision Theory," *Journal of the American Institute of Planners*, Vol. XXVII, No. 4 (November 1961), pp. 335–45.

A good survey of the relation between formal decision theory and planning practice.

Friedrich, Carl J., ed. *The Public Interest*, Yearbook of the American Society for Political and Legal Philosophy, Vol. V. New York: Atherton, 1962.

A key problem of decision-making theory is dealt with here in a highly critical manner. Most of the contributing authors deny the possibility of decisions "in the public interest" except as a rhetorical device. See also Kenneth Arrow's work. Together, these two books all but destroy the logical basis for central allocative planning, except where an agreement on the major value premises of the plan exists.

——, ed. *Rational Decision*, Yearbook of the American Society for Political and Legal Philosophy, Vol. VII. New York: Atherton, 1964.

A critical view of the rational decision-model. See especially the chapter by Judith N. Shklar on "Decisionism."

Gore, William L., and Dyson, J. W., eds. *The Making of Decisions: A Reader in Administrative Behavior*. New York: Free Press, 1964.

A useful compendium containing some of the key papers on decision theory.

Hickman, Bert G., ed. *Quantitative Planning of Economic Policy*. Washington, D.C.: Brookings, 1965.

The chapters, written especially for this volume, summarize the current "state of the art" of central economic planning.

Lindblom, Charles E. *The Intelligence of Democracy*. New York: Free Press, 1965.

A major statement by the leader of the "incrementalist" school of planning. His theory of "partisan mutual adjustment" finds here its most coherent formulation. The volume also contains a sustained attack on the logic of comprehensive central planning, based on a presumed capacity for synoptic decision-making. In his book, *The Active Society*, Amitai Etzioni formulates a third alternative of "mixed scanning." All three approaches, however, neglect the question of how decisions, once made, can be implemented.

Little, I. M. D. *A Critique of Welfare Economics*. 2d ed. London: Oxford, 1957.
    This fundamental critique put an end to a decade of search for an objective welfare function in economic analysis.

March, James G., and Simon, Herbert A. *Organizations*. New York: Wiley, 1958.
    Still the basic book in organization theory. Its chapters on planning make the useful distinction between routine and non-routine decision-making.

Margolis, Julius, ed. *The Public Economy of Urban Communities*. Washington, D.C.: Resources for the Future, Inc., 1965.
    Futher work on welfare approaches to public decision-making. See companion volume edited by Howard G. Schaller.

Raiffa, Howard. *Decision Analysis: Introductory Lectures on Choice under Uncertainty*. Reading, Mass.: Addison Wesley, 1968.
    A basic text on the subject.

Schaller, Howard G., ed. *Public Expenditure Decisions in the Urban Community*. Washington, D.C.: Resources for the Future, Inc., 1963.
    A "modified" welfare approach to the public problems of the American city. Contains a number of interesting individual contributions. See companion volume edited by Professor Margolis.

Shackle, G. L. S. *Decision, Order, and Time in Human Affairs*. Cambridge: Cambridge, 1961.
    An iconoclastic approach to the question of time and uncertainty in economic decisions. Introduces the important concept of subjective probability.

Simon, Herbert A. *Administrative Behavior: A Study of Decision-Making Processes in Administrative Organization*. 2d ed. New York: Free Press, 1965.
    The original formulation, in theoretical and behavioral terms, of the rational decision-making model. The second edition contains an important "Introduction," in which Simon modifies his earlier model in terms of a concept of "bounded rationality." This book

succeeded in dominating planning theory for over a decade. Its influence is still being felt in the newer systems analysis approaches to public policy (see Quade and Boucher).

Tinbergen, J. *Economic Policy: Principles and Design*. Amsterdam: North-Holland Pub. Co., 1964.
An epoch-making study, providing a theory and method for rational economic policy. Except in connection with short-run economic policy, faith in this method has declined in recent years.

PLANNING FOR SYSTEM CHANGE: INNOVATION

Argyris, Chris. *Organization and Innovation*. Homewood, Ill.: Irwin and The Dorsey Press, 1965.
Innovations in business firms: case studies and theory.

Boulding, K. E. "Toward a General Theory of Growth," in Joseph J. Spengler and Otis Dudley Duncan, eds., *Population Theory and Policy: Selected Readings*. New York: Free Press, 1956, pp. 109–24.
Identifies structural growth as a type requiring continuous structural modifications of a system as a condition for further growth. Parallels the work of Morse and Kuhn.

Diamant, Alfred. "Innovation in Bureaucratic Institutions," *Public Administration Review*, Vol. XXVII, No. 1 (March 1967), pp. 77–87.
Objects to the commonly held view that bureaucratic organizations are inherently conservative.

Campbell, Donald T. "Reforms as Experiments," *American Psychologist*, Vol. XXIV, No. 4 (April 1969), pp. 409–29.
Suggests methods for evaluating the results of planned reforms as a basis for redesigning them.

Fairweather, George W. *Methods for Experimental Social Innovation*. New York: Wiley, 1967. First corrected printing, May 1968.
Chiefly concerned with the methodology of "experimental evolution," a concept central to Edgar Dunn's recent book.

Halpern, Manfred. "A Redefinition of the Revolutionary Situation," *Journal of International Affairs*, Vol. XXIII, No. 1 (1969), pp. 54–75.
Halpern defines modernization as the ability continuously to generate and absorb change. This requires structural changes in the system of societal guidance. A major essay supporting the viewpoint elaborated in Morse's chapter (see below).

270   ANNOTATED BIBLIOGRAPHY

Kuhn, Thomas S. *The Structure of Scientific Revolutions*. Chicago: Univ. of Chicago Press, 1962.

A widely influential book which argues that major advances in scientific knowledge come about as a result of shifts in the paradigms of "normal" science. Most of the evidence is drawn from the history of science. Its basic argument, however, coincides closely with Chandler Morse's theory of the development process.

Maruyama, Magoroh. "The Second Cybernetics: Deviation-Amplifying Mutual Causal Processes," *American Scientist*, Vol. LI (1963), pp. 164–79.

One of the few articles dealing specifically with the phenomenon of positive feedback in cybernetic systems.

Morse, Chandler. "Becoming versus Being Modern: An Essay on Institutional Change and Economic Development," in Chandler Morse, et al., *Modernization by Design*. Ithaca: Cornell Univ. Press, 1969, pp. 238–382.

A major statement on the need for structural change in developmental planning.

Press, Charles, and Adrian, Alan, eds. *Empathy and Ideology: Aspects of Administration Innovation*. Chicago: Rand McNally, 1966.

A public administration point of view.

Ruff, Larry E. "The Economic Common Sense of Pollution," *The Public Interest*, No. 19 (Spring 1970), pp. 69–85.

Structural change in institutions influences the outcome of public policies. Contrasted with technological institutions and command planning.

Schoop, Jack, and Hirten, John E. "The San Francisco Bay Plan: Combining Policy with Police Power," *Journal of the American Institute of Planners*, Vol. XXXVII, No. 1 (January 1971), pp. 2–10.

Excellent case study of innovative planning.

THE USES OF THE FUTURE

Ayres, Robert U. *Technological Forecasting and Long-Range Planning*. New York: McGraw, 1969.

Methodologically interesting contribution. A good antidote to more metaphysical preoccupations with the future.

Bennis, Warren G., and Slater, Philip E. *The Temporary Society*. New York: Harper, 1968.
  The psychological stress of living towards a continuously evolving future. See Toffler, whose less scholarly book covers the same ground.

Boguslaw, Robert. *The New Utopians: A Study of System Design and Social Change*. Englewood Cliffs, N.J.: Prentice-Hall, 1965.
  Philosophical and social issues in the technocratic approach to human problem-solving.

De Jouvenel, Bertrand. *The Art of Conjecture*. New York: Basic Bks., Inc., 1967.
  Paradoxically, but significantly, a conservative French philosopher provides the ideological underpinnings for the "scientific" study of the future.

Forrester, Jay W. *Urban Dynamics*. Cambridge, Mass.: M.I.T. Press, 1969.
  Demonstrates the often counter-intuitive results of small present changes if rigorously projected into the distant future. Though his concrete application leaves much to be desired, the demonstration of the principle is itself important.

Helmer, Olaf. *Social Technology*. New York: Basic Bks., Inc., 1966.
  Helmer was among the avant-garde of long-range forecasters. This book describes his basic ideas and includes a long appendix on the Delphic method he, together with others, developed at the Rand Corporation.

Jantsch, Erich. *Technological Forecasting in Perspective*. Paris: Organization for Economic Cooperation and Development, 1967.
  A monumental survey of the current "state of the art."

Kahn, Hermann, and Wiener, Anthony J. *Toward the Year 2000: A Framework for Speculation on the Next Thirty-Three Years*. New York: Macmillan, 1967.
  A concrete application of "futurology" by two of its leading practitioners.

Lapp, Ralph E. *The New Priesthood: The Scientific Elite and the Uses of Power*. New York: Harper, 1965.

Michael, Donald N. *The Unprepared Society: Planning for a Precarious Future*. New York: Basic Bks., Inc., 1968.
  A short polemic arguing the need for long-range planning. In

view of the serious cognitive and political difficulties of effective long-range planning, the book's merits are questionable. It is nevertheless typical of much of the thinking in which futurologists engage when their minds turn from technological to social issues.

Mincer, Jacob, ed. *Economic Forecasts and Expectations: Analysis of Forecasting Behavior and Performance.* New York: National Bureau of Economic Research, 1969.
A dispassionate analysis of economic forecasting.

Moore, Wilbert E., and Tumin, Melvin M. "Some Social Functions of Ignorance," in Bernard Rosenberg, Israel Gerver, and F. William Horton, eds., *Mass Society in Crisis.* New York: Macmillan, 1964.
In view of the current obsession with knowing the future, Moore and Tumin address themselves to the question whether ignorance of the future is not desirable as an impetus to action. An early formulation of Hirschman's principle of the "Hiding Hand."

Ozbekhan, Hasan. "The Triumph of Technology: 'Can' Implies 'Ought,'" in Stanford Andersen, ed., *Planning for Diversity and Choice: Possible Futures and Their Relations to the Man-Controlled Environment.* Cambridge, Mass.: M.I.T. Press, 1968.
Identifies one of the principal fallacies of futurology and technocratic thinking generally. Because a "solution" is feasible technically, it *should* be used. Instances of the contrary, such as the refusal of the United States Congress to support further experimental work on the supersonic transport plane, stand out dramatically because of their rarity.

Perloff, Harvey S., ed. *The Future of the United States Government: Toward the Year 2000.* New York: Braziller, 1971.
The individual contributions to this symposium sponsored by the American Academy of Arts and Sciences are uneven, but the subject is intrinsically interesting, and the essays by Perloff, Orlans, Holden, Schon, and Barber are worth reading.

Toffler, Alvin. *Future Shock.* New York: Random House, 1970.
High-class journalism. Toffler is a perfect example of the bathos surrounding the whole field of "futurology." Nevertheless, he provides many concrete examples of the unsettling experience of living in an era of hyper-rapid change.

"Toward the Year 2000: Work in Progress." *Daedalus*, Special Issue (Summer 1967).

Papers and proceedings of a working conference chaired by Professor Daniel Bell. Several important contributions, especially by Fred Ikle ("Can Social Predictions be Evaluated?") and Donald A. Schon ("Forecasting and Technological Forecasting").

ON THE RELATION OF KNOWLEDGE TO ACTION

Archibald, K. "Three Views of the Expert's Role in Policy Making: Systems Analysis, Incrementalism, and the Clinical Approach," Rand Corporation, P-4292 (January 1970).

Excellent discussion of the role of the expert *vis-à-vis* his client. Comes out in favor of a synthesis of the three approaches reviewed.

Beneviste, Guy, and Ilchman, Warren F., eds. *Agents of Change: Professionals in Developing Countries*. New York: Praeger, 1969.

A review by well-known practitioners in a variety of professions of the problems encountered in advising foreign governments. One of the best general statements of the problem.

Horowitz, Irving Louis. "The Academy and the Polity: Interaction Between Social Scientists and Federal Administrators." *The Journal of Behavioral Science*, Vol. 5, No. 3 (July–September 1969), pp. 309–36.

Some structural problems in the relation of knowledge to action.

Kaplan, Morton A. *On Historical and Political Knowing: An Inquiry into Some Problems of Universal Law and Human Freedom.* Chicago: Univ. of Chicago Press, 1971.

An important critique of knowledge in the social sciences. Professor Kaplan emphasizes the importance of historical context in interpreting the findings of social science research.

Kissinger, Henry A. "The Policy Maker and the Intellectual," in Thomas E. Cronin and Sanford D. Greenberg, eds., *The Presidential Advisory System*. New York: Harper, 1969.

A lucid account of policy making by committees (leading to mediocrity) and the hapless role of the advisor to bureaucracy, who often falls into the same trap. An argument for creativity.

Lyons, Gene M., ed. "Social Science and the Federal Government," *The Annals of the American Academy of Political and Social Science*, Vol. 394 (March 1971), Special Issue.

Addresses the central issue of knowledge and power. Good articles by Lakoff, Green, Orleans, and Lyons.

Mannheim, Karl. *Ideology and Utopia*. New York: Harcourt, 1949.

——. *Man and Society in an Age of Reconstruction*. New York: Harcourt, 1949.

——. *Freedom, Power, and Democratic Planning*. New York: Oxford, 1950.

This trilogy encompasses Mannheim's most important works. The books appeared in their original editions in the order listed. In *Ideology and Utopia,* Mannheim lays the foundations for a sociology of knowledge and poses the critical issues with which his later work deals more exhaustively. *Man and Society* addresses the central question of rational knowledge as a basis for guiding change within society. In light of present conditions in America, this work gains new relevance. *Freedom, Power, and Democratic Planning* was written while Mannheim was living in exile in England. It is more attuned to the Anglo-Saxon temperament and stands out by focusing upon the question of educating for a society committed to guiding the course of its historical development through the application of reason and scientific knowledge.

Merton, Robert K. *Social Theory and Social Structure*. Rev. ed. New York: Free Press, 1957.

A major collection of writings by one of America's most notable sociologists. Merton not only makes a trenchant criticism of Mannheim's sociology of knowledge, but throughout provides some of the major theoretical undergirdings for a theory that endeavors to treat the relationship between scientific knowledge and organized actions.

——. "The Role of Applied Social Science in the Formation of Policy: A Research Memorandum," *Philosophy of Science,* Vol. 16, No. 3 (July 1949), pp. 161–81.

An early and still valuable methodological outline to the new field of policy sciences.

Michael, Donald N. "On Coping with Complexity: Planning and Politics," *Daedalus,* Vol. 47, No. 4 (Fall 1968), pp. 1179–93.

Contains an interesting suggestion for massive political participation in decision processes through decentralized access to central computer models.

Miller, George A. "The Magical Number Seven Plus or Minus Two: Some Limits on Our Capacity for Processing Information," *Psychological Review*, Vol. 63 (1956), pp. 81–97.
A famous finding of experimental psychology.

Millikan, Max F. "Inquiry and Policy: The Relation of Knowledge and Action," in Daniel Lerner, ed., *The Human Meaning of the Social Sciences*. New York: Meridian Books, 1959.
A thoughtful statement by a professor who has played an important part in shaping American foreign aid policy.

Morgenstern, Oscar. *On the Accuracy of Economic Observation*. Princeton, N.J.: Princeton Univ. Press, 1963.
A book not easily forgotten or ignored. Concerned with the problem of error in aggregate quantitative analysis, Morgenstern cautions against excessive reliance on quantitative measures without a full understanding of their validity. The book is filled with fascinating examples.

Norma, Donald A. *Memory and Attention: An Introduction to Human Information Processing*. New York: Wiley, 1969.
Important summary of current knowledge concerning this important aspect of societal guidance.

Piaget, Jean. *Genetic Epistemology*. New York: Columbia Univ. Press, 1970.
On the basis of experimental findings, Piaget argues that knowledge arises from the co-ordination of actions and is, therefore, prior to language. He also stresses the importance of beliefs that, in certain cases, are more powerful in guiding behavior than is knowledge. Theoretical basis for asserting, as I do, that action is in every case primary and that scientific knowledge, if it is to produce significant effects in guiding the course of society, must be closely joined to actions.

Polanyi, Michael. "Tacit Knowing: Its Bearing on Some Problems of Philosophy," *Review of Modern Physics*, Vol. 34, No. 4 (October 1962), pp. 601–16.
A fundamental critique and extension of cognitive theory. Tacit knowing is a conceptually more rigorous formulation of "personal" knowledge, which is basic to my own analysis of transactive planning.

Reichenbach, Hans. *Experience and Prediction: An Analysis of the Foundations and the Structure of Knowledge.* Chicago: Univ. of Chicago Press, 1938.

A classic of positivistic thinking. Contemporary science is still largely guided by this view. Polanyi's work (above) provides an important corrective.

Seers, Dudley. "Why Visiting Economists Fail," in David E. Novack and Robert Lekachman, eds., *Development and Society: The Dynamics of Economic Change.* New York: St. Martins, 1968.

Human problems in the "art of advice."

Wilensky, Harold L. *Organizational Intelligence: Knowledge and Policy in Government and Industry.* New York: Basic Bks., Inc., 1967.

One of the most important contributions to the subject. Sharply critical of most efforts to apply scientific knowledge to problems of public policy. Particularly interesting is Wilensky's analysis of information pathologies. The special merit of the book lies in its emphasis on information as the critical link between knowledge and action.

ALTERNATIVE MODELS OF ORGANIZATION

Crozier, Michel. *The Bureaucratic Phenomenon.* Chicago: Univ. of Chicago Press, 1964.

One of the most insightful excursions into bureaucratic behavior. The cases studied are French, but the results suggest a wider applicability. The study acquires special relevance for societal guidance by attempting to analyze the efficacy of bureaucratic systems for societal development and planning.

Downs, Anthony. *Inside Bureaucracy.* Boston: Little, 1967.

The American counterpart to Crozier's pioneering effort. Essential reading.

Grodzins, Morton. *The American System: A New View of Government in the United States.* Edited by Daniel J. Elazar. Chicago: Rand McNally, 1966.

Variations on the "marble cake" theme of American political and administrative organization. The most original and influential description of a system that escapes precise definition by virtue of its extreme complexity.

Hirschman, Albert O., and Lindblom, Charles E. "Economic Development, Research and Development, Policy Making: Some Converging Views," *Behavioral Science,* Vol. VII (1962), pp. 211–22.

A justly famous article that tries to link Hirschman's reform-mongering model with Lindblom's "mutual adjustment" model of policy making and both to organizational structures conducive to innovative behavior in research and development. Supporting evidence for a non-hierarchical form of organization.

Landau, Martin. "Redundancy, Rationality, and the Problem of Overlap," *Public Administration Review,* Vol. XXIX, No. 4 (July–August 1969), pp. 346–58.

Apparent organizational chaos may be beneficial from the standpoint of communication theory. An important and original contribution that supports looser organizational structures than those implicit in the rational bureaucratic model inherited from Max Weber. (See Merton's *Reader* below.)

Lawrence, Paul R., and Lorsch, Jay W. *Organization and Environment: Managing Differentiation and Integration.* Boston: Harvard University, Graduate School of Business Administration, Division of Research, 1967.

Empirical evidence for the proposition that optimal organizational designs vary with conditions in the relevant environment. Hierarchical forms are adapted to stable environments; increasingly differentiated forms are more suitable for "turbulent" and rapidly changing environments. The latter require less formal coordination but more explicit attention to the problem of integration of organizational behavior.

Lorsch, Jay W., and Lawrence, Paul R., eds. *Studies in Organization Design.* Homewood, Ill.: Irwin, 1970.

Further development of the theme that planning, in rapidly changing situations, becomes identical with integrative activities in highly differentiated (and decentralized) organizations. See especially the chapters by Fisher, Athreya, and Hampden-Turner.

Likert, Rennis. *The Human Organization: Its Management and Value.* New York: McGraw, 1967.

Explicit treatment of the innovative model of organization (here called participative), as well as of three variants of the bureaucratic (or authoritative) system of organization (exploitative, benevolent, consultative).

Marschak, Thomas A. "Strategy and Organization in a System Development Project," in National Bureau of Economic Research, *The Rate and Direction of Inventive Activity: Economic and Social Factors.* Princeton, N.J.: Princeton Univ. Press, 1962.
Empirical study of an alternative to the bureaucratic model. Ties into the Hirschman-Lindblom thesis mentioned above.

——. "Centralized Versus Decentralized Allocation: The Yugoslav 'Laboratory.'" *The Quarterly Journal of Economics,* Vol. LXXX (1968), pp. 561–87.
Does a decentralized system of decision making lead to accelerated economic development? The evidence is unclear, but there are important non-economic benefits that should be taken into account in a full evaluation.

Merton, Robert K., et al. *Reader in Bureaucracy.* New York: Free Press, 1952.
Although much work has been done in this field since 1952, the volume remains an excellent introduction to the major concepts in the study of bureaucracy.

Sjoberg, Gideon M.; Hancock, Donald; and White, Orion, Jr. *Politics in the Post-Welfare State: A Comparison of the United States and Sweden.* Bloomington, Ind.: Department of Government, Indiana University, 1967.
An obscure but nonetheless important theoretical formulation of alternate organizational models. A heuristic framework for further investigation.

White, Orion F., Jr. "The Dialectical Organization: An Alternative to Bureaucracy," *Public Administration Review,* Vol. XXIX, No. 1 (January–February 1969), pp. 32–42.
See Sjoberg, et al., above.

Wilcox, Herbert G. "Hierarchy, Human Nature, and the Participative Panacea," *Public Administration Review,* Vol. XXIX, No. 1 (January–February 1969), pp. 53–64.
A persuasive opinion that participatory management structures advocated by Argyris, Bennis, Likert, and others contain more ideology than empirical proof of efficacy. However, contrary empirical evidence is not presented.

Wilson, James Q. "Innovation in Organization: Notes Toward a Theory," in James D. Thompson, ed., *Approaches to Organizational Design.* Pittsburgh: Univ. of Pittsburgh Press, 1966.

Wilson maintains that the decentralized, non-hierarchical model is more likely to lead to stalemate than innovation. A closely reasoned essay, drawing on the author's experience with urban politics (Chicago model), but failing to take into account the crucial environmental factor in organizational design.

THE TRANSACTIVE STYLE OF PLANNING

Adizes, Ichak. *Self-Management: The Yugoslav Post-Reform Experience: The Effect of Decentralization on Organizational Behavior.* New York: Free Press, 1970.
A balanced evaluation of this important national experiment in participatory management.

Aleshire, Robert. "Planning and Citizen Participation: Costs, Benefits, and Approaches." *Urban Affairs Quarterly,* Vol. 5, No. 4 (June 1970), pp. 369–93.
One of the most cogent arguments favoring decentralized approaches to planning for urban development.

Alexander, Christopher. *Notes on the Synthesis of Form.* Cambridge, Mass.: Harvard Univ. Press, 1964.
A radical reconceptualization of the processes of problem solving and design. Partial solutions to small problems build up progressively to system-wide solutions.

Arnsberg, Conrad M., and Niehoff, Arthur H. *Introducing Social Change: A Manual for Americans Overseas.* Chicago: Aldine Pub., 1964.
The planner descends into the "foreign" world of his client group. Problems of cross-cultural understanding and motivation. The process of mutual learning is not explicated, however.

Arnstein, S. R. "A Ladder of Citizen Participation," *Journal of the American Institute of Planners,* Vol. XXXV, No. 4 (July 1969), pp. 216–24.
A rational appraisal of the possibilities of citizen participation in planning and community development at different levels of decision-making.

Bolan, Richard. "The Social Relations of the Planner," *Journal of the American Institute of Planners,* Vol. XXXVII, No. 6 (November 1971), pp. 387–96.
A penetrating "transactive" analysis of the planning process and the role of planners in American cities.

Buber, Martin. *Between Man and Man*. Boston: Beacon Press, 1955.

———. *The Knowledge of Man*. Edited by Maurice Friedman. New York: Harper, 1965.
Selected essays by the foremost exponent of the dialogic principle.

Davidoff, Paul. "Advocacy and Pluralism in Planning," *Journal of the American Institute of Planners*, Vol. XXXI, No. 4 (November 1965), pp. 331–37.
The first formal statement of what has become a major movement, turning the planning profession from "summit" planning to assisting local neighborhoods and communities to formulate and present their own plans to central authorities. The beginnings of the transactive style.

———. "Normative Planning," in Stanford Anderson, ed., *Planning for Diversity and Choice*. Cambridge, Mass.: M.I.T. Press, 1968.
First public recognition *by a planner* that the public-interest view of planning is untenable as a philosophical basis for the profession and that its members are not value-free technicians.

Friedman, Maurice. *Problematic Rebel: An Image of Modern Man*. New York: Random House, 1963.
An existential analysis of man. Philosophical anthropology at its best. Primarily literary sources. See Gehlen below.

Gehlen, Arnold. *Der Mensch: Seine Natur und seine Stellung in der Welt*. Bonn: Athenaeum Verlag, 1958.
The biological and behavioral approach to philosophical anthropology. Transactive planning requires that we have an adequate image of man. Very few studies have attempted to bring the experimental findings of the biological and behavioral sciences into a philosophical synthesis. Gehlen's work is probably the most ambitious attempt to date.

Goulet, Denis. *The Cruel Choice: A New Concept in the Theory of Development*. New York: Atheneum, 1971.
Of special interest is Chapter 7, "Development as Dialogue."

Hampden-Turner, Charles. *Radical Man: The Process of Psycho-Social Development*. New York: Anchor Bks., 1971.
Grounded in existential philosophy, Hampden-Turner proposes a participant cellular structure for the organization of corporate management and draws implications for the larger political scene.

May, Rollo. *Man's Search for Himself*. New York: Norton, 1953. A personalistic approach to man.

Peattie, Lisa. "Reflections on Advocacy Planning," *Journal of the American Institute of Planners*, Vol. XXXIV, No. 2 (March 1968), pp. 80–87.
Reflections on the experiences of a leading advocacy planner. Before advocacy is possible, the community must be organized. Problems in defining "community." Planners' traditional roles are radically changed under conditions of advocacy. The transactive element is implicit.

Schein, Edgar H. *Process Consultation: Its Role in Organization Development*. Reading, Mass.: Addison-Wesley, 1969.
Process consultation involves the client and the consultant in a period of joint diagnosis. Mutual learning lies at the heart of the consultant relationship, in which the processed knowledge of the expert is joined to the personal knowledge of the client. A major contribution to the theory of what I have called transactive planning.

Waley, Arthur. *The Way and Its Power: A Study of the* Tao Te Ching *and Its Place in Chinese Thought*. New York: Grove, 1948.
Transactive planning in ancient China. Portions of the Tao may serve as a useful guide to the aspiring transactive planner.

INDEX